MEMPHIS

—— AND ——

THE PARADOX OF

PLACE

NEW DIRECTIONS *in* SOUTHERN STUDIES

EDITOR

Charles Reagan Wilson

MEMPHIS

—— AND ——

THE PARADOX OF PLACE

GLOBALIZATION *in the*

AMERICAN SOUTH

WANDA RUSHING

THE UNIVERSITY OF
NORTH CAROLINA PRESS

Chapel Hill

Designed by Courtney Leigh Baker and set in Dante by Keystone Typesetting, Inc.
Manufactured in the United States of America

The paper in this book meets the guidelines for permanence
and durability of the Committee on Production Guidelines for
Book Longevity of the Council on Library Resources.

The University of North Carolina Press has been a member
of the Green Press Initiative since 2003.

Lines from Kate Campbell, "Visions of Plenty," and Don Share,
"Dilemma" and "At Forrest Park," have been reprinted with permission.

Library of Congress Cataloging-in-Publication Data
Rushing, Wanda.
Memphis and the paradox of place : globalization in the
American South / Wanda Rushing. — 1st ed.
p. cm.—(New directions in southern studies)
Includes bibliographical references and index.
ISBN 978-0-8078-3299-8 (cloth: alk. paper) · ISBN 978-0-8078-5952-0 (pbk.: alk. paper)
1. Memphis (Tenn.)—Civilization. 2. Memphis (Tenn.)—History.
3. Globalization—Social aspects—Tennessee—Memphis. 4. Globalization—
Economic aspects—Tennessee—Memphis. 5. Culture and globalization—
Tennessee—Memphis. 6. Place (Philosophy) I. Title.
F444.M55R87 2009
303.48'276819—dc22
2009003096

CLOTH   13 12 11 10 09   5 4 3 2 1
PAPER   13 12 11 10 09   5 4 3 2 1

CONTENTS

ACKNOWLEDGMENTS

I began this project five years ago, intrigued with a city that became my home in 1998. Many have supported me and encouraged me in this venture. I would like to thank the College of Arts and Sciences and the Department of Sociology at the University of Memphis for granting me a professional development assignment—a one-year sabbatical leave—during the 2005–6 academic year to work on the project. The time was instrumental in giving me the momentum to complete the manuscript. I am grateful for the resources and staff of the University of Memphis Library, especially the Mississippi Valley Collection, and the Memphis and Shelby County Room at the Benjamin L. Hooks Central Library.

Sian Hunter, my editor at the University of North Carolina Press, expressed an interest in this project from its conceptualization. I appreciate her leadership and support and the support of David Perry and UNC Press. I am grateful to Kaudie McLean for calling attention to missing details in the manuscript. I also want to thank Charles Reagan Wilson at the University of Mississippi, editor of the New Directions in Southern Studies series, for his comments, suggestions, and expressions of confidence in the manuscript. Wendy Griswold's insightful comments on the manuscript helped me sharpen the theoretical focus. Anonymous reviewers who read the book proposal and the manuscript advanced my thinking about globalization and place, as did Anthony Orum, editor of *City and Community*, who accepted my first publication on Memphis, and the anonymous reviewers of that article.

Locally, I want to thank friends and neighbors living in the Evergreen Historic District whose expressions of neighborhood pride and community awareness introduced me to life in Memphis. I thank Ed Galfsky for extending an invitation for me to attend the Business and Industry Luncheon for 2006 Carnival Memphis after helping me locate materials he had donated to the public library. I also thank Clyde Venson for sharing programs and personal recollections from Kemet Jubilee and Cotton Maker's Jubilee and Charles Newman for meeting to discuss the Overton Park Supreme Court case. My work has benefited from the attention of students at the University of Memphis—both undergraduate and graduate—who have listened to explanations of my work-in-progress in the classroom and have given feedback. Several graduate assistants supported by the Department of Sociology, in particular Jessica Abernathy, Abby Bennett Johnston, and Corey Twombly, helped me locate important research materials. Former student Zandria Robinson read parts of the manuscript and provided useful comments. Mary Katherine Levie, with support from the Women's and Gender Studies Program, helped with manuscript preparation.

Family members have made many sacrifices for this project. My parents, John Leroy and Fair Rushing, like many rural southerners who lacked opportunities to obtain university degrees, provided the means and encouragement for me to pursue higher education when I was growing up in North Carolina. My sons, Benjamin Edwards and William Edwards, enthusiastically supported my return to graduate school at the University of Tennessee in Knoxville, my relocation to Memphis, and my work on this book. My husband, Martin Levin, a transplanted Connecticut Yankee, has been very supportive of this project and has proved himself to be an excellent editor and a discerning reader.

I DEDICATE THIS BOOK to the memory of Dr. Jameson Jones, dean at Rhodes College (retired), my mentor and friend. Never one to elegize the past, Jameson nonetheless shared his reflections on his early years in Corinth, Mississippi, and his observations on Memphis through many stages of his long life. His joy in daily walks in Overton Park, his enthusiasm for art, and his affection for the written word—in poetry and in prose—have inspired many friends and admirers as well as former students and colleagues.

MEMPHIS

—— AND ——

THE PARADOX OF

PLACE

I'd rather be there than any place I know.

—W. C. HANDY, "Beale Street Blues"

INTRODUCTION

This book is about a place called Memphis. Its purpose is twofold. First, it aims to create a global / local context for developing a better understanding of the concept of place in the social sciences. It does so by relating accounts of confrontations and collaborations involving real people in a particular southern place to regional and global processes. The second aim is to bring about a better understanding of a specific place—Memphis, Tennessee. The Mississippi River city, typically marginalized by scholars and underestimated by its own residents, can be seen as a dynamic center of economic productivity, cultural innovation, and social change. The book is based on an interdisciplinary narrative case-study approach to capture the complexities of Memphis, a remarkable southern place, and explain its global significance.

Memphis is known in some circles as the "home of the blues" and "the birthplace of rock and roll." The title of Robert Gordon's book about Memphis music, *It Came from Memphis*, makes important connections between a place called Memphis and cultural innovation. Anyone who has listened to Johnny Cash's "I Walk the Line," Elvis Presley's "That's Alright, Mama," Jerry Lee Lewis's "Great Balls of Fire," Otis Redding's "Sittin' on the Dock of the Bay," Booker T. and the MGs' "Green Onions," or Sam & Dave's "Soul Man" may know that these recordings came from Memphis. Most people, however, who shop in a modern supermarket, spend the night at a Holiday Inn, take a Di-Gel tablet or St. Joseph's Aspirin, apply Coppertone sunscreen and Maybelline cosmetics, wrap a present in Cleo giftwrap, or receive an overnight package from Federal Express have no idea that these innovations also came from Memphis.

Until Federal Express came along, Memphis was never identified as a company town. Memphis still is not a company town. But it always has been a place associated with independently minded thinkers and entrepreneurs like Robert Church, the nation's first black millionaire; J. E. Walker of the Universal Life Insurance Company; Clarence Saunders of Piggly Wiggly; Kemmons Wilson, who started Holiday Inn; Sam Phillips at Sun Studio; Abe Plough of Plough Pharmaceuticals (later to become Schering-Plough); and Jim Stewart and Estelle Axton of Stax Records. These people achieved great success; some were toppled by great failures, but like many Memphians, most started from modest beginnings. Even Fred Smith, the founder and CEO of FedEx Corporation who grew up in Memphis, enjoys telling the story about his class project at Yale. His business plan for Federal Express earned him a grade of "C."

Memphis residents and city officials, like some Yale business professors, do not always recognize the value of the city or its resources. Who wants to brag about having the first modern supermarket in Memphis when the founder of Piggly Wiggly, Clarence Saunders, was forced into bankruptcy? By most local accounts, Elvis Presley was a nice young man, but why would anyone travel to Memphis to visit Graceland? It has become the second most visited home in America; only the White House receives more visitors. Who would have imagined that the city once identified as a yellow fever "pestilential mudhole" and designated the unhealthiest city in the United States would become the home of St. Jude Children's Research Hospital? St. Jude treats children from around the world without regard to their ability to pay. And it has become an international leader in the research and treatment of childhood leukemia and sickle cell anemia and research on avian flu, and is a vital part of a cluster of the newly emerging biomedical technology industry in Memphis.

Why would anyone value Memphis music? For years, Memphians and respected experts, such as University of North Carolina sociologist Howard Odum, warned about the dangers of the blues. Odum expressed shock at the impoverished lives of African Americans he observed in the Mid-South region in the 1920s. He wrote that the songs "tell of every phase of immorality and filth. . . . Openly descriptive of the grossest immorality and susceptible of unspeakable thought and actions, rotten with filth, they are yet sung to the time-honored melodies."[1] Recently, similar criticism was published about Academy Award–winning Memphis rappers Three 6 Mafia. Much to the embarrassment of some Memphians, the rappers thanked God and shouted out "MEMPHIS, TENNESSEE," when the 2005 Academy Award for best song was announced before millions of television viewers for "It's Hard Out Here for a Pimp." No media event has provoked as much collective embarrassment and condemnation in Memphis since Elvis Presley first performed on the *Ed Sullivan Show*, or perhaps since Jerry Lee Lewis announced that he had married his thirteen-year-old cousin.

Attitudes about some things have not changed very much, but Memphis has proved that it can learn from its mistakes. In the city that "turned its back on the river and ran away from its historic downtown"[2] after the 1968 assassination of Martin Luther King Jr., reconciliation, revitalization, and resurgence are under way. The city that refused to send an official representative to the funeral of Dr. King or to pay respects at the airport when his body was flown to Atlanta now supports the National Civil Rights Museum. Built on the site of the Lorraine Motel, the museum serves as a shrine to Dr. King, a commemoration of the civil rights movement, and a link between Memphis and the struggle for human rights around the world. Recently, the city named its stunning new Central Library in honor of a local activist who played a prominent role in the civil rights movement—Benjamin L. Hooks.

Downtown development is booming. New residential and commercial buildings now rise on landscapes formerly devastated by urban renewal. Restaurants, hotels, art galleries, nightspots, and sports arenas welcome people to a vibrant downtown. Overton Park and the Old Forest, slated by the city and the state for interstate construction, spared by citizen activism and a Supreme Court decision, and memorialized in a collection of short stories by Peter Taylor, welcome visitors to a natural woodland habitat and a modern urban zoo. The historic Evergreen neighborhood, partially torn down and bulldozed for the contested and never-completed interstate corridor project, has been rebuilt and restored. And the Overton Park Concert Shell, constructed in 1936, has undergone a $1 million renovation. The newly constructed Stax Museum of American Soul Music and Stax Music Academy now stand at the corner of College and McLemore, where Stax Records operated from 1960 to 1975, and the old Capitol Theatre building that housed it was razed. Today, the Stax Music Academy sponsors after-school and summer programs to teach children, especially at-risk children from low-income neighborhoods, about music and the value of education. In 2006, fourteen of those children participated in the first-ever Stax Music Academy Summer Tour presented by FedEx. They opened festivities for the nineteenth annual Porretta Soul Festival in Porretta Terme, Italy, held in a city park named for Memphis legend Rufus Thomas. Graceland, Sun Studios, and Lauderdale Courts—the public-housing project where the young Elvis lived with his parents—are now preserved on the National Register of Historic Places. The city that refused to negotiate with black sanitation workers in 1968 now elects black officials to serve as city mayor, county mayor, city council members, county commissioners, state legislators, and U.S. congressmen. In 2006, former congressman Harold Ford Jr., an African American from Memphis, ran for the U.S. Senate, narrowly losing in one of the nation's most closely watched Senate races.

The University of Memphis, formerly an all-white segregated campus, is racially diverse, with an African American undergraduate student enrollment of approximately 38 percent. The university's commitment to diversity also includes reaching out to international students and programs. In 2007, the university secured a prestigious Confucius Institute by submitting a winning proposal to the Chinese Embassy and the Office of the Chinese Language Council International. A cultural partnership between the University of Memphis and Hubei University promotes cultural understanding and international relations.

Today, downtown development, the growth of strong neighborhood associations, the expansion of educational opportunities, and the election of African Americans to public office indicate that Memphis is coming into a new era and acquiring a fresh identity. Nonetheless, current local institutions reflect old paradoxes regarding politics, race, geography, and wealth. There are two mayors, a city mayor and a county mayor; two school systems, a large, predominantly black city school system and a smaller, predominantly white county school system; and two economic and social landscapes, suburban sprawl and affluence outside the I-240 Expressway ring and urban poverty and prosperity within it. Racial and ethnic matters continue to be dichotomized as black and white despite the presence of a small but active Native American community, increasing numbers of Asians and Africans, dramatic growth in the Latino / Latina population, and a more visible Muslim community. High rates of crime and poverty and low levels of educational attainment continue to pose problems for social and economic success in the city. So does a lack of public trust. Suspicion lurks just beneath the surface and emerges periodically. In recent years the FBI brought charges of corruption against prominent officials in a sting investigation referred to as "The Tennessee Waltz." Several members of local and state government were convicted on bribery charges.

City matters ranging from preserving statues commemorating a Civil War general, funding park maintenance, supporting NBA basketball, legalizing casino gambling, prosecuting allegedly corrupt officials, and debating riverfront development make Memphis an interesting subject. But the complexity of the place does not lend itself to "normal" paradigms of social science analysis or easy measurement.[3] To see Memphis in perspective, as a place having global and local significance, requires interdisciplinary research and a bit of sociological imagination. The pages that follow consider various approaches to globalization and place, in search of the best theoretical and methodological framework for telling a story about Memphis—an interesting southern city with a turbulent past positioning itself for a promising future.

LOCATING MEMPHIS

Geographical and political boundaries and census data identify the city for official purposes but provide only a starting point for understanding Memphis. As of 2005, the U.S. Census Bureau ranked the incorporated city of Memphis with its population of 672,277 as the seventeenth-largest city in the United States and the largest city in Tennessee. The city's 63.1 percent African American population made it conspicuously different from a Tennessee state population that was 80 percent white. Memphis ranked eighth in the nation in percentage of population that was African American.[4] Beyond the city's incorporated boundaries, the Memphis Metropolitan Statistical Area (MSA) was the second largest in Tennessee, behind first-ranked Nashville-Davidson. As of 2005, the Memphis MSA population of 1,260,905 was 45 percent African American. The MSA ranked fifth nationally in percentage of population that was African American.[5] Based on current demographic trends, however, census projections suggest that in the near future, metropolitan Memphis will become the first large metropolitan area in the United States populated by an African American majority.

In land area, the Memphis MSA includes five counties in three states: Shelby, Tipton, and Fayette Counties in Tennessee; De Soto County in Mississippi; and Crittenden County in Arkansas. The Memphis ADI (areas of dominant influence) television market, according to Arbitron, covers a thirty-one-county area in western Tennessee, northwestern Mississippi, eastern Arkansas, and southeastern Missouri. The Memphis daily newspaper, the *Memphis Commercial Appeal*, serves the northern Mississippi Delta region. Circulation covers ninety-four counties in Tennessee, Arkansas, Mississippi, Kentucky, Illinois, and Missouri.[6]

Many refer to Memphis and the surrounding region as the Mid-South, a term that seems a more apt description of its geographic location—both midwestern and southern—than its identity.[7] Not surprisingly, observers often suggest that Memphis, at the intersection of so many geographical and political borders, suffers from an identity crisis.[8] Officially, Memphis, the central city of Shelby County, Tennessee, and the central city of the MSA, serves as the county seat of Shelby County. Symbolically, however, Memphis is thought of as the capital city of the Mississippi Delta. David Cohn's oft-quoted phrase is "The Mississippi Delta begins in the lobby of the Peabody Hotel in Memphis and ends in Catfish Row in Vicksburg."[9]

IDENTITY AND AMBIVALENCE

Memories and identities from the past and self-consciousness, pride, shame, and ambivalence about those identities give meaning and narrative coherence to Memphis as a distinctive southern *place* and shape *place* identity. Ambivalence about the kind of city Memphis ought to be now and in the future, as well as negative images from the past, seems to haunt the city. Observers have depicted Memphis as a "provincial river town," a "Southern backwater," or "an inland river city where cultures, rich and poor, black and white, urban and rural, Northern and Southern . . . collide."[10] For decades, writers have described Memphis as a city suffering from an identity crisis or an "inferiority complex."[11] Literary works by Memphis-born and -reared writers such as Peter Taylor and Don Share reveal how psychological and social identities, as well as family histories, are shaped and stigmatized by Memphis—the place. Taylor's novel *A Summons to Memphis* and several of Share's poems in *Union* portray Memphis and its inhabitants from the viewpoints of former residents who chose to leave the city and the region. Both authors transform their narrators into "outsiders" who describe individual self-consciousness or embarrassment regarding biographical, cultural, and historical ties to the Memphis past. These narrators relate changes in accents and region of residence to strategies for choosing new nonsouthern and non-Memphian identities. But returning to Memphis as outsiders, these narrators find individual meaning in their constructions of the past.

Taylor's narrator distances himself from Old South and New South characteristics of Memphis as symbolized by his father, the well-mannered, scrupulous attorney (Old South), and his sisters, who become independent businesswomen (New South). The narrator informs the reader that "there was nothing Deep South about our family—an important distinction in our minds"; yet his family suffers from unresolved conflicts related to their ambivalence about place.[12] The narrator reveals that his father was forced to move to Memphis from Nashville. The family never quite adjusted or recovered from the humiliation of the forced move and endured additional stress by being forced to cope with "the peculiar institutions of the place," for example, aspects of Memphis associated "with the cotton and river culture of the Deep South." He describes Memphis as a "land-locked backwater" and "land-oriented" place and contrasts his family's provincialism with his more cosmopolitan identity acquired by living and working in a different place—New York City.[13]

Actual Memphis residents, as well as fictional former residents, sometimes express defensiveness about local identity, place, and the past. Ambivalence about the past seems to rise whenever new projects are proposed for the city or unresolved historical conflicts resurface. Interestingly, this self-consciousness about place-identity and perceptions about the relative standing of Memphis vis-à-vis other cities is not a recent phenomenon. The identity crisis began with the city's nineteenth-century origins and continued through historical struggles associated with the Civil War, yellow fever, commission government, civil rights, and downtown revitalization. Periodic attempts to revise official public memories, refashion identities, and commemorate more suitable pasts or understandings of the past have fueled conflict and provoked controversy for generations.

Memphis is a place of innovation and tradition, poverty and power, as well as continuity and disruption. The city embedded in its own accumulated local history, and subjected to global flows of commerce and communication, continues to shape and be shaped by the people who live and work there. These people, many of whom are descendants of black and white rural migrants from the region, have produced a wealth of local, place-specific resources—typically undervalued ones—as well as conflicts that are misunderstood. With this book, I hope to contribute to new discussions and understandings about place, the South, and Memphis.

There are few spots on the globe as interesting as the South; and perhaps none so rich in startlingly poignant paradoxes. . . . The time has come . . . to see the region in perspective.— LILLIAN SMITH, *How Am I to Be Heard? Letters of Lillian Smith*

—— I ——

GLOBALIZATION & THE SOUTH

Memphis and the Paradoxes of Place

Memphis, Tennessee, is a remarkable city located in the southern United States, a region associated with a history of disruptions, traditions, cumulative disadvantages, and dramatic transformations. Memphis, like the region, has its own history of disruptions, traditions, and transformations, as well as paradoxes. More than one hundred years ago, nineteenth-century Memphis survived the Civil War with little damage, only to be decimated a few years later by recurring yellow fever epidemics. Memphis became an "iconic" American place in the mid-twentieth century because of the city's identification with an innovative popular music that crossed racial divisions. But the city suffered setbacks in its economic and political growth because of racial tensions and bitter conflicts associated with the 1968 Sanitation Workers' Strike and the assassination of civil rights leader Martin Luther King Jr. Today, Memphis occupies a unique status as a distribution center in the global economy, but the city continues to struggle with social and economic inequalities as well as its collective identity.

Memphis, the place, has been shaped by its history of cultural and economic innovation, political conflict, public policy decisions, class and racial tensions, migration patterns, and geographic location. This detailed case study of Memphis combines theories of globalization and place with a bit of sociological imagination to capture the complexities of one resilient city and to develop a better understanding of cities as sites of cultural continuity and disruption as well as nodes of global economic activity. This book shows not only how a study of a particular urban place and an understanding of the people who live there can enrich studies of globalization, but also how studies of the South benefit from analysis of global processes.

Five goals guide the project. First, the concept of place is brought into the foreground of discussions of global processes, local practices, and urban spaces. Place is recognized as part of an ongoing struggle for the social "production of locality" within global flows.[1] At a time when most social science research privileges the global over the local, leaving place in the background, this project reframes discussions about globalization, place, and the American South using an interdisciplinary approach. Second, the selection of a relatively understudied southern city typically considered inessential for commanding or controlling the work of globalization shows not only that place matters but, equally important, that Memphis matters. Memphis has been excluded from studies of the top tier of a global-cities hierarchy and from studies of cities deemed to be centers of "progress" in the Sunbelt region of the United States. But in a discussion of global flows and disruptions, Memphis matters. Third, this project uses a narrative case-study analysis as the best means of showing how "one place comprehended can make us understand other places better."[2] It reveals the complexity of global-local processes as being much more than binary opposites and shows how the South is positioned as an integrated part of those processes rather than as a national or regional exception. The fourth goal of this project is to call empathetic attention to place and the people whose lives have made a difference in Memphis, especially those who have been devalued as "people of little substance."[3] For two hundred years, generations of black and white rural migrants and their descendants, part of migratory flows, have produced a wealth of local, place-specific resources as well as tensions and conflicts in Memphis. Described by Richard Wright as the most "unprepared people [who] wanted to go to the city,"[4] the people of Memphis and their contributions have a history of being misunderstood and underestimated. Fifth, the project is organized to tell a story with narrative power and human interest by conducting an in-depth, holistic, historical-sociological investigation of a particular place in a global context. The literary-narrative case-study approach utilizes a theoretically informed generalized approach to understand place and uses particular details about place as a means to inform theory.

More than fifty years ago southern writer and activist Lillian Smith wrote: "There are few spots on the globe as interesting as the South; and perhaps none so rich in startlingly poignant paradoxes. . . . The time has come . . . to see the region in perspective."[5] Smith's words seem as appropriate now as they were more than half a century ago due to persistent interest in the South and new questions about the meaning of "place" in a global world. To paraphrase Smith, we could say that few places in the South are as interesting as Memphis or as rich in paradoxes. The time has come to see the city in perspective.

At first glance, any southern city may seem an odd choice to study a dynamic urban place. The South is the least urbanized region of the United States. Few scholars recognize southern cities as real "American" cities, much less as global players.[6] Indeed, fifty years ago, regional sociologist Rupert Vance categorized all southern cities as "unremarkable." More recently, scholars have identified a few remarkable southern cities transformed by intensive global flows of capital and people, for example, Miami and Houston. Interestingly, these particular cities have been described as globally significant but not very southern, or perhaps not even "places." Portes and Stepick attribute Miami's transformation to global forces, including decades of Latino immigration and U.S. foreign policy toward Cuba.[7] Feagin's study of Houston in the 1980s shows a city transformed by global capital. He describes it as "more than a place in urban space; it had become a symbol in a resurgent free enterprise ideology."[8]

Memphis is uniquely positioned in global flows of trade and commerce. The city serves the Mid-South region, the nation, and the world as a vital link to the global economy. The first event in the production of locality (at least from a nineteenth-century American perspective) involved the use of organized federal and state power by an expanding United States, enabling the state of Tennessee to acquire land from the Chickasaws, who had controlled the bluffs for ten thousand years. The Chickasaws, after defending the site from various French, Spanish, and English soldiers and explorers who had made claims on it since Hernando de Soto's mid-sixteenth-century visit, accepted a $300,000 payment and withdrew from West Tennessee into Mississippi. In 1819, one year after the Chickasaw Cession, Andrew Jackson, James Winchester, and John Overton founded the city of Memphis on five thousand acres they had purchased in the 1790s. The founders intended to develop the city's commercial and residential prospects, but their expectations for the production of locality were rife with contradictions. They founded the city to expedite commercial flows and to secure a physical boundary on the edge of the United States and the western frontier for maintaining control of the Mississippi Valley. At the same time, however, they reserved land along the riverfront for use as a "public promenade," recognizing the allocation of public space as an important part of place building. They expected this new locality to serve as an entrepôt for unencumbered flows of imports and exports and as a welcoming residential settlement for English-speaking migrants from other states as well as European immigrants. Within a few years the city also became a center for trading enslaved African American laborers to work nearby cotton plantations in Arkansas, Mississippi, and Tennessee.[9]

From its early-nineteenth-century settlement, Memphis acted as a center for the production, processing, and distribution of cotton and agricultural products traded in world markets. Midway between New Orleans and St. Louis, the city supplied thousands of towns and plantations in a multistate delta region, including the Mississippi Delta, the Arkansas Delta, the Louisiana Delta, the Missouri Bootheel, and western Tennessee. As an international center of cotton production and trade, Memphis became the home of the largest cotton warehouses in the world, the largest inland cotton market in the world, the largest producer of cottonseed products in the world, the largest hardwood market in the United States, and the nation's second-largest pharmaceutical market and third-largest grocery market.[10]

Governed by commercial elites who wanted to profit from the area's strategic geographical location on the bluffs of the Mississippi River and proximity to an abundance of natural resources, the city has continued to invest in its transportation infrastructure for nearly two hundred years. As global trade has intensified, the Memphis location and its transportation infrastructure have become increasingly advantageous. Today, Memphis operates the busiest cargo airport in the world. It serves as the international headquarters of Federal Express and operates as its primary distribution hub in the United States. Because substantial agglomerations of distribution and logistics activities have been drawn to the area, the city aptly describes itself as "North America's Distribution Center." Memphis occupies a crucial position in future North American trade because of the city's transportation infrastructure and its central location between Monterrey, Mexico, and Toronto, Canada. Proposed highway construction for the NAFTA corridor now routes 1-69 through metropolitan Memphis.

Memphis, uniquely situated in global economic and cultural flows, has experienced severe disruptions in the production of locality that distinguish it from other cities. The story of yellow fever epidemics provides an excellent example. Most southern cities trace economic devastation and social upheavals to the Civil War—an event involving one riverfront battle that disturbed the flow of commerce in Memphis for just one day. But yellow fever was more deadly and disruptive in Memphis than the Civil War, and this disruption provides an additional rationale for the selection of Memphis as a case study.

The yellow fever epidemics that swept southern cities in the 1870s can be seen as a product of the dynamic tension between globalization and place and as a disruption in the production of locality. Scientists now understand that global weather patterns in 1878—an El Niño—created tropical conditions in the American South. Records indicate that the region experienced unusually warm temperatures, a long summer "season," and rainfall at 150 percent above normal levels. Global flows of immigrants had brought many Europeans to the United States (and to Memphis) after the Civil War. These white Europeans especially lacked autoimmunity to the virus. Global trade meant that cargo ships loaded with ivory, copper, and other African imports, as well as the hidden cargo of mosquitoes and their eggs, carried infected passengers and insects to many port cities, including Memphis. But the combination of deplorable *local* sanitation with these unusual environmental conditions produced more human deaths and economic devastation in Memphis than any other American city and dramatically changed migration flows.[11]

Prior to the yellow fever epidemics, post–Civil War Memphis displayed remarkable resilience and growth. Although city leaders had supported secession and the Confederacy, the city surrendered without a fight after a brief river battle on 6 June 1862. Commercial trade, including contraband with the Confederacy, resumed almost immediately. One historian noted that "few Southern towns suffered as little from the four years of the war as did Memphis."[12]

After the war, Memphis recovered more quickly than most southern cities and displayed rapid and promising growth despite physical and economic devastation in surrounding rural areas of Arkansas, Mississippi, and Tennessee. The city's population nearly doubled between 1860 and 1870, increasing from 22,623 to 40,226. In 1870, the Memphis population was twice that of Atlanta's population of 21,789 and nearly double Nashville's population of 25,865 inhabitants.[13] With prospects for sustained economic and population growth, the city was poised to become a prominent commercial center of the "New South." But prospects changed when yellow fever moved up the Mississippi River from New Orleans. In three epidemics—1873, 1878, and 1879—more than 7,000 people died, an additional 19,000 or more suffered nonfatal attacks of the illness, and more than half the population fled, at least until the crisis abated. In a reversal of Civil War outcomes, no southern city suffered as much from yellow fever as Memphis.[14]

The racial composition of Memphis also changed dramatically. When Memphis fell to Union forces in 1862, the city became a destination for a large migration stream of African Americans from rural Mississippi, Arkansas, and Tennessee. Whereas blacks had comprised only 17 percent of the city's population in 1860, by 1870, they comprised more than one-third of the population. With the arrival of each yellow fever epidemic, affluent white citizens were most likely to leave the city because they had the resources to do so. All remaining residents faced potentially fatal health risks. Historians have expressed differences of opinion regarding whether whites were more vulnerable to contracting the disease and more likely to die from it.[15] But by 1878, as a result of higher rates of white out-migration and high death rates, blacks comprised a two-thirds majority of the 20,000 people who remained in the city. Consequently, black residents played essential roles in caring for the sick, burying the dead, and serving civil society as members of the police force and city council.[16] Throughout the 1870s, African Americans allied with ethnic residents—primarily Irish Catholics—in local politics. When the epidemics subsided and affluent residents returned to the city, blacks became scapegoats for the city's escalating debt. Returning residents led a movement for municipal reform to regain political control and repudiate debt by establishing a commission government and revoking the city's charter. Memphis was not the only city to create a commission government in response to crisis, but in January 1879, after petitioning the Tennessee legislature, Memphis became the only American city to surrender its charter and actually lose its name. Officially and legally, the city on the bluffs became identified as the Taxing District of Shelby County, Tennessee. The commissioners who governed the district kept taxes low and underfunded most public services, including public education. The name Memphis was restored in 1891, and home rule was restored in 1893, ending commission government. During this time, however, local elections changed from a ward political system to citywide elections. These actions concentrated power in the hands of upper-class white males and limited the influence of African American and minority voters for decades to follow.[17]

During commission government, and in the aftermath of yellow fever epidemics, the city lost momentum for "New South" development, the human and capital resources needed to sustain it, and the confidence of outside investors. One writer noted that "a great city which escaped the rolling thunder of the Civil War's guns practically unscathed was brought to its knees by a mosquito."[18] Meanwhile, as Memphis struggled to recover from a $100 million economic setback, loss of population, and disruption of urban life, Atlanta surpassed Memphis to lead the region in population growth and economic recovery and secured its status as the capital city of the New South.[19] And Nashville surpassed Memphis as the largest city in Tennessee. A January 1879 statement in the *Nashville American* read: "Then there will be no such place as Memphis, for she will be numbered among the things that were like the ancient metropolis from which she took her name. People will speak of her as the settlement on the Chickasaw Bluffs, or something of that sort, and Nashville will be the biggest city in Tennessee."[20]

When Memphis found itself suffering from a third yellow fever epidemic in 1879, city commissioners appealed to the National Board of Health for advice and financial assistance. Although scientists had not yet identified the precise cause of yellow fever as a mosquito-borne virus, public health officials associated recurrent epidemics with filthy local conditions and urged public sanitation measures to combat disease. The National Board surveyed Memphis and recommended installing a modern sewer system, a proper drainage system, paved streets, and a safe public water system. With financial assistance from the state of Tennessee, the city completed sanitation improvements by 1880. Artesian water was discovered and drilled successfully in 1887. With the expansion of artesian water supplies for residential and commercial use and successful implementation of scientifically managed public hygiene, Memphis dramatically improved health conditions and infrastructure needed for recovery and redevelopment.[21]

The rest of the country noted improved health and sanitation in Memphis, but negative attitudes about Memphis from outsiders lingered.[22] Because local officials did little to clean up the city before the National Board survey, some newspaper writers outside the region assumed that people in Memphis, and most southerners, lacked the knowledge and ambition to help themselves. Actually, a lack of capital more than a lack of knowledge or resolve stymied Memphis officials. But perceptions of local indifference and dependence on outside intervention angered many outside the region who attributed local inaction to ignorance or laziness rather than poverty.[23] One New England journalist viewed the recurrence of yellow fever epidemics in Memphis as the continuation of a long history of evils in the South. The *Boston Commonwealth* published these comments on 26 July 1879:

> A large sum of money was raised last year [1878] in the North for the relief of this city, but very little came from Southern communities. With all the warning that was given by the fever then, nothing has since been done in the way of drainage or purification. The fact is, Memphis is one of the filthiest towns in all the South, the garbage being thrown into the streets and allowed to fester and rot with all its disease-distributing influences. The yellow-fever scourge is one of the evils that follow in the train of slavery and an imperfect civilization. The worst feature of the sorrow is that the native inhabitants have no ambition to remove the cause, no heart to stand by and care for the sufferers, and no disposition to put their hands in their pockets for the relief of the poor.[24]

Designated the unhealthiest city in the nation, harshly criticized by the New York financial community for "scandalous acts of dishonesty" related to debt repudiation when the city surrendered its municipal charter in 1879, and criticized for indifference to debt and disease, Memphis suffered from a discredited and stigmatized identity.[25] When commission government ended, newly empowered city officials eager to proceed with the production of locality recognized that a spoiled identity would interfere with efforts "to attract commerce and capital to the newly purified, self-consciously progressive city."[26] They also feared that the continuing in-migration of a rural underclass, black and white, and the ratio of black to white residents would hamper redevelopment efforts.

The effects of the yellow fever disruption continued to plague the city after white elites returned to Memphis to reassert themselves—physically and ideologically—into the production of locality. As mentioned above, they regained control first by forfeiting the city charter and then by repudiating city debts. After regaining the city charter and improving local health and sanitation conditions, they established a distinctive urban park and parkway system to reposition the city within global flows of commerce and culture as a salubrious southern place deserving of national prominence. But place making after the disruption of yellow fever not only emphasized the importance of a healthy environment, beautiful landscapes, and public spaces but also involved reimposing racial segregation and institutionalizing a racial ideology that dramatically affected the production of locality for the next century and produced unintended disruptive effects.

PLACE AND THE SOCIOLOGICAL IMAGINATION

> Place absorbs our earliest notice and attention, it bestows upon us our original awareness; and our critical powers spring up from the study of it and the growth experiences inside it. . . . One place comprehended can make us understand other places better. Sense of place gives us equilibrium; extended, it is sense of direction too.—EUDORA WELTY, *The Eye of the Story*

Place matters. Writers, poets, historians, and musicians have recognized the salience of "place" for some time.[27] But despite its importance as a fundamental concept, place is often taken for granted or left in the background by social scientists.[28] In recent years, scholars from various disciplines have acknowledged that space and place "matter" more than was once thought, and perhaps in different ways.[29] One sociologist suggests that place "is not a setting or a background but an agentic player in the game—a force with detectable and independent effects on social life."[30] Others recognize that place gives shape and boundary to social inequalities, culture, personal identity, family history, economic development, and social change. And place affects our quality of life, "our access to jobs and public services (especially education), our access to shopping and culture, our level of personal security, the availability of medical services, and even the air we breathe."[31] Place also affects our location on the digital divide and whether we have access to global digital networks. In other words, "place mediates social life" and contributes to our understanding of global processes, social practices, and historical change.[32]

Typical globalization studies not only overlook less "essential" places but also ignore the impact of local places and local cultures on globalization processes. Countertheories of *localization* note the resilience of local culture, despite globalization. They explain how "the local resists, absorbs, and ultimately transforms the global" and trace the emergence of new localisms within global flows.[33] But many studies view localization as problematic because of its association with reactionary nationalisms, competitive localisms, ethnic cleansing, and obsessions with "heritage."[34] And, as is the case with globalization, localization perspectives typically view the global-local nexus as *oppositional*. Place itself is caught in the crossfire. Both perspectives treat place more as a bystander than as an agentic player in social life.

Place has been treated differently in scholarly discussions of "southern exceptionalism," which identify an entire region, for example, the U.S. South, as a unique American place. This perspective, as defined by C. Vann Woodward and others, characterizes the South as a distinctive region of the United States defined by military defeat, occupation, reconstruction, poverty, and the "burden" of history.[35] Southern distinctiveness is often explained by regional comparisons between southern and nonsouthern states, which show how one region is becoming more like the other. Other studies make historical comparisons of life in the contemporary New South and life in the Old South.[36] Political scientists describe a "solid South" when explaining regional realignment from Democratic to Republican.[37] Sociological studies of the "enduring South" explain the persistence of regional identity.[38] Historians and sociologists categorize some "places" as more southern than others using a variety of qualitative and quantitative measures.[39] All of these studies view the South as a *distinctive* place or exceptional region, despite the effects of globalization processes.

The southern-exceptionalism perspective is based on three assumptions that allow scholars to emphasize "internal" factors within a national context to explain regional distinctiveness. But these assumptions impede developing a global / local framework for understanding *place* in the urban South. First, they assume the South is inherently different from the rest of the United States and a bit out of step with the "modern" world due to "internal" historical and cultural factors that isolated the region.[40] If southern cities are different, it is because the South is different.[41] Second, they assume this distinctive place, shaped by historical internal factors, includes two homogeneous cultures—one white, one black.[42] Third, they assume that the preferred unit of analysis for examining place is the *region*—composed by states defined as southern by various criteria, often beginning with membership in the Confederacy—or the *subregion*, for example, the Delta, Appalachia, the Sunbelt, the Black Belt, or the Bible Belt, and not the *city*. In fact, the city is treated as antithetical to *place*, which is presumed to be rooted in the rural South.[43] Some observers employ the exceptionalism perspective to call attention to positive aspects of the region and view the South as an *imagined community*—a place that commands emotional legitimacy and stirs nostalgic longings.[44] Reed views the South not only as a place but also as a *province*. Citing Josiah Royce's definition of a province, he describes the South as "part of a national domain which is, geographically and socially, sufficiently unified to have a true consciousness of its own unity, to feel a pride in its own ideals and customs, and to possess a sense of its distinction from other parts of the country."[45] But for many observers, the southern-exceptionalism perspective emphasizes negative or problematic aspects of the South. Descriptions of persistent poverty, ignorance, violence, racism, insularity, disease, and "enclaves of backwardness"[46] pervade scholarly work and feed popular stereotypes. Television shows and films such as *The Beverly Hillbillies* and *The Dukes of Hazard* portray the foibles and eccentricities associated with babes, bumpkins, bubbas, buffoons, and backwardness. But many scholarly discussions of the prevalence of poverty, infant mortality, health care, racism, and other problems associated with southern states tend to reinforce widely held regional stereotypes. Hence, southern exceptionalism also calls attention to the South as a problem-ridden place, an American "other," and a regional suspect.[47] In either case, whether southern exceptionalism is viewed as a positive or problematic condition, it is a phenomenon attributed to so-called internal factors and usually associated with narratives of regional decline or progress. If globalization comes into play, it can be seen as a threat to southern distinctiveness. Consequently, the concept of globalization can be used to support narratives of progress or decline. With global transformations, the South becomes less distinctive (southern) or more cosmopolitan (nonsouthern) but is still an American "other."

The exceptionalism perspective does not adequately address the present analysis of globalization, place, and Memphis. First, its focus on internal factors neglects external institutions and processes, namely, those associated with global capitalism and inequality.[48] Second, the assumption of homogeneity ignores significant class, ethnic, gender, and racial dimensions of place, as well as contested meanings and identities. Subsequently, the exceptionalism perspective lacks a critical examination of "whiteness," ignores *global* processes of racial formation, and fails to explore the rearticulation of racial identity in specific places.[49] Third, it has little to say about cities, except those found in the "Sunbelt" South, usually deemed to be more "progressive" and less southern.

Challenges to the exceptionalism perspective look at the impact of external global processes on the South. Alternate investigations of the eighteenth, nineteenth, and twentieth centuries explain the regional impact of the South's incorporation into the capitalist world system through processes of colonialism and underdevelopment.[50] Looking at the developed world, these scholars argue that external global economic demands, not internal economic processes, fostered the plantation slave-labor system and its successors in sharecropping and tenancy and led to the region's subsequent concentration of low-wage peripheral industries. Wallerstein views the concept of the Old South as a useful mental construct brought into existence "only a short time before it was historically eliminated as a material construct."[51] Studies of uneven development tend to treat the Old South as a material construct and assert that "each developed country has created its own underdeveloped country within its own borders," drawing comparisons between the South and other underdeveloped regions.[52] Similarly, recent studies of the twenty-first-century South situate the region or specific southern communities— rural and urban—within global flows of wealth, information, and immigration to explain the regional impact of globalization and the transformation of local communities.[53] One scholar uses the term "grounded globalism" to demonstrate how regional, national, and global identities are being reconfigured and enhanced, thereby emancipating the South from burdens of the past.[54] A somewhat different approach to globalization—postcolonial studies —"looks away" from the developed world to view the South as a *space* in the southern hemisphere. This approach views the South in relation to Latin America and the Caribbean yet recognizes its distinctiveness. From this perspective, the South occupies "a space simultaneously (or alternately) center and margin, victor and defeated, empire and colony, essentialist and hybrid, northern and southern (both in a global sense)."[55] Each of these alternate approaches frees the discussion from assumptions made by the southern-exceptionalism perspective and suggests potential for developing a richer understanding of the South within a global context.

This project takes another step toward understanding globalization, the South, and place by using "the sociological imagination" to shift perspectives.[56] To define place as an agentic player, and not as a bystander or marginalized "other," it is possible to examine dynamic tensions between the global and the local in a specific urban location. We can think of "place" as uniquely situated in networks of *global* relations and cultural flows, as well as embedded in accumulated *local* history and culture. Hence, place mediates the impact of global and local processes. The characteristics of place include geographic location human population, and material form, as well as networks of social relations, collections of cultural symbols and historical memories, processes of iconological identification, and interpretations of meaning and value. But place is characterized by more than geographical boundaries, material structures, and compilations of population statistics. It is not just a background for transformative local and global processes. Place is also a site of imagination, constructed through symbolic work. Place exists in the mind as well as on the land.[57]

Place "is constructed out of particular interactions and mutual articulations of social relations, social processes, experiences and understandings" that integrate the global and the local in positive and negative ways.[58] Dynamic tensions between local features of place and global processes create new and sometimes unexpected place-specific resources that may appear as paradoxes. These paradoxes of place confound predictions that globalization processes produce uniformity or "generic" outcomes. Instead, outcomes vary in particular places, partly due to conflicting efforts to promote the intensification of global economic processes or to mobilize resistance to them, to perpetuate or challenge the power of the status quo, and to fuel racial conflict or collaboration. Indeed, conflicts and contradictions regarding the value and use of place-specific resources further contribute to the uniqueness of place.[59] Place is a repository of distinctive resources, "a privileged locus of culture," and a crucible of cultural and economic interactions.[60] Many cultural, social, political, and symbolic resources are place specific and cannot be digitized or duplicated in any other location, despite efforts to simulate places for mass consumption.[61] Whereas most theories of globalization predict the liberation of "social relations from local contexts of interaction"[62] by weakening local culture, in fact, the opposite sometimes occurs. Indeed, place-specific cultural and economic distinctiveness endures and persists in part because of global processes, not in spite of them. For example, cosmopolitan newcomers who acquire knowledge about local cultural and symbolic resources and adopt cultural practices, especially those associated with literature, music, and the arts, help reproduce local culture and perpetuate place distinctiveness.[63] Alliances between newcomers and "old-timers" may operate to preserve "authentic" local communities, cultures, practices, and places.[64] Moreover, newcomer participation in local rituals, embedded in social hierarchies and regulated by traditional boundary-maintenance activities, actually intensifies local contexts of interaction, sustains place-based class identities, reproduces upper-class privilege, and links local elites to transnational networks. These rituals not only help socialize the next generation for maintaining distinctions of wealth and power but also reproduce place distinctiveness.

Global flows of trade, communication, culture, and human migration have captured the attention of twenty-first-century scholars and observers. Explanations of global phenomena, such as the "flattening" of the world, the emergence of global cities, and the growth of capitalism in "Communist" China, pervade mass media and scholarly interpretations of rapidly accelerating social and economic change.[65] Theorists who focus their attention on the impact of globalization processes on cities typically emphasize the role of cities as centers of command and control, vital nodes of economic activity, interconnected points on digital networks of communication, or peripheral links to the global economy. They view the global era as an "epoch of simultaneity . . . of juxtaposition."[66] Consequently, within these transformative global processes, the annihilation or demise of place distinctiveness is considered part of the postmodern condition.[67]

Not surprisingly, the pervasive influence of theories of space-time compression and global connectivity means that social science research tends to focus more toward digitized financial and communication processes and away from studies of place and locality. Insistence that globalization's "eradication of space through the domestication of time" has "eroded the constraints" of local social and cultural arrangements privileges the scale of the global for understanding dynamic processes and downplays local places, treating them as spaces of stasis.[68] Similarly, studies of global cities tend to focus on the top tier of a global-cities economic and political hierarchy.

Abstract portrayals of cities as economic sites located in advantaged or disadvantaged regions of the world and poised for competition vis-à-vis each other within global flows tend to obscure the importance of cities as places that anchor human lives, histories, and relations. But some social scientists insist that social life—past, present, and future—cannot be comprehended "without understanding the arrangements of particular social actors in particular social times and places."[69] Assessments of the impact of globalization, as experienced by social actors in particular times and places, suggest that "flows" bring continuities and disruptions into social life, as well as economic specialization and cultural diversity.[70] Some suggest that as globalization processes intensify, human beings and their social relations experience more forceful disruptions and dislocations and respond to them.[71] Under disruptive circumstances, it seems possible that "place" could become more distinctive in particular time periods and more significant. Yet much of the discussion of global flows suggests that places are becoming more alike and less meaningful. Prominent theories of globalization fail to explain how "place"—materially and symbolically—anchors human life experiences within these flows and disruptions. Questions about the complexities of globalization and place call for further analysis of qualities of "place" that render it coherent, cumulative, distinctive, resilient, meaningful, and significant.[72]

GLOBAL FLOWS, PLACE, TIME, AND DISRUPTIONS

Concerned about the persistence of place within global flows, Appadurai recognizes the ongoing "production of locality" as an essential part of urban life.[73] Within global flows, locality (or place) can be seen as a social achievement maintained in opposition to various odds. Physical action, consciousness, and the assertion of organized power over settings are necessary for the ongoing task of producing locality against the odds. These actions start with the physical origins of locality, or place, and continue with efforts to maintain its material and symbolic existence. Consequently, global flows and disruptions can be seen as affecting ongoing human struggles to sustain the production of locality.

Disruptions are integral components of global flows and part of human lives and histories. Studies of diverse world cultures reveal oral and literary accounts of wars, epidemics, plagues, diasporas, droughts, and economic depressions, as well as catastrophic events such as hurricanes, floods, fires, earthquakes, tornadoes, and volcanic eruptions. All these occurrences constitute disruptions in the physical production of locality as well as economic and cultural activity. Disruptions affect conscious efforts to "invent culture, reflect on it, experiment with it, remember it (or structure it in some other way), debate it, and pass it on."[74] Disruptions also affect distributions of human and natural resources, threatening the sustainability of localities.

Whereas Appadurai focuses on connections between locality building and flows, Hannerz draws attention to the relation between flows and time.[75] He suggests that at specific times particular cities stand out within the context of global flows, and he concentrates on their unique cultural contributions, which he describes as the social organization of cultural meaning. Similarly, Hall identifies particular cities that emerge as cultural centers in periods of time he considers *belles époques*.[76] Interestingly, both Hannerz and Hall identify the 1950s as a significant time, each selecting an American city as a significant place of culture during that time with Hannerz selecting San Francisco, California, and Hall choosing Memphis, Tennessee. The two cities share certain similarities but display significant differences.

Hall reminds us that "no one kind of city, nor any one size of city, has a monopoly on creativity or the good life."[77] Nor does any city have a monopoly on cultural contributions. Throughout history a number of cities have emerged as sites of cultural creativity and innovation. For Hall, "places that ignited the sacred flame of the human intelligence and the human imagination"[78] include the Athens of Pericles and Socrates, the Vienna of Beethoven and Freud, the London of Shakespeare, and quite incongruously, the Memphis of Elvis Presley and Robert Johnson. Hall identifies Memphis in the 1950s as the only "place" in the South "before the civil liberties movement transformed the region" where black and white folk traditions—African American blues and white country music—could meld to produce rock and roll.[79] Hannerz identifies San Francisco as the center of an urban "Beat" culture in the 1950s, which became a center of flower power, acid rock, and student rebellion in the late 1960s and later became "the site of the greatest elaboration of gay culture."[80] Hannerz identifies the major figures in the "Beat" era as literary figures such as Jack Kerouac and Allen Ginsberg. Hall identifies the major figures who defined the rock and roll era as musical performers, including Elvis Presley.

In Memphis, the time period of the 1950s is significant, not only because of the flow of changing racial and economic circumstances (nationally and regionally), but also because of local class distinctions. San Francisco's Beat culture, as well as the hippie culture that followed, was produced by culturally sophisticated urban elites who intellectualized about alienation and anomie. Memphis's musical culture—blues, country, rock and roll—came from a rural-minded people who sang about alienation and anomie from the perspective of impoverished and poorly educated agricultural workers, schooled in an oral tradition. From a perspective of global flows, both the Beat / hippie / gay San Francisco culture and the blues / rock / soul Memphis culture made an impact during a time when many young people were experiencing alienation associated with post–World War II industrialization and the rise of the United States as a global power. But Memphis gave voice to a disadvantaged rural class whose cultural expressions were rooted in *oral* tradition, whereas San Francisco gave voice to a privileged urban class whose cultural expressions were rooted in *literary* tradition. Both cities and cultures stand out with regard to their contributions to the organization and expression of social meaning. But class, race, and regional differences influenced the local expression of these social meanings, as well as their contributions to global culture.

The fusion of blues, gospel, and country music in Memphis became rock and roll; hence, Memphis music, created by a rural underclass, transformed popular culture throughout the world. Its legacy attracts international attention to the city and inspires new generations of cultural innovators. In today's digitized flows when, "by definition, most of popular culture is disposable . . . Memphis music has refused to disappear."[81] Memphis, the place, has also refused to disappear despite a history of disruptions in the production of locality.

MEMPHIS MATTERS

No city has had more of an impact on modern culture.

—ROBERT GORDON, *It Came from Memphis*

It has been said that no city has left a greater *global* impact on modern culture.[82] Perhaps it is also true that no city has gone to such extremes to rebuff its history and discount its legacy of rural traditions and "low-down culture." Decimated by yellow fever in the 1870s and repopulated by rural migrants, Memphis often has been described as provincial. Historian Gerald Capers observed that in 1900, "Memphis presented a strange paradox—a city modern in physical aspect but rural in background, rural in prejudice, and rural in habit."[83] In the 1920s, journalist H. L. Mencken described Memphis as "the most rural-minded city in the South."[84] For most of the city's history, "men of substance"[85]—Memphis commercial and civic elites, including founders, landowners, cotton factors, and citizens who share their values—have discounted the civic and cultural contributions of rural migrants. Making unfavorable comparisons with those considered "people of little substance" enabled elites and "people of substance" to define "respectability" in a raucous riverboat town. Treating "others" as objects of surveillance and control helped elites secure their own status, shape their own identities, and maintain social order. But marginalized people, primarily black and white rural migrants and their descendants, have brought their own dreams and "visions of plenty"[86] to Memphis. These "people of little substance" are the men and women who tended the sick and buried the dead during the yellow fever crises, plowed cotton fields with mules and then tractors, picked cotton in eleven-foot sacks, loaded commodities on steamboats and trains, milled lumber, made tires and tractors, picked up the city's garbage, and sang the blues. Historically, and presently, they have come to Memphis to seek opportunity, forge new identities, and rise in status. Consequently, Memphis, the "inland river city where cultures, rich and poor, black and white, urban and rural, Northern and Southern, did not so much converge as collide," became a site of conflict that produced a wealth of local cultural and economic resources.[87]

Tensions between "people of little substance"—those who have endured low wages, undesirable labor, spatial separation, and surveillance—and "people of substance" have produced ambivalence and antagonism, as well as cultural innovation and political change. Local misunderstandings about these conflicts, and the value of cultural innovations, have left their mark on community relations as well as on the urban landscape. At certain historical periods, the city demolished key sites associated with cultural and social change as if it could remove the people, "sterilize the very soil"[88] that nurtured them, and make them disappear from public memory. At other times, the city worked to preserve those sites. Today, the Beale Street Historic District (1966), Sun Records (2003), and Graceland (2006) appear on the Department of the Interior's list of national historic landmarks. The newly built Stax Museum and Stax Music Academy stand on the site of the destroyed Stax Records. And a newly emerging entertainment industry welcomes visitors to the "home of the blues" and the "birthplace of rock and roll." But many mainstream Memphians—white and black, past and present—have had difficulty admitting or accepting that marginalized cultural outsiders—"people of little substance"—have left lasting cultural contributions to the city and the world.

This research shows Memphis, the largest city in the Mississippi Delta / Mid-South region, as much more than a designated cultural, historical, and economic crossroads on a southern map of regional exceptionalism or a digitized point on a global network. Memphis is a *place* defined not only by its geographic location and material form, but also by networks of social relations, collections of cultural symbols and historical memories, and investment with cultural meaning and value. Because Memphis occupies a prominent place in the global economy and kindles the artistic and political imaginations of people throughout the world, it offers a rich source for conducting case-study research on the processes of globalization, localization, and place.

RESEARCH MATTERS

> Whether or not the South needs more sociologists, I suspect sociology
> needs more Southerners, real ones or spiritual ones—not to take over, not to turn
> sociology away from universalism, but to divide the labor within our discipline, to tell
> sociological stories about particular people, particular groups, particular societies. And
> interesting stories they could be.—JOHN SHELTON REED, *One South*

This study uses a narrative, historical-sociological, case-study approach to investigate Memphis, globalization, and place. Its eclectic approach combines sociological theory, literary narrative, "thick description" of a specific case, and "new historical sociology" to create an alternative to the variables-oriented paradigm that now dominates social science research and is often criticized for losing touch with real people in real places.[89] This approach is intended, in part, as a response to John Shelton Reed's challenge to "place more value on descriptive interpretive, story-telling sociological work, for reasons both intellectual and (broadly speaking) political."[90] It honors the practice established by Howard Odum, and continued by Reed, of producing work with "narrative power and human interest."[91] Because this book is written by a southern woman (a native North Carolinian with deep family roots in the rural South) about a southern place, it may confirm Reed's suspicion that there is something "southern" about this way of doing sociology.[92] Also, it may counter various "grand narratives of globalization" that may imply that the South and southerners are disappearing, as well as "petite narratives" of particularistic and local resistance to globalization and universalism.[93] Written as a descriptive, interpretive, and narrative work of sociology, it is an in-depth, holistic, historical-sociological investigation of a particular place in a global context.

This approach also owes a debt to a very different sociologist who wrote about the South. W. E. B. Du Bois, in *The Souls of Black Folk*, published in 1903, identified the "problem of the color line" as the problem of the twentieth century. His words still resonate and inform twenty-first-century research. But in *Souls* Du Bois also writes a literary narrative about the lives of rural, southern African Americans and his own young adult years as a student at Fisk and a teacher in middle Tennessee. At the beginning of *Souls* Du Bois asks a question that is both rhetorical and sociological: "How does it feel to be a problem?" He answers the question from his own experience as an African American man who has lived and worked in the South and from the perspective of a sociologist who finds answers from quantitative analysis to be lacking. His literary-narrative approach reveals the richness of life and culture "beneath the veil" to demonstrate how members of a "poor peasant class," through gifts of story, song, and spirit, are interwoven with the woof and warp of America. And, in his empathetic narrative approach, Du Bois reframes the discussion of African American culture.

As stated above, this project aims to reframe scholarly considerations of cities, globalization, and the South. But this book also attempts to reframe scholarly discussions of Memphis. Much prior scholarship depicts the city as a source of problems and a setting for dramatic social crises, usually associated with racial conflict. Lynette Boney Wrenn's *Crisis and Commission Government in Memphis* depicts the city's problems associated with insolvency, yellow fever, and governance by white elites at the end of the nineteenth century. Other books examine twentieth-century problems. Keith Wailoo's *Dying in the City of the Blues* reveals the politics of race and health in the discovery and treatment of sickle cell anemia. Michael Honey's *Southern Labor and Black Civil Rights* studies interracial union-organizing in Memphis. Roger Biles examines machine politics during the Crump political era in *Memphis during the Great Depression*. Joan Beifuss chronicles the 1968 Sanitation Workers' Strike and the assassination of Martin Luther King Jr. in *At the River I Stand*. Cowie critiques the failures of industrial recruitment and the racial division of labor in one chapter about Memphis in *Capital Moves: RCA's Seventy-Year Quest for Cheap Labor*. Richard Moe and Carter Wilkie condemn Memphis urban renewal and downtown demolition in chapter 3 of *Changing Places: Rebuilding Community in the Age of Sprawl*. These studies contribute to our understanding of Memphis and problems the city faced at particular times in history. But the focus on problems limits our understanding of Memphis as a dynamic urban place, or agentic player, embedded in accumulated local history and intertwined in global processes.

NARRATIVE AND HISTORICAL SOCIOLOGY:
A SPACE FOR THE CASE STUDY

This study relies on a literary-narrative case-study method to tell a story about Memphis. The case-study approach, integral to classical social science research and appropriate for this project, differs from the methods that dominate contemporary social science research. At one time, case-study methods were taken for granted in conducting social science research; but today, they are used less frequently. Most research designs use logical-deductive methods modeled after natural sciences and widely considered to be more "scientific." However, proponents of case-study methods continue to point out their value for providing detail and historical context and informing theory in social science research.[94] A few prominent and award-winning case studies of cities and communities have made noteworthy scientific contributions. These include Kai Erikson, *Everything in Its Path: A Destruction of Community in the Buffalo Creek Flood* (1976); Anthony Orum, *Power, Money, and the People: The Making of Modern Austin* (1987); Joe Feagin, *Free Enterprise City: Houston in Political-Economic Perspective* (1988); and Alejandro Portes and Alex Stepick, *City on the Edge: The Transformation of Miami* (1993). Also, two classic studies of race and class in Indianola, Mississippi, conducted in the 1930s, have made lasting contributions to the study of the South. Sociologist John Dollard's *Caste and Class in a Southern Town* and anthropologist Hortense Powdermaker's *After Freedom: A Cultural Study in the Deep South* have had consequences for generations of scholars, policymakers, and critics.[95]

Case studies use information from a number of sources and over a period of time to produce a more holistic, or in-depth, study of complex social networks, processes, and meanings.[96] Whether case studies are used to study people in their own natural settings or to study the actual setting, or place, the best ones "deal with the reality behind appearances, with contradictions and the dialectical nature of social life, as well as with a whole that is more than the sum of its parts."[97]

The urban case study has been described as a "confrontation with complexity" because it "seeks to grasp the characteristics of all major institutions in a city, the interconnectedness among these institutions, and their links to other systems and seeks to illuminate changes in all these characteristics over time."[98] It views the city from levels ranging from individual experience to collective representation. Consequently, urban case-study research yields "fundamental sociological knowledge of human agents, communities, organizations, nation-states, empires, and civilizations" and the web of social processes that connect them.[99]

Case-study methods may be somewhat controversial, but they have been used since the early days of institutional social science research. The use of narrative in social science research is also controversial, and its connections to classical work are less obvious. But critical urban sociologists, as well as critical race theorists, use narrative to challenge dominant theoretical and methodological traditions, to create intellectual surprise, and to generate theoretical innovation.[100] Case studies use narrative in sociological research to tell a story, to give a detailed explanation about real people in real places: "The literary-narrative approach can be precise and disciplined—and at the same time graphic, readable, and imaginative. As with the novel, the narrative form permits the sociological researcher to tell a story with actors, action, and a background, even one that may possess a compelling plot. Vivid description is not the less scientific because it is descriptive."[101]

In fact, "a story can more readily provoke intellectual surprise by confronting settled ideas and paradigmatic theories."[102] The combination of narrative analysis and historical case-study research offers a means for relating specific historical events and contingent decisions to large-scale social processes and explaining how they change over time in a particular place.[103] Through the use of narrative and historical-sociological research, it is possible to explain connections between contemporary and past actions. Extensive dialogue between theoretical ideas and historical details provides a contextual analysis of place and permits further "theoretical generation and generalization."[104]

Keep in mind that it is not the "pastness" of events but the "representation" of events that makes them historically and sociologically important.[105] Consequently, "historical reality" is conceptualized not as "time-bounded snapshots" of events or explanations of cause and effect "but as stories, cascades of events."[106] The narrative explains how "complex actors encounter complex structures" producing dynamic confrontations, not stasis.[107] A focus on human agency and place, history and narrative permits us to merge the theorized description of the event with its explanation. Thinking about the social world "narratively" and "generalizing not in terms of 'causes' but in terms of narratives" adds to historical understanding and informs theory.[108]

SOURCES MATTER

I am convinced that the actual evolution of research ideas does not take
place in accord with the formal statements we read on research methods.
The ideas grow up in part out of our immersion in the data and out of the whole
process of living.—WILLIAM FOOTE WHYTE, *Street Corner Society*

Finally, it is important to note the significance of lived experience, as well as the use of archival materials and literary works, for this research. The ideas for this research came from my immersion in the richly textured life of Memphis, as well as a long-standing scholarly interest in the South. Ideas came from years of daily walks in Overton Park and conversations with Memphis residents. These ideas were reinforced by monthly visits to First Wednesdays at the Brooks Museum, Last Friday Art Trolley Tours on South Main Street, and annual visits to Memphis in May events in the spring as well as Memphis Music and Heritage activities in the fall. These ideas grew with visits to Chuccalissa, Stax, the Rock 'n' Soul Museum, the National Civil Rights Museum, Martyr's Park, the Pink Palace Museum, as well as the Center for Southern Folklore, Ballet Memphis, Beale Street, and the lobby of the Peabody Hotel. I have attended public debates over riverfront development, marched alongside students in the city parade celebrating Martin Luther King's birthday, and watched Latino / Latina immigrants gather for a rally at the Civil Rights Museum. I have listened to stories from students and neighbors, young people as well as octogenarians and nonagenarians. Their stories cover a range of topics, including cutting through the Memphis Zoo property to get back to the Southwestern campus (now Rhodes College) after venturing downtown and hearing jug bands in the 1930s; attending social events at Graceland in the 1940s—long before Elvis Presley bought the estate from the Cole family, who built and named it; visiting the zoo on "Black Thursdays" and missing school on "Black Mondays" to support the Sanitation Workers' Strike; and going to court to preserve Overton Park. I have heard personal stories about watching the King and Queen of Cotton Carnival arrive on a royal barge on the Mississippi River in the 1940s, and stories of watching tanks roll down Union Avenue in 1968. As an observer (and a surprised motorist), I have witnessed members of the Secret Order of the Boll Weevils, cloaked in green costumes and disguised by masks with long snouts, cruise through midtown Memphis in the back of a modified green school bus on their way to entertain patients at a local children's hospital or perform some other community service. Each year I read statistics on low-performing city schools in Memphis; and I have seen some of the students I teach at the University of Memphis, who come from city schools, excel and pursue graduate study at some of the leading universities in the United States.

While living and working in Memphis, I have become aware of the paradoxes of place and of the limitations of most social scientific perspectives to explain them. I have conversed with many residents who express ambivalence about the city of Memphis and a self-consciousness of their own "outsider" status in the city or the city's definition as "other" by the rest of the world.

More than one person has confessed to me, "I have a love-hate relationship with my city." Others have asked me how anyone from North Carolina could be so fascinated with Memphis and find it a desirable place to live. I have also conversed with friends and family outside of Memphis about my local discoveries, often to hear, "I had no idea that came from Memphis." Based on my own experiences, I could not help but turn to research to raise more questions about Memphis and the paradoxes of place.

Research for this book involved searching archival records stored in library collections, as well as reading literary and historical works about Memphis. Archival collections housed at the University of Memphis in the Mississippi Valley Collection, as well as in the Memphis and Shelby County Room at the Memphis and Shelby County Public Library, provided official public documents, city magazines, brochures, pamphlets, maps, newsletters, correspondence, and planning reports. Additional valuable sources came from oral histories conducted by the Memphis State University Oral History Project, as well as newspaper clippings and photographs from the morgue files of the now defunct *Memphis Press-Scimitar* and articles from the *Memphis Commercial Appeal*. Internet access to more recent documents from federal, state, and local government, as well as organizational activities of various citizen groups, and recent newspaper articles also informed this research.

Sources also include the works of four writers and one poet who have ties to Memphis—Eudora Welty, William Faulkner, Peter Taylor, Richard Wright, and Don Share. The novels of Eudora Welty, the Mississippi writer who once lived in Memphis and wrote obituaries for the *Commercial Appeal*, offer little insight into Memphis. But Welty's book *The Eye of the Story* captures important dimensions of place. Her novels, short stories, and autobiography—*One Writer's Beginning*—show how individual identities and family traditions relate to place. Another Mississippian, William Faulkner, described trips to Memphis from his fictional Yoknapatawpha County in several short stories and novels. The central place associated with Faulkner's fiction is found in northern Mississippi, but Faulkner treats Memphis as "a crucial site, almost a mythic site" in several works.[109] It is certainly the case with *The Reivers* that Faulkner depicts Memphis as "the Big City, the promised land of sin and delight."[110]

Tennessee writer Peter Taylor's Pulitzer Prize–winning novel, *A Summons to Memphis*, and his short story "The Old Forest" inform us about Memphis, identity, and place. The poetry of Don Share, a prize-winning poet and senior editor of *Poetry* magazine in Chicago (formerly curator of the Poetry Room at

Harvard University) who grew up in Memphis, expresses many tensions between Memphis past and Memphis present, much like the novels and short stories of Peter Taylor. A few pages from Richard Wright's autobiography, *Black Boy*, give the perspective of a young African American man who lived, worked, and read books in segregated Memphis in the 1920s, en route from the Mississippi Delta to Chicago. These three writers deal with the tensions of race, class, gender, identity, and place in different historical eras. Wright's experiences occur in the early twentieth century. Taylor describes Memphis in the mid-twentieth century. Share's poetry describes late-twentieth-century conflicts and experiences.

The combination of sociological imagination, archival research, literary works, and lived experience informs this account of Memphis as a dynamic urban place. As a site of creativity, innovation, imagination, and entrepreneurialism, as well as power and conflict, Memphis is a place of drama that appeals to human interest. This narrative case-study analysis of the remarkable southern city of Memphis, and the people involved in the ongoing negotiations of defining it, reveals much about the processes of globalization and the paradoxes of place.

Need sent me through unanealed wilderness · To one of the dole-fullest spots of ground
on the whole earth: Memphis. · Where the past still hurts, and gets sung about. · Where
the Mississippi flows by without anguish.— DON SHARE, "Dilemma"

2

NEITHER OLD SOUTH NOR NEW SOUTH

Memphis and the Paradoxes of Identity

Memphis lies in the far southwest corner of Tennessee on the east bank of the
Mississippi River. The city gets its name from the ancient capital of Egypt on
the Nile River and has been described as the "Metropolis of the American
Nile."[1] Egyptian-themed symbols ornament a few prominent public spaces
reminding residents of the city's namesake. The Pyramid, a 321-foot-high
pyramid-shaped stainless steel sports and concert arena, with a statue of
Ramses positioned in front, overlooks the Mississippi River, where nearby, the
M-shaped Hernando de Soto Bridge carries I-40 traffic from Tennessee to
Arkansas. At the Memphis Zoo, located in Overton Park, Egyptian hiero-
glyphics welcome visitors at the front gate. In 2006, the Tennessee city established a new relation to Ancient Egypt. Archaeologists from the Institute of
Egyptian Art and Anthropology at the University of Memphis received international attention for their discovery of a new tomb in the Valley of the Kings
in Egypt, a few feet away from Tutankhamen's Tomb.

The collective identity of Memphis, however, is not based on the discovery
of Egyptian antiquities, nor is it represented by Egyptian-themed symbolic
displays in public spaces. Instead, the city's identity is entwined with the

ongoing struggle for the social production of locality and efforts to sustain its material and symbolic existence. Periodic disruptions and changes in global flows have affected local efforts to shape place identity. As Memphis grew from a frontier outpost to a commercial center and recovered from yellow fever, tensions formed concerning Old South and New South ideas, urban and rural culture, and black and white racial differences. Nineteenth- and twentieth-century disruptions, and ensuing tensions, continue to influence twenty-first-century identities. Consequently, Memphis "has come to see itself as an amalgam of characteristically southern urban traits, where close proximity to rural culture bred innovative cultural expression and also fomented vicious racial tension, where the influences of the rural delta still mix uncomfortably with cosmopolitan ideals."[2]

This chapter shows how past disruptions and identities, self-consciousness about them, and concerns about public image give meaning and narrative coherence to Memphis as a distinctive southern place and shape place identity. Symbols of past disruptions and conflicts, installed in public spaces to shape collective identity at particular times, represent decades of investment and conscious design to reposition Memphis as a place of regional, national, and international significance. These symbols, representing "memories" of disruptions and conflicts, are embedded in race, class, and gender relations. Consequently, they exemplify "the quintessential sociological issues of power, stratification and contestation."[3] Once "memories" become objects of com-memoration and collective identity, they operate by a logic and force of their own. Subsequently, these objects limit the range of things that can be done with them by later generations.[4] Over time, they accumulate on the urban landscape, define social hierarchies, affect sociobiographical memories, shape individual identities, and evoke feelings about place. As part of the city's "community of memory," these objects capture "complex interactions between structure, agency, and contingency"[5] and contribute to the unique characteristics of place.

PLACE, SPACE, AND OBJECTS OF COMMEMORATION

Poet and Memphis native Don Share describes Memphis as one of the "dole-fullest spots of ground on the whole earth . . . where the past still hurts, and gets sung about."[6] The blues musical tradition reflects the painful past from the perspective of people at the lower end of the social hierarchy. Also, reminders of the doleful past can be found in commemorative objects installed in public spaces. These objects include statues, monuments, museums, parks, and ritual observances. Like the narratives told through poems and songs, these objects have proved to be "transmissible, cumulative, and received differently from one group to another."[7]

Placement of objects of commemoration on the Memphis landscape began at the end of the nineteenth century with designs for an urban parkway system and fund-raising for a commemorative statue to celebrate the city's recovery from the disruptions of yellow fever, debt, and commission government. Paradoxically, the city lacking Old South traditions and aristocratic pretensions, as well as New South achievements, found itself at the turn of the century being governed by white political leaders who drew on selective "memory" of a glorious southern past to bolster their authority, advance their own self-interests, and create new identities for the city and themselves.[8] Leaders hoped to establish continuity between the city's newly achieved "progressive" status and "established" southern tradition. They did so by developing a modern urban landscape and by creating symbolic public spaces to shape collective social memory.[9] These physical and symbolic changes enabled leaders to instill a sense of authority, stability, and permanence, which had been lacking since the epidemics, and to stimulate recovery from the stigma of disease and debt. Strategies to convince the nation and the world that Memphis was a clean, safe, and progressive city worthy of outside investment for future growth, and not a disease-ridden, uncivilized place burdened by an unhealthy and unsuccessful past, were necessary but not sufficient for recovery. Additionally, leaders perceived a need to embody collective memory in public spaces, permanent monuments, and commemorative ceremonies to remind residents of continuity with significant people of substance and historic events. These physical and symbolic changes associated with "place" not only gave the city a new identity, which leaders intended to settle political, social, and economic questions of their time, but also set the stage for unintended future economic and political conflicts. Disputes about the city's image and identity associated with those public spaces have lasted into the twenty-first century.

ECONOMIC PROGRESS AND SOCIAL REGRESS:
MEMPHIS REINVENTS A SOUTHERN PAST

Evidence of economic progress and modern infrastructure dominated the Memphis landscape in the 1890s. The city opened the first bridge across the

Mississippi River south of St. Louis—the Frisco Bridge—introduced electric streetcars, provided local railroad service to nearby towns, and dramatically changed the public promenade on the riverfront by opening the new Federal Building and the first public, albeit segregated, library—the Cossitt Library. Additional improvements included more paved streets, reorganized public utilities, and expansion of the artesian water supply and modern sewer for residential and commercial use. The Peabody Hotel, a number of large churches, bank buildings, the Grand Opera House, and numerous commercial or entertainment establishments graced downtown. The building boom lasted until the 1920s.[10] In 1900, the new municipal government, which carried over the concentration of elite power from the era of commission government, established a park commission. City officials intended to enhance the city's urban landscape by providing salubrious settings for recreational outings and ceremonial gatherings. They also expected parks to increase property values and tax revenues, to help improve the city's national image, and to attract desirable new residents. The park commissioners aspired to gain national and international attention for progressive urban development. By consulting renowned landscape architectural firms and joining other cities as participants in the culture of landscape design, city leaders also hoped to expand their economic and political influence in the city and region.[11]

At the turn of the century, many American cities, inspired by broad boulevards and parks in Paris and other European cities, designed their own. New York created Central Park; Kansas City, Boston, St. Louis, Philadelphia, New Orleans, and Atlanta also established public parks; but Memphis had set aside only six acres of parkland and needed to acquire additional space to compare favorably with other cities. The Memphis Parks Commission acquired more land by using state and local funds, seeking donations from property owners who would benefit by living near the park or parkway, and threatening to invoke condemnation procedures. Amazingly, by 1906, the commission had acquired and designed more than 1,750 acres of parkland.[12] The first Parks Commission obtained the services of Kansas City landscape architect George Kessler, a German-born and -trained American architect. Kessler, and others influenced by the work of Frederick Law Olmsted, who designed New York's Central Park, preferred using wide boulevards flanked by tree-lined parkways and walkways to create desirable urban communities for attracting business and residential growth. Following recommendations by Kessler and John C. Olmsted, nephew and adopted son of Fredrick Law Olmsted, to connect two large parks by a parkway system, the park commission took dramatic steps to transform the Memphis urban landscape. Their accomplishments included redesigning the city's original four public squares downtown—Court, Auction, Market, and Exchange; developing two new small urban parks—Forrest and Confederate; and designing two large parks on the city periphery—Overton and Riverside.

The first three park commissioners were appointed by the mayor. The first chair of the commission, L. B. McFarland, a prominent judge, had served four years in the Confederate army as an enlisted man. For the remainder of his long life, he participated in regional Confederate memorial organizations and promoted use of public spaces to commemorate the Lost Cause. Robert Galloway, who acquired the honorary title of "colonel," had served as a city commissioner during the era of commission government. The son of Scottish immigrants, Galloway made a fortune in the coal business and in real-estate development and developed the first subdivision near what became Overton Park. John R. Godwin, prominent cotton factor, financial intermediary in the global circuit of capital and cotton, and state representative, served as the third member of the first parks commission.[13]

The park commissioners, like their contemporaries in many American cities, embraced the ideals of the City Beautiful reform movement, which viewed landscape design as a means to inspire civic loyalty and reduce social disorder.[14] Like their peers in many southern towns, however, they supported "history" and "education" projects advocated by Confederate memorial organizations. These organizations, formed throughout the South in the 1890s, promoted an exclusively white southern view of the Civil War and the Lost Cause.[15] Functioning as reputational entrepreneurs, members of these organizations built commemorative parks, commissioned statues, and held public ceremonies to celebrate military leadership and the personal sacrifices of Confederate veterans, living and dead. The city of Richmond, Virginia, unveiled an equestrian monument of General Robert E. Lee in 1890. The lavish ceremony followed a twenty-year campaign to memorialize Lee and legitimate his status in national memory as an American hero, not a traitor.[16] One year later in Memphis, the Forrest Monument Association began fund-raising for a monument to honor its favorite son, General Nathan Bedford Forrest.[17]

For Memphis park commissioners and other city leaders, the design of parks and parkways not only promoted economic growth and a more progressive image but also imbued the urban landscape with a sense of authority, purpose, and southern "tradition."[18] The combination of local, regional, national, and international goals in urban landscape projects was not uncommon. Although reputable landscape architects such as Kessler and Olmsted used nationally and internationally venerated designs, they also modified their designs to fit local preferences. In Lexington, Kentucky, the Olmsted brothers noted the local interest in horses and increased the park areas needed for pleasure riding.[19] In Memphis, Kessler accommodated his clients' wishes to establish Forrest Park in the center of the city and erect an equestrian monument in honor of General Nathan Bedford Forrest.

The Forrest Monument Association, organized in 1891, predated the repeal of commission government and appointment of the Parks Commission. L. B. McFarland, chairman of the Parks Commission, previously chaired the committee that placed a Confederate monument in Elmwood Cemetery in 1871, after he failed to convince city leaders to locate the Confederate monument on the public promenade on the riverfront at the core of civic public space. The public promenade, a gift from founders Overton, Winchester, and Jackson to the people of the city of Memphis, runs from Union Avenue on the south to Auction on the north. The city rejected McFarland's plan and used the public promenade on the riverfront to build the U.S. Customs House there in 1876, the Cossitt Library in 1888, and a city dump. Thirty years later, McFarland persuaded leaders to clean up the dump and build Confederate Square on the riverfront promenade. He also convinced them to locate Forrest Park at the center of the city, as defined by the new park system and parkway. He wrote: "It is the design of the commission to subordinate everything except its utility as a park in the treatment of these grounds to the fact that it is Forrest Park and to the accentuation of the monument itself."[20] Kessler's 1902 landscape drawing of Forrest Park clearly subordinates the placement of pathways and plants to the position of the Forrest Monument. The drawing creates a highly visible memorial landscape on nine acres at what became the center of the city and a focal point for place building and identity construction.[21]

Planning for Forrest Park and the equestrian monument took place during a period in European and American history described as "statuemania—the rage for commemorative statues."[22] The rage peaked between 1870 and 1914, and Forrest Park was built in 1905. Statues of *past* military or political heroes, built of bronze and marble, were designed to build consensus for common "ideals" and to legitimate authority for *present* political and social arrangements. For example, the city of Winchester in the United Kingdom erected a bronze statue of King Alfred the Great in 1901. In France, Alise-Sainte-Reine erected a statue to Vercingetorix. Typically, these didactic monuments, the most conservative of commemorative forms, depicted a heroic human form from another time as an allegorical allusion and a symbol of the community. They were carefully sited to underscore their symbolic role at particular places. And they were expected to last forever to stabilize the physical and political landscape.[23]

In many southern cities, including Memphis, political leaders selected Civil War heroes as subjects of commemorative statues in public spaces. The Forrest Monument Association received donations and pledges from veterans' organizations and women's auxiliaries to collect $32,359.53 to pay for a statue and public installation ceremonies honoring General Nathan Bedford Forrest. The association commissioned the statue and laid the cornerstone for the monument in 1901. Obtaining permission from Forrest's son in 1904, the association disinterred the remains of Forrest and his wife Mary from the historic Elmwood Cemetery and reinterred them in Forrest Park. In 1905, they installed and dedicated the equestrian statue of Forrest over the graves and placed markers at the base of the pedestal. The 9,500-pound bronze statue was produced in Paris and shipped via New York and Savannah to Memphis. Reportedly, thousands of people—estimates range from 18,000 to 30,000—filled the park and lined the streets to watch the spectacle unfold. Confederate veterans paraded, and Forrest's granddaughter unveiled the monument at official dedication ceremonies. A *Memphis Commercial Appeal* editorial praised Forrest as a military genius and added, "There need be no apology for erecting this striking monument to commemorate his splendid deeds. Memphis can at last point with genuine pride to this enduring recognition of the achievements of one of her greatest citizens."[24] There was no mention of the human labor, presumably contributed by African American males, who lifted the statue from the dockyards on the Mississippi River, transported it with wagons and mules to the center of town, and hoisted it atop the pedestal over the graves in Forrest Park.

Ostensibly, officials and supporters of Confederate veterans' organizations created the Forrest Park memorial as a "lasting and official record of the past, above political bias and worthy of civic admiration."[25] Alternatively, however, Forrest Park and Confederate memorials can be seen as the "invention of tradition" designed by elites at the end of the nineteenth century to show continuity with a "suitable past" and legitimate their own authority.

> "Invented tradition" is taken to mean a set of practices, normally
> governed by overtly or tacitly accepted rules and of a ritual or symbolic

The Nathan Bedford Forrest statue in Memphis's Forrest Park is an object of commemoration and conflict. Photograph by Mike Brown.

nature, which seek to inculcate certain values and norms of behaviour by repetition, which automatically implies continuity with the past. In fact, where possible, they normally attempt to establish continuity with a suitable historic past. . . . However, insofar as there is such reference to a historic past, the peculiarity of "invented" traditions is that the continuity with it is largely fictitious.[26]

WHY FORREST?: SELECTIVE HISTORY, COLLECTIVE MEMORY, AND PLACE

In 1905, Forrest Park, its equestrian monument, and the graves of the general and his wife stood in a public space in the center of Memphis and dominated the city's memorial landscape. The ceremony took place four decades after the Civil War ended in a city that had not been strongly identified with a traditional southern aristocracy or any major military or ideological Civil War battles. This "paradox of memory" shows how "the past structures the present through its legacy, but it is the present that selects this legacy, preserving some aspects and forgetting others, and which constantly reformulates our image of this past by repeatedly recounting the story."[27]

The selection of Forrest to represent the city's Old South traditional identity was by no means a neutral, consensual rendering of the Memphis past. The Forrest Memorial came into being as a product of contemporary politics in a time of dramatic social change at the end of the nineteenth and beginning of the twentieth century. The memorial, and its establishment in a prominent public space, served powerful interests who sought to establish an official public memory and a collective identity. Like the Lee Memorial in Richmond, the Forrest monument became a powerful representation "of the elite culture of the New South."[28] Both monuments stood for a process of commemoration and reconciliation "that everyone knew but no one said was for and between whites."[29] Ceremonies and monuments in public spaces reminded whites, of all social classes, of the "wages of whiteness," which rewarded all whites with deference at public ceremonies and in daily interactions. It also bolstered white hopes of upward mobility despite the economic reality of low wages or limited educational opportunities.[30]

The dedication of a public space, the disinterment and reburial of the remains, and the installation of the 9,500-pound bronze monument showed the primacy of post-Reconstruction social relations in the city and symbolized its race, class, and gender hierarchy. The reburial of General Forrest, and his wife "Miss Mary" by his side, symbolized the salience of patriarchy and traditional gender roles in the newly emerging social order. The monument's physical likeness to Forrest stressed the values of idealized, or a "culturally exalted" version of, southern masculinity linked to institutional power.[31] The statue's Anglo-Saxon good looks, athleticism, and heroic bearing, poised on a pedestal, require that everyone look up to him. Savage points out that the selection of the equestrian format for Civil War monuments represents a classical allegory of power.[32] There is no display of overt force, and none is needed to convey authority. Forrest's horse, like Lee's, stands with all four feet on the pedestal. Forrest rides in the saddle holding the reins gently but firmly in his hands, making light contact with the horse's mouth. His sword is sheathed, not drawn. The absence of a representation of overt force in the statue suggests that the general is in control and needs only a touch on the reins to exercise power. The pose provides a symbol of idealized master-slave, male-female relations of the past, as well as a model of elite hopes for modern, regulatory power in the future.[33]

The memorial landscape in Memphis, as in other places, shows "the historical south that exists today is the consequence not of some innate regional properties, but of decades of investment, labor, and conscious design by individuals and groups of individuals."[34] Throughout the South, members of the United Daughters of the Confederacy raised scholarship funds, influenced textbook selection, and built memorials to teach generations of schoolchildren to "remember" the Confederacy and the Lost Cause.[35] In Memphis, McFarland and others invested decades and dollars in developing memorials in Elmwood Cemetery, Confederate Park, and Forrest Park to show the city's continuity with a "suitable historic past" and socialize future generations of Memphians to accept their position in the social hierarchy.

Throughout America, not only the South, "in the decades just before and after 1900, political and cultural elites drew on the imagery of past golden ages to shape public memory in ways that supported their authority."[36] During the "Gilded Age," leaders selectively perused local "attics of memory" in search of collectively held, ideologically charged versions of the *past* to promote *present* social arrangements.[37] Significantly, they drew on group identity and social context to remember or create the past and to develop new readings of the past in terms of the present.[38] In the South, efforts to shape public memory involved white understandings, experiences, and privileges. White leaders selected symbols and created public spaces that excluded images of the black experience and valorized the Lost Cause to legitimate the exclusion of African Americans from public life.[39]

In Memphis, leaders strategically discounted memories from what they deemed to be an unsuitable past, including yellow fever, fiscal ruin, and heroism of the martyrs of yellow fever. But the city's "attic of memory" yielded very few symbols of wealth, grandeur, social progress, "high" culture, notable individual achievement, or a "suitable" past for those who were seeking to "invent tradition" to fashion new identities for the city and themselves. As late as the 1930s, historian Gerald Capers described modern Memphis as possessing "no aristocracy, no tradition and little interest in its past." In his view, shared by many others, the Civil War "disrupted a *petite noblesse* in the processes of aging," and yellow fever "destroyed a second embryonic aristocracy before it was born."[40] Moreover, the city suffered not only from the loss of a nascent aristocracy but also from the loss of a more diverse population. Capers portrays Memphis in the decades before yellow fever as heterogeneous and cosmopolitan and Memphis after 1880 as homogeneous and provincial.[41] He regretted the high death rate of the Irish, a loss of influence of the Catholic Church, the out-migration of "influential" Germans, and the loss of new foreign immigration due to yellow fever. He added: "The cost of the fever is not to be reckoned by the number of victims, but by the intelligent and solid citizens it drove elsewhere."[42]

In Capers's view, shared by many, the repopulation of the city by native-born farm folk, namely, a rural underclass that included a high percentage of African Americans, neither enhanced the city's image nor provided evidence of a suitable past for the "invention" of tradition. Often unschooled and unskilled, and devoted to fundamentalist or Pentecostal religion, rural migrants captured the attention of journalist H. L. Mencken, who caustically referred to Memphis in the 1920s as the "most rural-minded city in the South" and the "buckle of the Bible belt."[43] These rural folks, much like the martyrs of yellow fever who cared for the sick, buried the dead, and maintained civil society, were discounted and marginalized by local leaders and national observers. In the words of Foucault, they were considered "people of little substance," to be treated as objects of surveillance and control, not as role models or heroes worthy of admiration or public commemoration.[44]

In Memphis, the South, and the nation, 1890–1920 was a period of growth and opportunity for some whites, but for blacks, it was a time of exclusion, disfranchisement, racial violence, and the establishment of Jim Crow laws. A new era of race relations emerged, supported by the 1896 U.S. Supreme Court decision in *Plessy v. Ferguson* to uphold "separate but equal" facilities. The period has been described by one historian as a nadir for African Americans.[45] Another historian describes the time (the turn of the century) and place (the South) as the "crucible of race."[46] In Memphis and Shelby County, where the population was nearly equally divided between blacks and whites, community leaders wanted to maintain white hegemony. This meant eliminating blacks from public positions, imposing racial segregation in public facilities, and using violence or the threat of racial violence to curtail democratic participation. They succeeded. African Americans, politically active from the 1870s until the 1890s, had served as members of the city council and the police force. The last black police officer retired in 1895, and the last African American was elected to the city council in 1896.[47] More than half a century passed before African Americans served again in public civic positions. The first Memphis Parks Commission designed the city's "public" parks for whites only. Segregation laws denied African Americans entry to white "public" parks[48] until 1963 with the U.S. Supreme Court desegregation decision in *Watson v. City of Memphis*. Despite legal and extralegal forces of political exclusion, however, rural African Americans continued to migrate to Memphis. Census data indicate that blacks continued to be a significant factor in population growth for the city of Memphis and for Shelby County and a threat to white hegemony.

Efforts to create a new social order did not mean that blacks automatically accommodated to racial norms and expectations; hence, the time period also included an escalation of violence against blacks throughout the South. Accounts of several incidents in Memphis received national and international attention. In March 1892, a group of black Memphians established the People's Grocery Store in South Memphis, which angered the white competitor across the street. Disputes escalated and led to the arrest of thirty armed black men who took positions outside the People's Grocery in response to threats of a mob attack; instead, they shot and wounded three deputies who arrived at night to serve warrants on the store owners. Four days after the arrests, nine white men took store proprietors Tom Moss, Calvin McDowell, and William Stewart from the jail and shot them to death. Ida B. Wells, a friend of the victims, wrote about these events, referred to as the Lynching at the Curve, and other acts of violence in the *Free Press and Headlight*.[49] Wells, editor and co-owner of the newspaper, published accounts of meetings in the African American community where resolutions were passed to urge blacks to go

West. Wells described Memphis as a place "which will neither protect our lives and property, nor give us a fair trial in the courts, but takes us out and murders us in cold blood when accused by white persons."[50] It is believed that about two thousand black Memphians relocated to Oklahoma in response to the resolution.

Wells wrote an editorial castigating Memphis's white public officials for tolerating, encouraging, and participating in lynchings. She further outraged whites by suggesting that rape was an excuse for lynching and that white women welcomed the advances of black men. The publication of that report led to the destruction of her newspaper office by a mob of whites who intended to lynch her. Away on a trip to New York and Philadelphia at the time these statements appeared in print, Wells never returned to Memphis. A witness in Memphis reported:

> She was branded by her own people here as a courageous and brave woman. When the news was circulated, a mob had planned, as her punishment, to take her to Court Square and tie her to a tree, without clothing and whip her to death, but she was too wise to stay here and eluded the mob. They searched everywhere for her but as I understand she was in the East when they went to her office looking for her. They smashed up everything in her place for revenge. After all, she did well to have left Memphis. Memphis was no place for a woman of that caliber.[51]

Relocating to Chicago, Wells became a "Crusader for Justice" whose anti-lynching campaign gained attention in northern states and Great Britain. Eventually, her campaign prompted Memphis newspapers to denounce lynching when local leaders discovered that the national and international publicity drew attention to negative images of the city and was bad for business.[52]

These community-sanctioned attacks on the black community were part of a larger movement in the South to use extralegal means to enforce a legal system of segregation and disenfranchisement embodied in the concept of "separate but equal." Blacks feared for their lives. Whites feared the consequences of failing to "keep blacks in their place." Southern state legislatures disenfranchised black voters and sanctioned separate school systems. In Memphis, separate public accommodations, disenfranchisement laws, intimidation, and racial violence followed the pattern established throughout the South.

But violence and intimidation cannot be sustained indefinitely. The use of regulatory power in modern societies is less likely to be based on the application of force and more likely to rely on disciplinary regimes, systems of surveillance, and normalizing tactics to maintain social control.[53] Dominant political groups employ state political structures to organize the use of *coercion* or force to gain control, but they rely on "educative processes" in the larger sense—schooling, media, political parties, and collective memory—to produce ideological *consensus* for maintaining social control and establishing hegemony.[54] This ideological consensus works more effectively than any police force or lynch mob. It mystifies public issues, mythologizes historical events, conflates private interests with public ones, engenders fatalism and passivity, and justifies status inequalities.[55]

The selection of Nathan Bedford Forrest for public commemoration ceremonies shows how memories from the past helped city leaders establish ideological consensus nearly forty years after the Civil War ended and how they used it effectively through the first half of the twentieth century. Forrest became central to the "invented tradition" of the Lost Cause for several reasons. First, Forrest was a Confederate general and war hero with connections to the city and the region. Born in Mississippi and a Mississippi plantation owner, he made his fortune as a Memphis slave trader before the Civil War and became part of the Memphis business establishment afterward. Second, he was one of the original thirteen founders of the Ku Klux Klan in Pulaski, Tennessee, in 1865. He served as the Klan's first grand wizard from 1867 to 1869, although he later repudiated the Klan. Third, Forrest's acts of "heroism" included allegedly ordering the murder of surrendered black soldiers at Fort Pillow, Tennessee, on 30 April 1864 and riding his horse through the Peabody Hotel in a show of bravado when General Grant quartered Union troops there.

Memphis leaders, as well as members of Confederate memorial organizations, endorsed the Forrest Park project to legitimate their authority at the turn of the century and made Forrest a central figure in the broader educative and ideological processes regarding the Lost Cause. Forrest appealed to veterans, widows, and families of Civil War veterans who saw Forrest as the richest symbol of the Confederate past.[56] The dedication of Forrest Park gave them an opportunity to honor family, friends, and ancestors. But Forrest's legacy also appealed to people who were sympathetic to white supremacist ideology and members of white supremacy organizations. Anyone familiar with accounts of Forrest's involvement with the Fort Pillow Massacre and the Klan must have viewed Forrest as a symbol of white supremacy. Forrest evoked memories from the past that could be used to legitimate white supremacist sentiments in the present and reproduce white supremacist ideology in the future.

At the Forrest Park dedication ceremonies, the Confederate flag flew alongside the U.S. flag. Typically, throughout the South, dedication ceremonies allowed city officials and members of memorial organizations to proclaim their allegiance to the United States while publicly honoring memories of a Confederate past.[57] These ceremonial displays of sectional reconciliation and allegiance to the United States confirmed the successful exclusion of African Americans from meaningful public life and symbolized abandonment of social justice as a national goal. These organizations succeeded not only by influencing white southerners but also by shaping the national consciousness about racial segregation.[58] For the next half century, public ceremonies that celebrated the mythic past, as well as racially segregated public schools and adoption of texts and curricula advanced by the United Daughters of the Confederacy and other southern heritage groups, continued the educative project. Official public memory failed to recognize any countermemories, especially from the black community.

Interestingly, in 1965, in the midst of the civil rights struggle, when African Americans resumed participation in public life in significant ways, the Memphis city council took action to acknowledge countermemories of the city's past. They designed a new memorial landscape in a public space to recognize the sacrifices made by martyrs of the yellow fever epidemics, nearly one hundred years after the disruptions occurred. Actions to create Martyr's Park on the bluffs of the Mississippi River south of the downtown business district and to commission a monument to honor the marginalized and forgotten heroes of the yellow fever epidemics began during another period of dramatic social change. Plans for the nine-acre park and memorial were conceived during a time of public challenges to white hegemony that ended de jure segregation, just as plans for the Forrest Park memorial were conceived at a time of justifying white hegemony. Between 1965, when the memorial was planned, and 1971, when dedication of the monument—an abstract artistic representation without a pedestal—took place with little fanfare, the 1968 assassination of Martin Luther King Jr. had created a new identity crisis for the city. Downtown Memphis was scarred by urban renewal and abandoned by white middle-class flight. Paradoxically, by 1971, many people and businesses that could afford to leave downtown had done so, just as people of means had evacuated Memphis during the epidemics. Now, for more than three decades at the time of this writing, the park and the memorial have been ignored. In

2000, quietly and without controversy, the city transferred Martyr's Park, and all riverfront parks, from supervision of the Parks Commission to the non-profit Riverfront Development Corporation. Martyr's Park stands by waiting for new development to reach the riverfront in the area south of downtown.

FORREST PARK: A CENTURY LATER

You are stuck here forever,
  General Forrest,
Without so much as a ghost to talk to.
  Memphis
is sick and tired of the past.
— DON SHARE, "At Forrest Park"

Today, one hundred years after the dedication of Forrest Park, the now ill-kept park and its weathered bronze statue no longer stand in the *center* of the sprawling city of Memphis, but some observers believe they stand in the way of progress and reconciliation. Located near downtown, surrounded by the University of Tennessee Medical Science Campus and nearby hospitals, with ongoing construction for new biomedical research facilities, the park and the statue face Union Avenue on the south. On the north, the park borders Madison Avenue, where vintage trolley cars pass from downtown to Cleveland Avenue and where local commuters, mostly African American, wait for buses or trolleys. Annually, when the national membership of Sons of Confederate Veterans meet at the Peabody Hotel, Civil War reenactors gather at the park to celebrate the birthday of Nathan Bedford Forrest. But the city has not flown the Confederate flag in the park since 1969, when the park commission decided to remove it after the assassination of Martin Luther King Jr.[59] Occasionally, employees from nearby hospitals hold picnics in the park. A few tourists stroll past the statue, but most of them are more likely to visit Sun Studio, one block west of the park. City maintenance crews mow the grass, prune the trees and bushes, and pick up litter rarely, so the park has become an eyesore for commuters and tourists who drive by on congested Union Avenue on their way downtown. In the eyes of many residents, the park has become a ghostly symbol of an unsuitable past.

In the summer of 2005, the neglected park became the focus of several controversies and spirited debates related to city identity and image. These controversies included the financial expense and social obligation of maintaining city parks; changing the names of city parks; expanding and upgrading the University of Tennessee Medical Science Campus and biotechnology research facilities; recruitment of the corporate headquarters of International Paper; and the contested historical legacy of Memphis in terms of identity crisis and image. The city council received proposals from different groups and individuals, including the Center City Commission, the mayor, a University of Tennessee trustee, and park supporters. One proposal suggested renaming Forrest Park as well as Confederate Park and Jefferson Davis Park to remove names from public places that identify the city with a Civil War legacy. Another proposal suggested turning Forrest Park over to the University of Tennessee Medical Science Campus. Relocating the statue and the grave would permit UT Memphis to create a more appealing street life as part of the revitalization of Union Avenue and construction of biotechnology research facilities near the medical campus. Other proposals suggested keeping the park, leaving the statue and graves, changing the name of Forrest Park to Civil War Park, and adding statues of prominent African Americans, including Ida B. Wells.[60] Paradoxically, proposals that mentioned renaming parks, removing monuments, and disinterring the remains of Forrest and his wife for reburial in Elmwood Cemetery provoked vigorous opposition to disturbing the graves and "rewriting history."

The debate about Forrest Park added fuel to existing power conflicts between the mayor and the city council and prompted strong statements from prominent African Americans, from black and white descendants of Forrest, and from members of southern heritage groups. The dispute raised familiar questions about identity, heritage, racial polarization, and economic development. The Reverend Al Sharpton visited Forrest Park and rallied against Confederate memorials to a small gathering of supporters. The Sons of Confederate Veterans (SCV), based in Columbia, Tennessee, launched a campaign to save the three Confederate parks and pledged $10,000. They also organized a Forrest Park maintenance day. Under the scrutiny of media attention, the SCV cancelled a minstrel show that had been planned as part of the annual celebration of Forrest's birthday. A new citizens group formed to save the park. Numerous southern heritage websites posted appeals for supporters to write city officials asking them to protect their heritage.[61] Meanwhile, the mayor and the city council battled over who had the legal authority to rename the parks or enter into maintenance agreements with other parties.

Eventually, Willie Herenton, the first African American to be elected mayor of the city of Memphis, while serving his fourth term and preparing to run for a fifth, ended the debate. The city council left things unchanged. Herenton decided to maintain the three Confederate parks as symbols of city history and official public memory. He pointed to his own position as an elected official as a symbol of progress, stating: "As mayor of Memphis, I am mayor of all the people. And these parks represent the Old South. . . . I am interested in moving toward a New South."[62] Mayor Herenton referred to another period of history that left a lasting impact on the city's identity and image. "In the aftermath of the tragic assassination of Dr. Martin Luther King, Jr. in our city we do not need another event that portrays Memphis nationally as a city still racially polarized and fighting the Civil War all over again."[63] City council member Myron Lowery agreed: "We don't want people to have the image of Memphis in 2005 as they did in 1905."[64]

Yet the kind of image that officials did not want was precisely the image captured by an Associated Press photograph published in the *New York Times*. In the background, the photograph shows the statue of General Forrest on its pedestal. In the foreground, a black man wearing bib overalls leans against a tree.

Many think the decision by the mayor and city council to leave the monument, the graves, and the park names helped avoid an embarrassing and potentially violent confrontation with the Klan. An Imperial Klaliff of the KKK had written a letter promising to "show up in full KKK Regalia and conduct a KKK funeral at Elmwood Cemetery . . . all at the city's expense if Gen. Forrest and his wife are removed from their resting place at Forrest Park."[65] No one in public office wanted to risk international media coverage of a KKK funeral procession accompanying the remains of General Forrest and Miss Mary from disinterment in Forrest Park to reburial in Elmwood Cemetery. No one wanted to stir up images of the "Old South" circa 1905. Nor did they want to create reminders of the racial conflict of 1968. Instead, local officials were eager to promote a progressive image of the city. They also wanted to close a "New South" deal pending with International Paper to relocate its company headquarters from Stamford, Connecticut, to Memphis. Later in the summer, International Paper announced its decision to move its corporate headquarters to Memphis.

A media image of the Nathan Bedford Forrest statue in Forrest Park aroused public controversy again in 2008. The Forrest statue appeared in a local television campaign ad for congressional candidate Nikki Tinker, who is black, in her Democratic primary challenge to first-term Ninth District congressman Steve Cohen, who is white. The ad featured a black former city council member who was a proponent of moving the graves and the statue and renaming Confederate parks in 2005. In the ad, he strongly criticized Cohen for casting a vote on the Center City Commission advising the city council to leave the statue in place, despite the fact that even Mayor Herenton agreed with Cohen's position. The campaign ad, which included images of a hooded Klansman as well as a photo of Cohen, who is Jewish, provoked local criticism of the ad among blacks and whites and generated additional national media attention. Democratic presidential candidate Barack Obama and former congressman Harold Ford Jr. denounced the ad. Cohen won the Democratic primary with 79 percent of the vote. Afterward, Cohen spoke of the progress Memphis has made since 1968 and viewed the outcome of the election as evidence of a postracial era in Memphis and in the United States. In November 2008, voters re-elected Cohen to serve a second term.

THE NATIONAL CIVIL RIGHTS MUSEUM:
COMMEMORATING A DIFFICULT PAST[66]

Forrest Park, the graves, and the equestrian statue remain as enduring symbols of nineteenth-century disruptions, attempts to create a new but contested identity for the city, and physical and symbolic reminders of continuity with the past. But reminders of a more recent disruption and painful past also appear on the urban landscape. The National Civil Rights Museum, located downtown at the site of the Lorraine Motel, reminds Memphians of events associated with the 1968 Sanitation Workers' Strike and the assassination of Martin Luther King Jr. The city, which experienced little suffering as a Civil War battlefield, not only suffered from yellow fever but also suffered a great deal as a result of resistance to the civil rights movement. In 1968, city leaders failed to negotiate a settlement with sanitation workers, who went on strike over inhumane working conditions and low wages. Martin Luther King Jr., Nobel Peace Prize laureate and advocate of nonviolent social change, had traveled to Memphis to march alongside the striking sanitation workers. At the time of the tragic shooting, many civil rights activists and media reports blamed the city of Memphis—the *place*—for King's death. At the 1969 sentencing of convicted killer James Earl Ray, Judge Preston Battle tried to exonerate the city of Memphis, saying: "Memphis has been wrongfully blamed for the murder of Martin Luther King, Jr. Neither the victim nor defendant lived in Memphis. Their orbits merely intersected there."[67] In his defense of the city, the judge argued that Memphis was not at fault because the city was only an innocent bystander, not an agentic player. It was an ordinary point for the intersection of two lives; hence, the city, as a place, should not be held responsible for the consequences of that catastrophic intersection. But Memphis can be seen as culpable precisely because Memphis *was* an agentic place and not a point of intersecting orbits. Place shapes conflict over race, class, and gender; hence, it was Memphis where the Sanitation Workers' Strike occurred, it was Memphis where the protracted ideological and administrative struggle could not be resolved, and it was Memphis where King lost his life.[68]

Judge Battle's disclaimer failed to change the negative image of Memphis held by the outside world. *Time* magazine characterized the strike as "a minor labor dispute in a Southern backwater" and indicted "the decaying Mississippi river town of Memphis" for King's death.[69] The news magazine's treatment of the tragedy, like many other Cold War–era discussions of U.S. racial conflict, attributed racial violence to local and regional places. From this view, both the strike and King's assassination resulted from antiquated, and backward, regional problems in an "exceptional" southern "place." Place mattered, for purposes of international impression management, because the culpability of Memphis, and other "backward" southern places or regional "others," symbolically absolved the "progressive" United States from national and international responsibility for racial injustice.[70] The judge's comments failed to exculpate Memphis in the eyes of the world or to mitigate the tragedy's local impact. The strike and the assassination accelerated the city's downtown decline, which was already in progress.[71] Additional white flight and deindustrialization ensued in the 1970s, and critics dubbed Memphis "the dark spot of the Sunbelt South."[72] At a time when some places in the "Sunbelt South" received accolades for social progress and economic development, Memphis remained a stigmatized regional "other" in the eyes of the outside world. City residents experienced another disruption in the production of locality and another identity crisis.

The Lorraine Motel, site of the assassination, also experienced disruption followed by years of decline. But thousands of visitors found themselves drawn to the historic downtown location despite deteriorating conditions in the privately owned building and decline in the surrounding neighborhood. Visitors noted the city's failure to create a suitable memorial, which further damaged the city's reputation. In 1979, local activist and museum supporter D'Army Bailey editorialized about city plans to revitalize Beale Street and criticized the lack of attention paid to the Lorraine: "Now there is encouragement that Beale Street will be rebuilt and be revived. But leaders in the black and white communities have not done much to preserve the world-famous King assassination site at the Lorraine. It is one of the key places that concerned visitors want to see. . . . Some of those who visit are surprised and disappointed by what they see."[73]

Finally, in 1982, despite more than a decade of failed attempts to maintain business operations, preserve the hotel, and memorialize Dr. King, the hotel went into foreclosure. It was sold at public auction on the steps of the Shelby County Courthouse. The Martin Luther King Memorial Foundation[74] purchased the deteriorating property for $144,000, and supporters struggled to obtain financial support for building a museum. That same year, 1982, the Vietnam Veterans Memorial was dedicated in Washington, D.C. Conceived in a period of controversy and conflict, the Vietnam Veterans Memorial presented a model for commemoration and coming to terms with a difficult past.[75] But nearly a decade passed before the dream of a civil rights museum in Memphis became reality. The project obtained widespread *national* support but encountered *local* criticism and resistance on ideological and practical grounds. Some opponents preferred outright removal of the city's notorious symbol of shame and overt racism and suggested creating a monument to King at a different location. Others believed that King's legacy would be better served by funding a job training center, building a school, or financing affordable housing rather than fund-raising for a $9 million cultural complex.[76] Some opponents voiced fears that another city museum would siphon support from existing local museums. But others objected to the expenditure of taxpayer dollars on another "failed" tourist attraction such as Liberty Land and Mud Island.[77]

Supporters insisted on preserving the actual site of King's murder to promote an "authentic experience of the past" and rejected proposals to erect a statue or abstract memorial at an alternate location. Some political activists hoped that preservation of the historic site would protect the movement's legacy from co-optation and dilution and motivate future generations to continue the struggle. Other Memphians supported the museum as a means for the city to come to terms with a difficult past. In either case, museum supporters viewed preservation of the site as the best means for connecting visitors with the visceral quality of place to "produce the sense of a tangible and immediate past."[78]

Initially, supporters who raised funds to purchase the property included attorney (now circuit court judge) D'Army Bailey; Charles Scruggs of radio station WDIA; Jesse Turner, president of the black-owned Tri-State Bank; Paul

Shapiro, businessman and philanthropist who owned Lucky Hearts Cosmetics located across the street from the Lorraine; and Local 1733 of the American Federation of State, County, and Municipal Employees (AFSCME). AFSCME represented the sanitation workers in 1968 and had invited King to Memphis. Schoolchildren supported the fund-raising drive with coins from their piggy banks, and senior citizens donated their pension checks. Then, between 1983 and 1988, white business leaders as well as state, county, and city governments committed themselves to the project that had already won popular support in the African American community. J. R. "Pitt" Hyde III, founder of AutoZone, personally donated $400,000 to the project and raised another $925,000 from corporate donors, including Federal Express, First Tennessee Bank, Promus Corporation, Donovan Enterprises, and Plough.[79] Public and private cooperation made it possible to create a museum at the Lorraine Motel.

By transforming the actual site of the assassination into a public space for reflection, reconciliation, and commemoration, the coalition of black and white community leaders and ordinary citizens preserved a valuable part of the city's past and helped rehabilitate the city's image. They also hoped that by coming to terms with its past, Memphis would heal and move forward into a progressive era. They expected the museum to give a boost to economic development in the surrounding neighborhood—an abandoned warehouse district and historically black residential area several blocks from the downtown central business district. Ultimately, a museum would help the city deal constructively with its past, reduce racial tensions, improve community relations, and cultivate a better national and international image.[80]

CIVIL RIGHTS MUSEUM: PRESERVING THE LOCAL PAST,
FORESEEING THE GLOBAL FUTURE

————

The National Civil Rights Museum for a long time has been perceived as a local or regional museum. We're not only a national museum, we're also an international museum. We are going to start living that.— BEVERLY ROBERTSON, Executive Director, quoted in D. Haynes, "Civil Rights Museum Grows into Second Decade," *Memphis Commercial Appeal*, 23 September 2001

The National Civil Rights Museum, at the site of the Lorraine Motel, first opened for tours in September 1991. Approximately 850 people attended opening ceremonies, where the museum's original organizers, or their children, "cut symbolic chains of oppression blocking the entrance and the struggle for equality" and released white doves.[81] The 10,000-square-foot museum structure extends from the façade of the original motel. Since the museum's opening, more than 2 million visitors have filed past the rooms where Dr. King and his associates spent the night and the balcony where King was shot. Permanent exhibits document the history of civil rights and the struggle for equality in the United States from 1619 until the 1968 assassination. Visitors walk past a timeline of historic events, then proceed to interactive exhibits that showcase civil rights movement experiences. Life-sized gray plaster figures represent "footsoldiers" in the civil rights movement—standing at Little Rock High School, sitting at a lunch counter, and holding a sign next to a garbage truck.[82] A plaster representation of Rosa Parks sits on the bus where visitors can take a seat near her and listen to the bus driver shout harsh orders to move to the back of the bus. Exhibits take visitors through the Montgomery bus boycott, Mississippi voter registration, freedom rides, and lunch counter sit-ins; across the Pettus Bridge in Selma; to the March on Washington and the Sanitation Workers' Strike in Memphis. The tour concludes with a solemn presentation of rooms 306 and 307, the rooms occupied by Dr. King and his associates. The rooms are furnished with rumpled beds, unfinished cups of coffee, and used room-service dishes and have access to the balcony. The rooms and balcony recapture the scene as it appeared on 4 April 1968 and evoke powerful sentiments. Near the rooms, video presentations show Dr. King delivering his final speech at the Mason Temple. The sound of a Mahalia Jackson recording of "Precious Lord Take My Hand" reinforces the somberness of the view.

The museum re-creates iconic images of 1968. Outside, automobiles parked in front of the Lorraine Motel look like those shown in photographs of the day of the assassination. Inside, there are no bronze statues or plaster mannequins to represent Dr. King. A bronze sculpture titled *Movement to Overcome* stands in the museum lobby. Its depiction of people climbing the mountaintop is a visual representation of the metaphor used in King's last speech, "I've Been to the Mountaintop." Posted on a wall facing the sculpture is a quote by the artist who created it. Michael Pavlovksy says: "This grouping of figures suggests a movement or progression across time, boundaries and obstacles . . . the untold stories of thousands of people who lived—and are still living—the Civil Rights Movement and what it stands for and stands against." The monument rises up from the floor. The monument does not capture recognizable human faces or privilege any racial or ethnic group. There are no powerful horses and no pedestals. The monument commemorates the collective struggle for human rights. It represents an arduous climb for human equality, from the ground up, where no one has reached the top, and no individual can reach it without bringing others along. It has been described as a precarious place and a site of revelation.[83]

In 2001, while celebrating the museum's tenth anniversary, staffers and directors considered ways to overcome perceptions that the museum is a local or regional museum with a limited focus on the 1960s in the "exceptional" South.[84] They wanted to increase attendance at the museum, make the site more accessible, and address events that have happened since 1968 to connect the American struggle for civil rights and the global struggle for human rights. Much earlier, in fact, soon after the museum opened, board members began to think about expanding its local physical space and defining its global vision. In 1998, the Center City Commission ranked plans for expanding the museum at the top of its list of seventy downtown improvement projects. With assistance from the Hyde Family Foundations, the museum acquired two buildings across the street, including the rooming house at 420 Main Street, where the gunman aimed and fired shots at King. These buildings became the site of an $11 million expansion project to house "Exploring the Legacy," which opened in 2002. The museum extension adds 12,800 feet of exhibition space. It uses digital technology, as well as artifacts, to explore the legacy of the civil rights movement and relate past historical events to the ongoing contemporary global struggle for human rights.[85]

The design of the expansion dramatically changes the urban landscape, breaks down physical barriers between Mulberry Street and the city, and creates an aesthetic sense of breaking down social barriers. A tunnel and a pedestrian plaza link the former Lorraine Motel on Mulberry Street to the two buildings on South Main. The plaza increases accessibility and visibility from South Main Street, the trolley, and downtown. The design of the expanded facility transforms a formerly marginalized space into a public space of commemoration and integrates it into a revitalized downtown. The room where the assassin took aim at the Lorraine Motel balcony has been preserved, but the interior of the buildings has been remodeled to create a modern steel and glass structure. Color videos of King, as well as color videos of Memphis leaders and events since 1968, explain changes in the city and the world.

The National Civil Rights Museum has increased its visibility in many ways. Today, the museum's stated mission is "to inspire participation in civil and human rights efforts globally, through our collections, exhibitions, and educational programs." Each year, weekend activities scheduled in honor of the Martin Luther King Jr. national holiday attract thousands of people to the museum. But regular museum hours as well as community outreach programs, special exhibits, and traveling exhibitions operate all year and address timely topics. One exhibit, "Americanos," depicted Latino life in the United States. In April 2006, an estimated ten thousand people, most of them Latinos / Latinas, gathered in front of the museum to protest U.S. immigration legislation. Peace and justice organizations have rallied there to protest the U.S. involvement in Iraq. At a global level, the museum participates in the International Coalition of Historic Site Museums of Conscience, established in 1999.[86] Other members of the coalition include the District Six Museum in Capetown, South Africa; Gula Museum at Perm-36 in Perm, Russia; Liberation War Museum in Dhaka, Bangladesh; the Memoria Abierta in Argentina; and the Martin Luther King Jr. National Historic Site in Atlanta, Georgia. Their goal is to transform historic site museums into activist institutions dedicated primarily to tackling "pressing social issues" and promoting "humanitarian and democratic values."[87] They have identified state terrorism, children as victims of war, sweatshops, genocide, racism, and poverty as important issues for activism and education.

The program that has created the highest profile for the museum—both locally and globally—is the Freedom Awards program. From the first year of operation, the museum has presented Freedom Awards to honor significant individuals—nationally and internationally—whose accomplishments embody the spirit of the civil rights movement. The first honorees in 1991 were Rosa Parks, Coretta Scott King, and James Farmer. International honorees have included Elie Wiesel, Mikhail Gorbachev, Desmond Tutu, Nelson Mandela, Yitzak Rabin (awarded posthumously), Bill Clinton, and Bono. National winners include Julian Bond, Benjamin Hooks, Harry Belafonte, Maxine Smith, Sidney Poitier, and John Lewis.[88] A few awards have been presented posthumously, but most awards recognize the lifetime accomplishments of living leaders. Honorees are contacted in advance and must agree to come to Memphis to receive the award and participate in related community activities. They receive awards from $25,000 to $50,000, donated by corporate donors and foundations.

In 2005, the museum honored Oprah Winfrey with the $25,000 National Freedom Award, funded by the International Paper Foundation. Paul Rusesabagina received the $50,000 International Freedom Award, funded by the Hyde Family Foundations. Ruby Dee and her late husband, Ossie Davis, received the first $25,000 Lifetime Achievement Award, funded by FedEx.[89] The honorees traveled to Memphis to receive their awards, tour the museum, and participate in community events. Oprah Winfrey, who began life in rural Kosciusko, Mississippi, addressed a public forum at the Temple of Deliverance Church of God in Christ before an audience of 10,000 people. In award ceremonies held downtown at the Cannon Center, all honorees spoke about the ongoing struggle for freedom. Oprah Winfrey and Ruby Dee spoke of the history of the civil rights movement in the United States. Winfrey added that one reason she accepted the award was to get the chance to meet Rusesabagina, who saved 1,200 people from the Rwandan genocide by housing them in the Mille Collines Hotel in Kigali for one hundred days. Rusesabagina, whose story was featured in the movie *Hotel Rwanda*, explained the history of Rwanda and the civil war that led to the 1994 genocide of nearly 1 million Tutsi and moderate Hutu. He also urged the audience to be aware of genocide and war in Congo and Darfur.[90]

The Freedom Awards program at the National Civil Rights Museum brings globally recognized leaders and activists to Memphis and sends those leaders back into the world with a new way of thinking about Memphis. The award presentations attract international media attention to the city and its accomplishments. Because of the museum, Memphis is recognized as a place of honor. Significantly, the Freedom Awards not only recognize achievements of exemplary individuals but also provide a forum for telling painful stories of shared suffering. As a result of this program and others sponsored by the museum, opportunities emerge for understanding and reconciliation. Six months after receiving her award, Oprah Winfrey returned to the museum for a surprise visit with her camera crew to create material for her television show and perhaps begin a new level of visibility for the museum.[91]

Museum activities also inspire a young generation to work for social change. Nonprofit education groups, such as Facing History and Ourselves, encourage students and faculty to visit the museum.[92] Some Memphis high school students take spring break tours of historic sites in Memphis and other cities associated with key events in the civil rights movement. Some students return to see the Civil Rights Museum, and other commemorative sites, with new eyes.[93] But students visit from other parts of the country as well. Some groups hold community fund-raisers to pay expenses and finance a weekend trip to visit the Civil Rights Museum, Beale Street, Sun Studio, and other historic sites.[94] Others observe the national holiday of Martin Luther King's birthday at the museum.

In 2007, the National Civil Rights Museum once again became a site of controversy. The Lorraine Civil Rights Museum Foundation, which operates the museum, asked the State Building Commission of the state of Tennessee to extend its rent-free lease. A number of local activists contested the museum's request, voicing opposition to what they described as corporate control of the museum, calling for improvement of routine maintenance, and criticizing the museum's mission. Spokesman D'Army Bailey, one of the museum's founders, argued that the board had become too corporate and too white. Therefore, he preferred reconstituting the board memberships by filling positions with local civil rights activists and union organizers. Judge Bailey, removed as chairman by a foundation-board decision shortly after the museum opened in 1991, contended that in establishing a museum he "didn't envision . . . a facility where people could look at the past. My idea was to provide a facility that would incite and spur people to action."[95] Board member Gregory Duckett, an executive with Baptist Memorial Health Care Systems, disagreed, saying the museum "was never designed to be an activist institution."[96] The controversy abated when the state approved a fifteen-year lease to the foundation. The new agreement required the museum's board to increase its African American membership from the previous 50 percent to 60 percent and agree to hold annual public meetings.[97]

In April 2008, the museum marked the fortieth anniversary of King's death with a series of events designed to "give the city and an international audience a chance to reflect on the civil rights movement" and showcase the city's progress since 1968.[98] Preservation and expansion of the museum at the site of the Lorraine Motel have helped improve understanding about the legacy of the civil rights movement and the challenge of human rights in the twenty-first century. Its success as a public-private endeavor has become a model for other communities interested in commemorating their civil rights histories and dealing with difficult pasts. Yet the museum, like other objects of commemoration, is received differently by members of different groups. Part of the legacy of the Civil Rights Museum is that its symbolic role is contested. Some prefer to view the museum as a sign of progress and stability, while others prefer to envision it as a symbol of an unfinished social movement and a rallying point for activism. In either case, the museum is a commemorative object established to focus local, regional, and global attention on a period of significant disruption in city history as well as ongoing community efforts to bring about progress and reconciliation.

CIVIC MEMORIAL SPACE:

COLLECTIVE MEMORY AND THE COMMON GOOD

> There was a huge library near the riverfront, but I knew that Negroes
> were not allowed to patronize its shelves any more than they were the parks
> and playgrounds of the city.— RICHARD WRIGHT, *Black Boy*

Today, Memphis is not the place it was in 1865, 1878, 1905, or 1968. But memories from the hurtful past, and the accumulation of commemorative objects, especially those found in public spaces, give meaning to the place Memphis has been and will become. In October 2005, one hundred years after dedication of the memorial at Forrest Park, commemoration of a new public space occurred in Memphis. The central branch of the Memphis–Shelby County Public Library, a newly built $45 million facility, held public ceremonies to name the library after a prominent city and national leader, a living, local connection to the civil rights movement—Benjamin L. Hooks.

The futuristic design of the five-story, 330,000-square-foot steel and glass structure expresses "a sense of permanence and civic monumentality," according to Frank Ricks, principal architect.[99] The structure of the building and its computer technology connect the community to the digital age, cyberspace, and the twenty-first century. But naming the building after an exemplary individual associated with the American civil rights movement also expresses permanence and monumentality. The name—the Benjamin L. Hooks Public Library—creates a powerful symbolic resource in civic space for establishing a community of memory and retelling the constitutive narrative of the city. Naming a prominent public civic center after an exemplary individual associated with the civil rights movement permits the community to recall stories of a painful past. But the narrative of segregation and opportunities denied now includes stories of individual achievement, family and community struggles, and the community impact of dramatic social change. And the central location—in the library system and in the city—moves African American history from the margins of civic space to the center.

City officials, business leaders, family, and friends attended ceremonies honoring Hooks, the Memphis octogenarian whose biography and history is tightly woven with city history and the national struggle for civil rights. Hooks, a Baptist minister and attorney, served as national executive director of the NAACP from 1977 until 1993. He was a civil rights activist who became the first black criminal court judge in Tennessee since Reconstruction when he was appointed in 1965. In 1968, his friend Martin Luther King Jr. visited the Hooks home after giving his last speech at the Mason Temple. In 1972, Hooks became the first black member of the Federal Communications Commission. In 1996, the nonprofit Hooks Institute was founded at the University of Memphis to support the university's urban research mission and to honor Benjamin L. Hooks. In 1998, Hooks received a National Freedom Award from the National Civil Rights Museum. In 2007, President George W. Bush awarded Hooks the Presidential Medal of Freedom for distinguished civilian service in peacetime.

Before Hooks was born, his grandmother, Julia Britton Hooks, was forced to leave the Cossitt Library downtown when she attempted to check out a book. Hooks was born in 1925 in segregated Memphis, at the time Richard Wright discovered his own personal strategies for resisting and circumventing segregation laws in Memphis to read books from the Cossitt Library that ousted Hooks's grandmother. In *Black Boy*, Wright's autobiography, he explains being driven by his hunger for knowledge to borrow a white office worker's library card and forge the white man's name to borrow books. Wright's autobiographical account is no less compelling than that of civil rights activist Benjamin Hooks. By the time the young Ben Hooks was old enough to read, the city opened a small underresourced library for blacks on Beale Street. Hooks complained to his father that the library was "small and ill-equipped," but his father told him to use what was available.[100] Then, in 1960, Hooks's niece, Carol Hooks Higgs, followed the family tradition and tried to use public library services. She was arrested and jailed with other black college students who tried to use the main library. The incident took place at a structure that had replaced the Cossitt Library as the main branch but preceded construction of the new Benjamin L. Hooks Library.

More than forty years have passed since the desegregation of public facilities opened public libraries to African Americans and members of all racial and ethnic groups in Memphis. But the naming and dedication of a prominent civic space in honor of an African American is a significant "first" in Memphis. At the dedication ceremonies, Benjamin Hooks reflected on his family history and personal biography, saying: "You have to be grateful for the struggles my niece and my grandmother made. To have the library named in the honor of a black person and for it to be named in my honor is a mighty great achievement. I never thought it would happen."[101] The public library that denied privileges to Richard Wright and generations of Memphians has become a space of commemoration and validation. The library serves as an important resource for the transmission of knowledge. But it also serves as a symbolic resource that helps Memphis remember its past by "retelling its story, its constitutive narrative," to bring about reconciliation and acceptance.[102]

COMMUNITY AND COMMEMORATION

The past? It is going, or gone.

Yet this isn't the end of it.

— DON SHARE, "Dilemma"

Local and global changes, along with the city's history of disruptions and struggles over collective identity, continue to shape understandings about the use of public spaces and the commemorative objects installed in them. These disruptions, understandings, and contested memories become part of the ongoing "production of locality" in urban life. Residents of the city of Memphis experienced disruptions with yellow fever epidemics and events related to an American civil rights tragedy. From time to time, city leaders and reputational entrepreneurs have attempted to come to terms with these disruptions and difficult pasts by creating objects of commemoration. Paradoxically, objects of commemoration are intended to convey authority, stability, and permanence, but they serve as reminders of disruptions, discontinuities, and divisions. Because these objects are perceived differently at different times by different people, they become objects of contention as well as commemoration. Despite local social change, and the prevalence of global cultural and economic flows, local disputes about commemoration and public space continue to affect the production of locality. In so doing, they bring new opportunities to create community understanding and reconciliation by retelling the city's constitutive narrative. As part of the city's "community of memory," these objects capture "complex interactions between structure, agency, and contingency"[103] and contribute to the unique characteristics of place.

Our human landscape is our unwitting autobiography, reflecting our tastes,

our values, our aspirations, and even our fears, in intangible, visible form.

—PEIRCE F. LEWIS, "Axioms for Reading the Landscape," in *The Interpretation of*

Ordinary Landscapes: Geographical Essays, edited by Donald W. Meinig

——— *3* ———

URBAN SPACE & PLACE

Memphis and the Paradoxes of Power

Downtown Memphis, situated on the bluffs of the east bank of the Mississippi River, overlooks the river and a floodplain on the west bank. Because of natural, geographic barriers west of the city, growth, development, expansion, and annexation have followed an eastern course. Currently, the city's land area encompasses approximately three hundred square miles of sprawl and includes core areas known as downtown, midtown, North Memphis, South Memphis, and East Memphis. Suburban communities north, east, and south of the city extend into and beyond Shelby County, crossing county and state borders. Consequently, space relations between the downtown riverfront and the city, suburbs, and metropolitan region have been remade many times by public policy and transportation technology, including steamboats, trains, automobiles, highways, and bridges. These policies, technologies, and spatial relations affect urban landscapes, neighborhoods, population migrations, and identities.

Two federal programs—interstate highway construction and urban renewal—have profoundly shaped U.S. urban landscapes in the post–World War II era. Both programs have been widely (and justly) criticized for creating generic places by demolishing historic architecture, displacing poor people, disrupting public spaces, and destroying urban cores. Yet despite the supposed effacement of difference by "generic" external processes,[1] urban landscapes actually display important differences between and within American cities. In other words, "place" still matters and mediates the impact of global, national, and local processes on urban landscapes.[2]

Variations in urban landscapes suggest that "place" means more than a physical space or setting for global and national processes to unfold and more than the "persistence" of local tradition. Variations in urban landscapes reflect tensions among diverse interests involved in "place building" and the production of locality, as well as memories of those conflicts. These tensions and memories create new and sometimes unexpected place-specific resources that may appear as paradoxes and confound predictions that external processes produce "generic" local outcomes. These paradoxes are *reflective* of past tensions over material and cultural resources and *constituent* of future tensions.[3]

This chapter defines "place building"[4] as promoting or bolstering specific features of place, while diminishing or extinguishing other features, to promote development and the production of locality. Place building is organized by powerful institutions to impose the "architecture of social class, gender, and race relations" on the urban landscape.[5] Place building entails decision making about infrastructure and image and uses the rhetoric of progress, that is, building better roads, better communities, or a better future, to justify selective development. Specific features of place, including public spaces and landmarks, may be created, selected, and reformulated in material form or symbolic representation as a part of efforts to modify, destroy, or rebuild urban landscapes. Attachments to landmarks and resistance to place building may lead to claims making by competing interests. Attempts to preserve and protect landmarks and to participate in the process of defining or redefining cultural meanings attached to them create conflict. Consequently, the ability to control or manage the material form and meanings attached to landmarks, and other specific features of place, says a great deal about urban development and the use of power in the production of locality.

This chapter focuses on one urban landmark that has been part of the Memphis landscape for more than one hundred years—Overton Park. It looks at tensions surrounding park creation, preservation, and development and how these tensions influence contemporary strategies to develop a new "twenty-first-century park" in metropolitan Memphis—Shelby Farms Park. For more than one hundred years, changing views of space and place, conflicting values of "progress" and preservation, as well as divisions of race, class, and gender have affected the physical and symbolic production of urban landscapes in Memphis.

The politics of federally funded and locally routed interstate highway construction never quite worked as intended by supporters of the 1956 Highway Act.[6] At the national level, the legislation supposedly met Cold War–era national security needs by providing the means to evacuate American cities in the event of nuclear attack. At the local level, most city officials and downtown business leaders sought federal interstate funds to support "place-building" strategies.[7] They expected expressway construction to move traffic more quickly and efficiently, to enhance economic development and industrial recruitment, and to revitalize declining downtowns. We now know that interstate enthusiasts at all levels miscalculated the economic, social, environmental, and political impact of the engineering juggernaut. Generally, interstate highway construction promoted growth of retail and residential property in the suburbs and accelerated the decentralization and decline of American downtowns. But responses to interstate construction and level of citizen resistance varied locally. New Orleans saved the historic French Quarter from interstate routing in 1969, and Portland, Oregon, deleted part of the interstate route in 1975.[8] Other cities, such as Kansas City, created interstate routes that isolated and bypassed black neighborhoods, often provoking local resistance from interracial grassroots coalitions.[9] In some communities, environmentalists contested interstate construction to preserve natural landscapes and protect wildlife habitats.

Urban renewal also produced varied results and unintended consequences. First defined as the Federal Housing Acts of 1949 and 1954, then redefined as community development in 1974, urban renewal followed a similar model of federal funding and local decision making. Local governments designated "blighted areas," used the power of eminent domain to clear them, and received federal funds for urban redevelopment. Generally, urban renewal projects destroyed some historic architecture, displaced poor and minority families, and replaced communities with public-housing projects associated with concentrations of poverty and crime. Although urban renewal produced increased redlining and white flight, it also motivated local citizens to form historic preservation organizations, nonprofits, and community development corporations to preserve, restore, and rebuild homes and businesses, often after considerable community losses had occurred.

In Memphis, the supposedly generic processes of interstate highway construction and urban renewal collided with unique local features of "place" in Overton Park to create a number of paradoxes. First, *white* citizens mobilized to oppose interstate highway construction plans to bisect a public park, threaten a public zoo located in the park, and demolish privately owned houses in nearby *affluent white* neighborhoods. During the same time period, the local NAACP pursued court cases to desegregate public facilities, including the city zoo, but endorsed routing the interstate through the public park. No interracial coalitions formed to oppose the plan.

Second, the escalation of racial and class tensions in Memphis and civil unrest associated with the Sanitation Workers' Strike in 1968 coincided with pressures on the city council to "sell" park acreage (or not) and make a final decision approving the interstate corridor route. They cast the final vote on 5 April 1968, the day after Martin Luther King Jr. was assassinated in Memphis, to expedite approval for interstate construction through Overton Park in midtown and to accelerate the demolition of Beale Street downtown. Black investors and business leaders, including the Memphis chapter of the National Business League supported urban renewal plans for Beale Street, whereas local white storeowners on Beale opposed urban renewal.[10]

Third, past tensions associated with the transformation of these urban landscapes influence current and future debates about space, place, and place building. The material form of the landscape, as well as historical events and cultural meanings associated with it, has become part of collective memory.[11] In twenty-first-century Memphis, these memories inform debates and affect outcomes concerning a number of place-building efforts involving public parks, interstate highways, and downtown development.

OVERTON PARK: EARLY-TWENTIETH-CENTURY PLACE BUILDING

Overton Park, established in 1901, is a 342-acre park located approximately five miles east of the Mississippi River and the Memphis downtown business district and inside the I-240 expressway ring. The park, originally known as Lea Woods and purchased by the Memphis Parks Commission from the heirs of city founder John Overton, now consists of 170 acres of old-growth forest, a nine-hole golf course (added in 1904), a zoo (1905), the Brooks Museum of Art (1916), and the Memphis College of Art (the Memphis Academy of Arts, founded in 1936 and moved to Overton Park in 1959), as well as walking and riding trails and picnic areas and playgrounds. Occasionally, local musicians performed in the Overton Park Shell until it closed in 2004. Following a $1 million renovation sponsored by the city and the Mortimer Levitt Foundation, the shell that was constructed as a 1936 Works Progress Administration project reopened in 2008, offering community concerts once again. One of the shell's most famous performances occurred on 30 July 1954 when newcomer Elvis Presley performed a few weeks after recording "That's Alright, Mama," at Sun Studio in downtown Memphis.[12]

Overton Park, designed by landscape architect George Kessler of Kansas City, provided a woodland retreat on the city periphery for early-twentieth-century white Memphians. A twelve-mile horseshoe-shaped parkway system, recommended by John C. Olmsted, nephew and adopted son of Frederick Law Olmsted, connected Overton Park, then northeast of the city, to Riverside Park, then south of the city. Riverside Park, now Martin Luther King Jr.–Riverside Park, originally consisted of 445 acres and overlooked the Mississippi River. But Riverside Park never achieved the popularity of Overton Park or won neighborhood support due to its more remote location, its lack of convenient access by road or streetcar, and its proximity to lower-income white and African American neighborhoods and riverfront industrial sites.[13] Consequently, utilitarian encroachments on Riverside Park, such as taking land for construction of I-55, aroused little public (white) opposition. But organizers used the slogan "Look what happened to Riverside—don't let it happen to Overton Park," along with photos of the results of bulldozing and clearing land through Riverside, to rally neighborhood opposition to the I-40 corridor in Overton Park.[14]

Development of Overton Park, the parkway system, and the Evergreen neighborhood occurred simultaneously in the early 1900s. Early residents included Robert Galloway, who built what is now known as the Galloway mansion, served as an elected commissioner when Memphis lost its municipal charter and became a state taxing district, served on the first parks commission, and opened one of the first subdivisions in the Evergreen neighborhood.[15] Galloway and other investors recognized the business potential of developing privately owned land adjacent to a publicly owned, professionally landscaped park. But development of the park and the residential neighborhood, like the conversion of any physical space to an urban landscape, proceeded "with its own ideology and rhetoric."[16] In Memphis, the ideology and rhetoric of early-twentieth-century place building reflected a number of regional, national, and international influences that shaped local ideas about "progress," public works, and urban development.

First, the Memphis landscape, like most other southern urban landscapes, reflects the city's rural, agrarian connections—both economic and aesthetic.[17] Southern cities—large and small, colonial and frontier, past and present—typically display a close relationship with nature in tree-lined town squares and parkways. Also, the late-nineteenth- and early-twentieth-century rhetoric of "place building" typically contains references to natural or rural environments. Second, late-nineteenth-century Memphis business boosters sought ways to reassure local residents and outsiders that the city was safe for returning residents and new investors after disease and debt devastated the city and damaged its reputation. Designated the unhealthiest city in the nation after its yellow fever epidemics, and harshly criticized by the New York financial community for "scandalous acts of dishonesty" related to debt repudiation when the city surrendered its municipal charter in 1879, Memphis needed to recover from disease, debt, and loss of dignity and to improve its image.[18] For Memphis, establishing its national reputation as a modern, progressive early-twentieth-century city required making improvements in public health and sanitation and winning public confidence. The city improved basic infrastructure by installing a sewer system and tapping artesian wells for clean drinking water. These public utilities proved to be long-term assets for the city's economic development.

But place building involves image building as well as infrastructure. To restore the city's dignity and win public confidence, Memphis leaders, like other upper-middle-class white males in late-nineteenth-century American cities, endorsed the norms of the City Beautiful reform movement and its goals for beautification and social order. They believed that enhancing the beauty of the city through Beaux Arts–inspired architectural designs for buildings and creating professionally landscaped public parks and parkways as urban "focal points" would inspire civic virtue and loyalty, reduce social disorder, and help American cities achieve cultural parity with their European competitors.[19] They expected to bolster their own power to shape the urban landscape, but they could not have foreseen how establishing an urban focal point would shape the social identities and political consciousness of future generations, empower citizens to resist city place-building strategies, and influence debates about developing urban spaces for more than a century.

Memphis commissioners turned to Kansas City and George Kessler, a German-born and -trained American architect, to design an "urban focal point" for the city. Kessler's plans for highways, parks, and fountains in Kansas City and other cities in the United States, China, and Mexico combined elements of European design and American naturalism. Kessler, and others influenced by the work of Frederick Law Olmsted, viewed wide boulevards, flanked by parkways lined with trees and walkways, as a means to separate homes from factories and shops, reduce congestion on streetcars, and create desirable urban communities that reminded residents of the aesthetics of rural life.[20] Kessler adopted Olmsted's vision of the urban park as an artfully contrived "natural" setting, an antidote to the "degeneracy" of city life, and a substitute for the "familiar domestic gathering."[21]

Overton Park and the parkway system attracted investors who subdivided the area west of the park and began selling lots in 1902 and 1903. This desirable residential community, known as Evergreen, became an early-twentieth-century Memphis streetcar suburb. City leaders intended the park and the old forest to inspire civic pride and loyalty to the *city*; perhaps unintentionally, these urban focal points created opportunities for a new generation of urban residents to identify with the *neighborhood* and form place attachments in a newly developed urban place.[22]

A number of scholars and writers have written about attachment to rural places for southerners who remain in rural locations or long for them from afar.[23] Little has been written about attachments to southern urban places. But Memphis residents who lived near Overton Park formed attachments to an urban place. The nearby park and the old forest reminded residents of their family connections to rural places and personal commitments to rural values —especially the aesthetics and stewardship of nature. Women who lived near the park, like other southern women, "focused much of their attention on the proper use of public spaces."[24] These gendered activities, along with proximity to the park and the parkway, helped define their "place" in the hierarchy of race, class, and gender. Initially, neighborhood attachment reinforced civic pride and loyalty to the city because place attachment of neighborhood residents was compatible with the interests of local officials and developers. Decades later, when those interests diverged, place attachment interfered with place-building strategies of urban growth elites but enhanced preservation efforts.

Overton Park, the forest, the parkway, nearby Rhodes College (formerly named Southwestern College), and the neighborhood are memorialized in Peter Taylor's short story "The Old Forest."[25] Taylor's descriptive account of class and gender divisions in white Memphis society in the late 1930s and early 1940s associates proximity to the park, connections to rural communities, and attention to public spaces with class privilege, gender differences, and social identity. He contrasts higher-status women who live near the park and have "old family connections back in the country on the cotton farms in West Tennessee, in Mississippi, in Arkansas . . . or Virginia" with lower-status women, that is, "city girls," who lack refinement and rural family connections. The higher-status women thought of themselves as "heirs to something," whereas the city girls did not.[26] The privileged women described in Taylor's story subscribed to "traditional" norms governing appropriate gender behavior and marriage. They helped protect the social reputations of men who threatened those norms and jeopardized privileges based on race, class, and gender by engaging in meaningless and potentially disastrous flirtations with "city girls." Taylor points out that these were the same women who later saved the park and the old forest from the axes of "modern" men, a reference to the interstate dispute in Overton Park. In his view, the higher-status women maintained "place" in both senses of the word—traditional social position and a physical location, connected to collective and individual identities and memories.

The formation of these identities attached to "place" indicates that Overton Park and the Evergreen neighborhood became physically and symbolically significant in the lives of the city's actual residents as well as Taylor's fictional ones. Neighborhood residents, like the young women in Peter Taylor's story, came to believe that they too were "heirs" to something. The heirs included not only the legal "heirs" of city founder John Overton, who agreed to sell the Lea Woods property to the city for the park, but also neighborhood residents who developed a social identity and a sense of responsibility for maintaining the park and the forest for future generations. The park and the old forest became a "place" for shaping the social identities and political consciousness of future generations of people living there. Attachment to "place" allowed neighborhood residents to feel good about themselves and their city due to their proximity to a "natural" setting, their membership in a cohesive community, and their participation in the "symbolic ecology of the metropolitan landscape."[27] Attachment to place helped residents form a covenant with the past and the future.

Events associated with World War II, the Cold War, and the civil rights movement dramatically changed Memphis, its urban landscape, and its traditional social order. Also, the demise of the streetcar, the rapid growth of automobile ownership, and the development of sprawling suburban shopping centers and residential communities changed Memphis and other cities.[28] Increasing traffic congestion and decreasing revenues limited commercial and residential development in downtown business districts, while suburban growth, fueled by favorable interest rates from VA and FHA loans, and a postwar baby boom attracted Memphians to move beyond the parkways into sprawling residential communities east of Overton Park.

Convinced that an interstate highway system would reduce congestion, boost downtown business growth, and improve national security in the Cold War era, federal, state, and local officials endorsed an interstate highway system. Local officials and developers viewed an expressway system as a means for Memphis to gain a competitive advantage over its rivals in economic development and industrial recruitment. The Chamber of Commerce adopted an expressway title and logo devoid of any local place-specific context to promote Memphis. "Expressways to Prosperity," a pamphlet published by the Memphis Chamber of Commerce in 1958 to review its 1957 accomplishments and forecast 1958, features an expressway graphic design on its cover, complete with yellow lines and ramps. Throughout the pamphlet, the expressway graphics and title appear next to key subheadings. The chamber pledged full cooperation with local, state, and federal agencies "leading to *early realization* of the Memphis expressway system."[29] Ironically, the realization of the Memphis expressway system occurred much later than anyone imagined. The process dragged on for decades.

Initial plans for a transcontinental I-40 to connect North Carolina to California included a section linking Memphis to Nashville, Tennessee, to the east and to Little Rock, Arkansas, to the west. Plans for the interstate involved constructing a new bridge[30] across the Mississippi River in Memphis. To move traffic from Nashville to Little Rock, engineers proposed a bridge north of downtown Memphis and a "high speed corridor" through Overton Park. Officially, planning began as part of the city's application for federal funds with adoption of the Comprehensive Plan by Harland Bartholomew and Associates from St. Louis, Missouri.[31] It proposed building a circumferential ring through predominantly black residential areas of the city, bisecting Overton Park with a six-lane corridor, and locating a busy interchange through the adjacent white residential neighborhood. Plans for another highway, north-south I-55, sacrificed acreage in Riverside Park, but these plans, like the circumferential highway, attracted less public opposition.

In 1957, local newspapers published maps of the proposed routes through Overton Park and provoked a public outcry. Neighborhood residents organized to oppose the proposed three-mile east-west corridor and interchange, which they viewed as a threat to "public enjoyment" and the "ecological integrity of the park," as well as a source of "community disruption."[32] Although a number of alternative east-west routes were proposed over the next few years, none garnered serious consideration from city hall. City engineers, citing professional values over sentimental attachments, preferred the Overton Park plan. The growth elite, including the Chamber of Commerce, business boosters, both local newspapers, and the city council, endorsed the original plan, citing "progress." More than half a century had passed since Overton Park's founding on the outskirts of the city as a symbol of progress. In that time, city boundaries and the population had moved beyond the park and the parkways. By 1957, the park had been redefined as an obstacle to connecting East Memphis and the suburbs to downtown and a barrier to progress.

Some business boosters felt that discussion of a more northern location for the east-west interstate route put Memphis at risk of losing federal funds for building a new Mississippi River bridge north of downtown. In their view, locating the bridge and the interstate to a site farther north of the city would hasten downtown decline. One alternative proposed locating the corridor through the northern end of the park, a strategy that avoided bisecting the park but involved moving the zoo away from the northern end of Overton Park to a southern park site. A third alternative followed creek beds and railroad tracks north of the park, but it threatened several small parks, water supplies, and a racially integrated neighborhood. This alternative route also provoked the greatest resistance from the African American community, which opposed relocation.

Neighborhood residents organized the Committee to Preserve Overton Park in 1957 and then changed the name to Citizens to Preserve Overton Park (CPOP) in 1964. Often dismissed by city leaders as little old ladies in tennis shoes, CPOP members never included more than a hundred people, but they made phone calls; attended public hearings; organized protests; pursued letter-writing campaigns; lobbied local, state, and national leaders; and circulated petitions. The city council voted its final local approval for the route on 5 April 1968 (the day following the assassination of Martin Luther King Jr.).

Because citizen efforts failed to persuade city officials to negotiate a political compromise, CPOP pursued litigation to force a legal resolution. Ultimately, CPOP won its legal battle to spare the park with a U.S. Supreme Court victory in 1971. But the legal victory came too late to prevent considerable damage to *private property* because of the city's use of its power of eminent domain to clear land for approaches to the corridor. Throughout the litigation process, the city continued its condemnation procedures and cleared 56 acres of right-of-way, devastating neighborhoods east and west of Overton Park. These actions destroyed more than 400 houses, 266 apartments, 44 businesses, 5 churches, and 1 fire station and demoralized many residents, who moved away.[33]

Attorney Charles Newman, who represented CPOP in the landmark Supreme Court case, criticized the city's demolition strategy:

> They had deliberately jumped the gun and torn down those houses at a time when they knew or should have known that they might not be able to complete the highway through the park. Although the courts refused to let them use this as an excuse to eliminate alternatives, many political leaders and members of the public bought this argument. . . . I've always believed that the main reason we were able to win this fight was that the Memphis establishment was overconfident, believing to the end they could ignore the law and simply refuse to give alternative routes the consideration the law required.[34]

In 1971, Justice Thurgood Marshall wrote the majority opinion in the Overton Park U.S. Supreme Court decision, which has become one of the most frequently cited administration law cases in the nation.[35] The court found that the secretary of transportation failed to find a "feasible and prudent alternative" to disturbing public parkland and remanded the case to district court. But the state never pursued the corridor plan. Instead, the northern loop of the circumferential highway—I-240—also serves as I-40 through Memphis. But the city of Memphis waited ten years to request withdrawal of the designated property from the interstate highway system. It has taken more than twenty years since the state of Tennessee returned the "corridor" land to the city of Memphis for neighborhood recovery and restoration. The Evergreen Historic District Association, which promotes historic preservation, neighborhood restoration, and tree planting, as well as oversight for commercial development, celebrated completion of the last new house constructed in the restored neighborhood in 2005. The celebration took place fifty years after the interstate process began.

Efforts to save the park and rebuild the neighborhood united citizens across generational, class, race, gender, and ideological divisions. Initially, a small group of affluent white female residents worked to save "our neighborhood" and "our" park for "our children." In making claims on the park, these women did not challenge traditional class, race, or gender boundaries. In fact, a few petitioners used class rhetoric to rebuke developers and city officials for their nouveau riche disdain of tradition and lack of appreciation for European-style park grandeur. Eventually, as the conflict continued, the class rhetoric changed. Appeals to elected officials in state and national capitals, as well as to local officials, dropped the elitist rhetoric and adopted a more democratic tone to defend the public interest.[36]

Decades of sustained legal and political efforts to preserve the park and restore the neighborhood, in the wake of bulldozers and eminent domain, required input from new generations of motivated residents, men and women willing to form alliances with experienced "old-timers" to live in an "authentic" community.[37] These allies may not have shared 1950s ideologies concerning class, gender, or race boundaries, but they did share common concerns about the public good. At various times, especially during the 1970s, opposition to these allies created negative media attention, which alternately described them as obstructionists to growth and progress, participants in "Hippie Sundays" at Overton Park, or decadent inhabitants of "Sodom and Gomorrah"—a reference to the declining inner city.[38] But the allies prevailed against declining property values, white flight, and local media criticism. Eventually, a more culturally and racially diverse community emerged. Now, diverse community residents share a common identity as "midtowners" or "Evergreeners"; feel a sense of responsibility for the neighborhood, the park, and the forest; and enjoy rebounding property values.

Today, the cultural memory of saving the park, and recognizing the value of protecting it, extends beyond the local neighborhood. Overton Park is now protected by its 1979 designation as a national historic landmark, and community efforts to preserve it have been institutionalized. Environmentally conscious organizations such as the Friends of the Park, as well as residents who are members of the Evergreen Historic District Association, share responsibility for watching the park and monitoring local government. Moreover, diverse local groups including growth elites, preservationists, neighborhood "old-timers," newcomers, midtowners, downtowners, and suburbanites all share a common cultural memory of the park dispute and neighborhood restoration. For preservationists and community residents, the memory serves as a positive reminder of how a few people can succeed in preserving and maintaining public spaces. For growth elites, the memory serves as a caveat that a few vocal opponents can obstruct or change development plans. Consequently, memory of the conflict involving Overton Park and the old forest can be invoked for any development controversy by any interested party. Recently, a public outcry over clear-cutting trees to build a Shelby County subdivision prompted city and county officials to reexamine local subdivision and zoning codes to protect wooded areas in the future. The *Memphis Commercial Appeal*'s account of the loss of trees on the site drew comparisons to Overton Park, describing the 150-acre forested site as "more than four-fifths the size of the woods in Overton Park."[39] For the site in question, private developers moved quickly. Public property was not at stake.

In 2008, city action to remove trees in Overton Park for expanding the Memphis Zoo provoked controversy. To prepare the site for constructing a $13.5 million exhibit, Teton Trek, the zoo removed 139 trees after gaining approval from the Memphis and Shelby County Office of Planning and Development. Although these trees grew on zoo property, and not in the old-growth forest, some park advocates objected to removing any trees from the park and disturbing the local environment. They disagreed with a decision made without their input that allowed the zoo to encroach on the natural, local habitat, creating a man-made showcase featuring an ecosystem that exists more than 1,500 miles away in Wyoming.[40] Future conflicts over aesthetics and stewardship of local habitats are likely to occur because the zoo's long-term master plan calls for developing another 17.5 acres of the forest as part of its twenty-five-year, $96 million overhaul. It remains to be seen whether a few watchful citizens will raise community awareness to contest further encroachment on the natural ecosystem.

As a significant urban landmark for more than one hundred years, Overton Park exists in material form, cultural meaning, and collective memory. This physical and cultural existence is reflective of past tensions and constituent of future ones, as demonstrated by a number of controversial urban development projects and the struggles of place building in twenty-first-century Memphis. Three significant projects exhibit similarities and differences with the Overton Park controversy, including commuter-highway construction and commercial development of land in Shelby Farms, a 4,500-acre park located just east of the I-240 expressway ring; a downtown riverfront development project on public property, bequeathed to Memphis by city founders who intended it to be reserved for public use; and another interstate corridor project slated to go through midtown Memphis or bypass it—the I-69 NAFTA Superhighway from Monterrey, Mexico, to Toronto, Canada.

PLACE BUILDING AND SHELBY FARMS PARK

Shelby Farms, located in the middle of Shelby County, just east of the I-240 expressway ring, is a popular site for picnics, hiking, horseback riding, fishing, bird watching, and other recreational activities. Its 4,500 acres, an area larger than the combined total acreage of New York's Central Park, San Francisco's Golden Gate Park, and Chicago's Lincoln Park, includes a nature preserve— 700 acres of wetland and hardwood forest, recreational areas, and 20 bodies of water.[41]

Used as a county penal farm from 1929 until 1964, Shelby Farms became part of the county recreation system in 1973 in response to a citizen mandate to protect it from development.[42] In 1975, the county approved a park plan by consultant Garrett Eckbo but never implemented it. Once rural, peripheral, and east of the Memphis city population, Shelby Farms is now at the center of suburban growth and sprawl and the focus of twenty-first-century place building and economic development efforts for metropolitan Memphis. Ongoing debates about the future of Shelby Farms raise a number of questions about infrastructure, image, specific forms of development, and the promotion of selected features of place.

In recent years, plans for highway construction in Shelby Farms provoked a public response similar to the 1950s-era conflict over building the I-40 corridor through Overton Park. County officials proposed building a north-south corridor through the western side of the park to expedite commuter traffic and relieve congestion, but all proposals encountered opposition from environmentalists and area residents who wanted either to avoid splitting the west side of the park between the Lucius Burch Natural Area and Patriot Lake or to limit the width of the proposed parkway. Following years of controversy, in 2003, the Tennessee Department of Transportation sent the county's proposed highway project back to local officials with instructions to consider using a "context sensitive design" that takes public involvement into account. Subsequently, Shelby County mayor A. C. Wharton appointed a seventeen-member advisory team, consisting of supporters and opponents of previous routes, to develop a compromise road plan by 15 November 2005. Because of the legacy of Overton Park, city and state officials have been more willing to pursue political negotiation, encourage citizen input, and avoid litigation. But in 2002, county commissioners reversed a decision to create a nonprofit organization to manage the park. Failure of county officials to agree on a master plan to protect the park, manage development, or declare a moratorium on development continued to fuel local activism, especially in light of pressure to sell or lease park land for development.

At times, county officials have considered selling or leasing one hundred acres of the parkland bordering Germantown Parkway, a major suburban artery, for commercial development. Opponents of development included Friends of Shelby Farms Park, which worked to inform and educate the general public about environmental protection and planned development of the park and served as an umbrella organization for a number of environmental and civic groups. The one thousand–member organization involved a more diverse array of interested parties than the Citizens to Preserve Overton Park and accessed modern communication techniques. It used the internet to publish newsletters and reports and to solicit donations. Also, it hired the professional services of a traffic and road engineering consultant and an environmental attorney to oversee the planning process.

Supporters of selling or leasing part of Shelby Farms include many traditionally minded developers who see the large expanse of land as a waste of "space" that could be used to recruit superstores such as Bass Pro Shops and generate revenue for the financially stressed county government. They view the park as a tax liability and insist that a revenue-strapped local government cannot afford to maintain "under-used public assets."[43]

But proponents of new economic development view the preservation of park land as an asset for economic growth and recruitment, not a liability. From their perspective, natural amenities drive location decisions made by individuals and companies.[44] A number of business and civic groups, including Mpact Memphis and the Shelby Farms Park Alliance, promote the idea that if Memphis expects to be more competitive in the "new economy," the city must recruit a "creative class" of young professionals, artists, and knowledge workers and cannot do so without urban amenities.[45] They also compare Memphis to rival cities that are investing in urban parks, including Charlotte, Raleigh, Atlanta, New Orleans, and Nashville, claiming that Shelby Farms Park is necessary for Memphis and Shelby County to gain a competitive advantage in the knowledge-based economy. According to Richard Florida: "Shelby Farms Park is more than incomparable parkland. More to the point, it is a unique competitive advantage for Memphis and Shelby County. There is no question that creative workers in the knowledge-based economy place high value on outdoor assets and on a distinct sense of place. In this way, the future of Shelby Farms Park is also the future of the region."[46]

The Shelby Farms Park Alliance, a self-described broad-based group of business and civic leaders, assisted by a locally based public relations firm, produced a briefing paper on the park's potential for generating economic development titled "The Case for Shelby Farms Park: Creating a Great American Park."[47] The alliance treats Shelby Farms Park as a metropolitan focal point to attract growth, much like Memphis developers viewed Overton Park and the parkways as an urban focal point more than one hundred years ago. Its internet brochure, featuring green pages and photographs of horseback riding and canoeing, contrasts sharply with the Chamber of Commerce "Expressways to Prosperity" brochure of fifty years ago. Rejecting the mid-twentieth-century emphasis on building roads, preferring to focus on nature, aesthetics, and quality of life, the brochure adopts place-building strategies more consistent with those used by early-twentieth-century Memphis developers.

The brochure lists six key points to make the case for the park. Point #1 notes the park's potential "to improve community health, increase property tax revenues, protect our water, teach healthy lifestyles, celebrate diversity, teach life skills to youth, fight crime and improve life."[48] The alliance brochure identifies modern-day threats of diabetes, obesity, heart disease, unhealthy lifestyles, environmental pollution, crime, and low property values. Preserving the 4,500-acre park and planning future development will improve human health outcomes and increase county revenues by fighting air pollution, filtering drinking water, providing recreational and health education programs, attracting desirable new residents, and increasing property values.

In a similar strategy, one hundred years ago, the city created Overton Park and a public water system as remedies to the public health and revenue crises precipitated by yellow fever. Today, the greatest threat to public health is not posed by mosquito-borne yellow fever; instead, a sedentary lifestyle, a product of contemporary life, is more deadly. According to the Centers for Disease Control, more than two-thirds of Memphis city residents are overweight enough to face significant health risks. In 2005, *Men's Fitness Magazine* rated Memphis the fourth fattest city in the United States and noted the city's fourth-lowest ratio of city parks to residents of any city in their survey.[49] In 2007, *Forbes* magazine ranked Memphis in first place as the most obese city in the United States and the nation's most sedentary city. Attributing the obesity epidemic to high poverty rates, high frequencies of fast-food consumption, and a local culture of southern hospitality and generous helpings of fried chicken, fish, and okra, the magazine recommended taking a community approach to improving health.[50] Interestingly, in both time periods—1900 and 2007—proposed remedies for public health problems included building more urban parks.

Point #2 explains how parklands help attract new business growth and give competitive advantages for recruiting members of the "creative class" to relocate in Memphis. Point #3 discusses conservation, stewardship, and the need for a master plan. Points #4 and #5 emphasize the need for visionary planning and leadership. These points include references to the Louisville Olmsted Parks Conservancy, Kansas City, and New York's Central Park as models. Interestingly, the original design of Overton Park and the parkways was an adaptation of Olmsted's urban park vision, and preservation efforts of the 1950s and 1960s that opposed the interstate compared Overton Park to great European and American parks.

Point #6, compatible with traditional southern rural values, reemphasizes the value of stewardship and the importance of planning for the future: "Decisions made today about Shelby Farms Park must be made in the names of Shelby Countians a century from now, because we act as stewards for their park. A credible master plan and an environmental protection agreement are the embodiments of this stewardship."[51]

Despite obvious similarities between the Shelby Farms and Overton Park controversies, such as publicly owned land surrounded by a predominantly white middle-class residential area, plans to bisect the park with a highway, and conflicts between developers and preservationists, there are significant differences between past and present place-building efforts involving these two landmarks. First, today, unlike fifty years ago, there is a lack of consensus among progrowth and development interests. Some proponents of growth prefer to permit private interests to develop "unused" public space; alternatively, others want to manage park lands and other public resources as part of selective development. It is uncertain whether environmentalists and growth-oriented leaders who value urban amenities for recruiting members of the creative class will prevail, especially in light of city and county revenue needs and media criticism of publicly owned "parks and white elephants."[52] It is also unclear how much and what type of park development might be recommended as part of a long-term master plan. Indeed, a master plan designed by outside experts might gain support from "new economy" interests but provoke opposition from environmentalists and lead to further conflict. The city's $200 million master plan for the Memphis riverfront, for example, is the basis of conflict between the Riverfront Development Corporation and Friends for Our Riverfront in downtown Memphis.[53] Both sides favor improving the existing Riverfront Promenade, but they disagree on development plans.[54] Meanwhile, in 2008, the city began work on the Beale Street Landing project for docking excursion and cruise boats. Beale Street Landing is the first step in a more extensive plan to create riverfront amenities that has been revised and delayed in response to the demands of some citizen groups and environmentalists and to conform with Tennessee historic preservation requirements.

A second difference concerns neighborhood attachment to place. Most twenty-first-century residents east of the I-240 expressway lack neighborhood attachments to Shelby Farms, and they make no historical claims as "heirs" of the property. Indeed, because Shelby Farms previously existed as a penal farm associated with the bottom of the status hierarchy and not an urban focal point or landmark with higher status connections, it is not a historical landscape associated with a physical and symbolic "place." In other words, Shelby Farms is a park without a "place" attached to it.[55]

A third difference relates to gender. Today, very few high-status women who live near the park are stay-at-home mothers and grandmothers who view Shelby Farms as central to maintaining their "place" in terms of social position or physical location. Today, many more venues are open to women— socially, politically, and economically. Fourth, and last, no nearby residents are facing the immediate threat of bulldozers and eminent domain to force them from their homes and neighborhood to raze private property for building the road through Shelby Farms. Plans to develop Shelby Farms, whether they originate in short-term local decisions or long-term visions of external experts, are unlikely to provoke the same kind of resistance as occurred fifty years ago. Any resistance efforts, however, may invoke the cultural memory of the Overton Park conflict to bolster their own claims making.

In 2007, following months of discussions, the Shelby County government agreed to award authority over the 4,500-acre park to the Shelby Farms Park Conservancy, a 501(c)(3) nonprofit organization. The conservancy, which replaces the Shelby Farms Park Alliance, has responsibility for day-to-day management and for overseeing the master-planning process. The Shelby Farms Park Conservancy Board involves representatives of prominent families and businesses in Memphis who have participated in various sports and cultural initiatives. County mayor A. C. Wharton announced the partnership agreement with the conservancy, stating that it "represents the fulfillment of Shelby County's 30-year dream for this special place at the heart of our community. With this conservancy in place, we have now begun our journey to transform Shelby Farms Park into one of America's great urban parks."[56]

In September 2007, the conservancy, in consultation with planning consultancy Alex Garvin and Association, issued a request for quotation to initiate a global search for landscape architects and urban designers interested in creating a master plan for a twenty-first-century park. Clearly, the conservancy envisioned something different from Olmsted's bucolic view of urban parks as a return to nature and the tranquility of open spaces. Garvin said: "A 21st-century park is something very different from what Frederick Law Olmsted imagined when he won the competition for Central Park in the 19th century. We have the Internet, we have computer games, we have people flying to Hawaii for vacation, so a park in the 21st century has to be a wholly new kind of thing."[57]

The conservancy board conducted a comprehensive campaign to seek citizen input by holding public forums and administering an internet survey to learn what kinds of park features were preferred. Thirty-three teams submitted proposals for Shelby Farms Park. From those submissions, the designs of three internationally known finalists were selected and announced in March 2008. The models submitted by those finalists—field operations, Hargreaves Associates, and Tom Leader Studio—went on public display at three Shelby County locations for public review. The board posted a web exhibition of the three designs along with another survey for public input.[58] One firm, field operations, was selected and hired from the three finalists. Final approval of the master planner and the final master plan was made by the Shelby Farms Park Conservancy Board, the Agricenter Board, and the Shelby County Commission.

This research shows that place still matters and mediates the impact of global, national, and local processes on urban landscapes. In Memphis, two public parks—Overton Park in midtown and Shelby Farms Park in Shelby County—show how variations in urban landscapes are *reflective* of past tensions and *constituent* of future tensions among diverse interests involved in place building.

Overton Park continues to exist more than one hundred years after its founding and has become part of the cultural memory associated with place, as well as part of the physical landscape. Mid-twentieth-century leaders underestimated the extent of meaning and value that residents associated with Overton Park and the surrounding neighborhood and overestimated their ability to achieve their desired objective through the use of force. Because they saw the park as a *space* for the most efficient use of engineers in pursuit of progress and failed to see it as a *place*, they underestimated the economic and social value of the park and the importance of the neighborhood for place building.

Today, efforts are under way to assure that Shelby Farms Park will continue to be valued as a unique feature of the Memphis / Shelby County metropolitan landscape one hundred years from now. The new slogan, "One park, one million trees," links community building and conservation efforts. Hyde Family Foundations announced a $20 million challenge grant to launch fundraising to support new designs for the park that are expected to cost $100 million. But proponents of new economic development, who view Shelby Farms as central to twenty-first-century place-building strategies for a metropolitan area, may be overestimating the value of international expertise in planning for a world-class park and underestimating the importance of local place attachment for preservation. It has been shown that place attachment to the physical landscape and the "symbolic ecology of the metropolitan landscape"[59] influence local decisions concerning place building and claims making for decades. It remains to be seen whether the last thirty years of community activism to find a compromise between developers and environmentalists to promote public use of park amenities have fostered local attachments, inspired pride and loyalty among old and new residents, and enhanced the formation of place-specific cultural memory. At any rate, conflicts over preservation or development of Shelby Farms, and comparisons to Overton Park, suggest that conflicts and cultural memory regarding urban landscapes reveal a great deal about the historically constructed city of Memphis as a distinctive place.

Sometimes when that Delta sun comes beating down · Well I swear those rows of cotton shine like gold · Visions of plenty · Roll across my mind · Still my hands are empty · And the system's going dry.— KATE CAMPBELL, "Visions of Plenty"

——— 4 ———

COTTON FIELDS, CARGO PLANES,

& BIOTECHNOLOGY

Memphis and the Paradoxes of Development

Geographic location is one characteristic of place fundamental to understanding the economic structure of Memphis and the city's role as a major distribution node in the global economy. Memphis plays a prominent role, not only because of the city's central east-west geographic location in the continental United States and its north-south location equidistant between Toronto, Canada, and Monterrey, Mexico, but also because of its two-hundred-year history of place-specific decisions, activities, and transformations. The city's geographic location on the bluffs of the Mississippi River near the rich cotton-producing region of the Mississippi Delta and an abundance of hardwood forests and natural resources, along with a tradition of entrepreneurialism and a history of labor-intensive human productivity, supplied the means to drive economic development related to agricultural and industrial production. But a history of selective strategies to promote or invest in some features of place, including geographic location, and to diminish or underinvest in others, such as commitments to public education, has affected the city's approach to economic development in the postindustrial era and its prospects for success as a "comeback city."[1]

Local development initiatives for producing and marketing agricultural products, enhancing distribution infrastructure, recruiting industry, and promoting professional sports and entertainment have created mixed economic and social outcomes. Some strategies that focus on geographic location have enhanced the city's comparative advantages in transportation and distribution and have generated wealth. But the consequences of those decisions, and others, especially those connected with "selling" Memphis by offering typically southern industrial recruitment incentives, marketing cheap land and natural resources, and maintaining a low-wage labor market, have generated and reproduced inequality. The use of public subsidies and tax abatements to recruit industry and finance downtown redevelopment projects also produces mixed results.

Paradoxically, each new wave of development strategies tends to reproduce old patterns of inequality, generating wealth and power for a few and maintaining the structure of poverty and inequality for many. Patterns of poverty, lack of educational attainment, and limited access to economic opportunities have become enduring characteristics of place. In Memphis, nearly one-fourth of city residents live below the poverty level, a number almost double the U.S. average. When compared to other southern cities, the Memphis poverty rate of 23.5 percent is the same as Atlanta's and greater than the New Orleans 20 percent rate documented before the diaspora set in motion by Hurricane Katrina.[2] In public education, the Memphis city schools report a high school graduation rate of 48.5 percent, one of the worst in the United States. Ranked fortieth in graduation rates among the fifty largest public school systems, the Memphis school system lags behind those of Nashville, Charlotte, Raleigh, Atlanta, and pre-Katrina New Orleans.[3] The city's high level of poverty and low level of educational attainment are deeply rooted in the city and regional economic structure, as well as historic patterns of rural-urban migration and ties to agricultural and industrial development.

These numbers conflict with the stated goals of present-day development efforts to create a niche for Memphis in the globally competitive biotechnology industry and to attract "knowledge workers" to live and work in Memphis. Focusing on appeals to the "creative class," the city now promotes its rich musical heritage, which includes the blues, rock, soul, and rap, and the Beale Street entertainment district in a revitalized downtown to attract tourists, as well as potential residents.[4] City business leaders and government officials raise expectations that Memphis will become a "world-class" city with references to enhancing the dynamics of distribution, promoting a revitalized downtown, building sports arenas, expanding the zoo, redeveloping the riverfront, and promoting the city's future as an internationally recognized biomedical research industry.

In terms of infrastructure, city leaders have always treated geographic location as the city's greatest asset. For some time, they have agreed to invest in transportation and logistics. Historically, however, ambivalence about the value of place-based resources, including the downtown urban core, the natural environment, and the labor force, has created local tensions. Today, many Memphis residents and city leaders are reassessing the value of the city's cultural and economic resources for transforming a distressed urban core into the kind of place where people want to live. Efforts to redefine Memphis as a "world-class" city now include public-private partnerships and an array of community-based organizations. New strategies for local economic development raise old questions about social inequality and the regional history of investments and expectations for public education and economic prosperity. Debates continue about how best to allocate and utilize place-specific local material, cultural, and natural resources, to develop an economic structure based not only on the benefits of geographic location and the spirit of entrepreneurialism but also on investments in human capital to enhance economic opportunities and improved life chances for all Memphians.

NORTH AMERICA'S DISTRIBUTION CENTER

Today, the city's most recognizable symbol of the global economy is Federal Express, headquartered in Memphis. The *Fortune 500* Blue Ribbon company[5] serves as a local and global icon of entrepreneurialism and the twenty-first-century synergies of technology, innovation, and wealth. Last year, the $36 billion global transportation and logistics giant moved more than 7.6 billion tons of cargo through the Memphis airport on 200-plus daily flights and pumped more than $9 billion into the local economy. Moving products in response to global demand, Federal Express handles more than 1 million packages each night through its Memphis superhub, approximately one-third of FedEx packages shipped worldwide. Because the company dominates the overnight delivery market, Federal Express and the Memphis airport serve as a magnet for high-tech / value-added distribution companies to locate operations in Memphis and the Mid-South.[6] The presence of Federal Express also

HONG KONG
BEIJING
TOKYO
OSAKA
ANCHORAGE

VANCOUVER

LONDON
AMSTERDAM
PARIS

MEMPHIS

GUADALAJARA
MONTERREY

CANCUN

SAN JUAN

SANTIAGO   SAO PAULO

Northwest Airlines Non-stop Flights

FedEx International Flights

MICHAEL GALLIS & ASSOCIATES © 2008

This Gallis map shows Memphis at the center of global trade.

influenced Northwest Airline's decision to establish a Memphis hub for passenger flights. For more than a decade, Memphis International has been the busiest cargo airport in the world. Local officials credit the airport as being responsible for 166,000 jobs, one out of every four in the region. FedEx employs 32,000 of those transportation workers. The airport drives more than $20 billion in economic activity in the Mid-South region, an impact greater than Atlanta's Hartsfield Jackson International, the busiest passenger airport in the world.[7]

Less visible than cargo planes flying in and out of Memphis, however, is the transportation and distribution infrastructure that connects Memphis to global markets through a confluence of transportation routes. The port of

Memphis is the largest still-water harbor on the Mississippi River and the fourth-largest inland port in the United States. Memphis handles more foreign import tonnage than any inland port in the United States and forms a vital link in the 2,600-mile inland waterway connecting the United States to Mexico via the Mississippi River and the Gulf of Mexico.[8] A Memphis–Shelby County Port Commission–supported project, Super Terminal Memphis, is a $350 million multirail freight project designed to streamline rail and truck distribution in the Mid-South and is expected to play a major role in global intermodal container shipping.[9] The 155-acre facility is being built in the Frank C. Pidgeon Industrial Park on 3,000 acres of undeveloped land located south of downtown Memphis between I-55 and the Mississippi River. The new terminal will provide a direct route from Memphis to Asia via Canadian National and Prince Rupert City.[10] Already, the city is the third-largest rail center in the United States and operates as a hub for five U.S. Class I railroads: Burlington Northern–Santa Fe, Canadian National (which purchased Illinois Central), CSX, Union Pacific, and Norfolk Southern. All major truck lines operate in Memphis. Located at the intersection of I-40 (east-west) and I-55 (north-south), Memphis is positioned at a strategic interstate crossroads in the middle of the United States, midway between Monterrey, Mexico, and Toronto, Canada. A new interstate highway, I-69, the NAFTA superhighway now under development, is mandated to pass through Memphis. Another interstate highway, I-22, will connect Memphis to Birmingham, Alabama. Plans are under way to add a third bridge to cross the Mississippi River at Memphis, serving rail and vehicle traffic.

The city's transportation and distribution infrastructure existed long before FedEx. But in 1973, when Federal Express founder and CEO Fred Smith moved his then-struggling fourteen small-plane delivery service from Little Rock, Arkansas, to his hometown of Memphis, the city experienced local difficulties associated with global processes of deindustrialization and a climate of changing labor relations. Decisions to sell bonds to enhance the area's transportation and distribution infrastructure to recruit FedEx produced benefits for the city and the Mid-South region, as well as the company. In 2007 FedEx signed a new thirty-year lease (the first was signed in 1979) with the Memphis–Shelby County Airport Authority. FedEx now leases 30.5 million square feet at the airport for hub operations. Substantial agglomerations of distribution and logistics activities have been drawn to the area to take advantage of having the latest possible drop-off times for FedEx overnight delivery and to utilize a concentration of logistics-industry providers in an area that contains more than 155 million square feet of warehouse space and employs more than 10 percent of the workforce in the warehousing and transportation sector. Strategically positioned as the urban center of regional distribution and transportation activities, Memphis claims the sobriquet of "North America's Distribution Center."

WHEN COTTON WAS KING

Earlier in city history, Memphis made similar claims regarding its prominent role in the global economy. Before the Civil War, Memphis described itself as the "Biggest Inland Cotton Market in the World." After the Civil War and the founding of the Cotton Exchange in 1873, the city became known as the "Largest Spot Cotton Market in the World," the "Largest Hardwood Capital of the World," and the "World's Largest Mule Market."[11] These descriptive names show how Memphis has evolved as a commercial center for warehousing, transportation, and distribution.

Historically, the city's advantageous riverfront location on the Fourth Chickasaw Bluff was first controlled by the Chickasaws, then occupied by Spanish soldiers, then held by U.S. soldiers, then ceded to the United States, and finally opened as a gateway for western expansion. The first attempt to "sell" the city's geographic location as its most valuable economic asset began with the city's founding in 1819. Early-nineteenth-century American settlers and speculators found the geographic location of Memphis and its natural port at the Wolf and Mississippi Rivers to be advantageous for shipping cotton, slave laborers, and commodities. After the Civil War and the yellow fever epidemics of the 1870s, city leaders invested to expand the transportation infrastructure beyond the waterways. Adapting to economic and technological changes, the city expanded transportation resources to accommodate trains, trucks, and planes by building airports and interstates and adopted new information technologies to increase the city's capacities in transportation and logistics.

Until very recently, cotton served as the most recognizable symbol of local business ties to the global economy, as well as a symbol of local social and economic relations to a plantation agriculture–based political economy.[12] In fact, despite significant social and political change in Memphis, the Old South images of a cotton boll and a steamboat still remain on the seal of the city of Memphis. Prospects for the expansion of cotton farming west of the Mississippi River and proximity to cotton plantations in the Mississippi Delta attracted early-nineteenth-century investors—Andrew Jackson, John Overton, and James Winchester—who acquired the Chickasaw trading site on the bluff of the Mississippi River with visions of making money from cotton marketing and real-estate development. The region offered rich natural resources for producing, processing, and marketing cotton, hardwoods, and other agricultural products. At Memphis, commercial interests developed the natural inland port, midway between St. Louis and New Orleans, for exporting these commodities to New York, London, and other parts of the world and for importing basic provisions as well as the amenities of planter life into the Mid-South region. In the 1840s, as riverboat trading and transnational railroad construction increased, Memphis took steps toward becoming a major distribution center. Orgill Brothers, the city's oldest wholesale enterprise, founded in 1847, distributed hardware products throughout the agricultural region and supplied building materials for constructing railroads. Other wholesale firms followed Orgill Brothers to Memphis—before and after the Civil War—selling groceries and provisions.[13]

Cotton factors, and the nineteenth-century cotton factorage system,[14] played a significant role in the expansion of cotton production. Because of their entrepreneurial activities, as well as their business connections to cotton, factors influenced the development of Memphis as a distribution center. Cotton factors represented planters and served as financial intermediaries in the global circuit of capital and cotton. Factors financed crops from planting to harvest by advancing credit, providing groceries and plantation supplies, receiving cotton from plantation owners, storing cotton in warehouses (sometimes waiting for prices to rise), and selling and exporting it to world markets. In Memphis, many cotton factors also invested in the wholesale and retail grocery business, railroads, insurance, real estate, and banks. As the local banking industry developed, factors became bank presidents and board members of banks. By 1925, when the Memphis Social Register was published, the families of cotton factors enjoyed an elite social status.[15]

Memphis cotton commissioners and factors established the Memphis Cotton Exchange in 1873, for the purpose of trading cotton, and the Memphis Merchants' Exchange in 1881, to trade in grains, cottonseed oil, and other agricultural products, not including cotton. The Merchants' Exchange also promoted the economic development of Memphis and compiled statistics on the local economy to keep track of commercial progress. As an additional benefit, the city's cotton men also actually owned local facilities for compress and storage. The Builders' Exchange, organized in 1900 to promote "mechanical and industrial" interests, succeeded in establishing building codes and raising architectural standards. Members of these institutions, and others who agreed with their business goals and priorities, became part of the "commercial-civic elite" who exerted powerful influence over the economic development of the city.[16]

One cotton factor and member of the Cotton and Merchants' Exchanges was Napoleon Hill of Williamson and Hill Grocers and Commission Merchants. An antebellum grocer and cotton factor, Hill became one of the city's richest and most powerful men by the end of the nineteenth century. Sometimes referred to as "the merchant prince," Hill owned real estate in downtown Memphis, as well as in rural Tennessee, Arkansas, and Mississippi. He invested in the Memphis and Little Rock Railroad, coal mines, and cotton warehouses. He held important positions in Memphis as a founder and president of Union and Planters Bank and head of the Merchants' Cotton Press and Storage Company.[17] Investments by Hill, and others involved in cotton, groceries, and wholesaling, strongly shaped the direction of the local economy and the spirit of entrepreneurialism.

For Hill and other members of the commercial-civic elite, plans for developing the local economy focused on promoting the city's geographic location, increasing the city's "economic identity with cotton," and building "Memphis into a place of dominance in cotton trading among Southern cities." Civic elites emphasized the comparative advantages of Memphis's central location and transportation networks and strengthened river and rail facilities to support the city's cotton-based economy.[18] With limited access to outside capital from the Northeast, Memphis leaders pursued strategies that attracted local traders and financiers. Based on their collective knowledge of local resources, they made investment decisions to enhance areas of specialization related to cotton factoring, cottonseed oil, cotton warehousing, wholesale groceries and provisions, railroads, banking, and regional retail trade in the Mid-South region of Tennessee, Mississippi, and Arkansas.[19]

Today, cotton is no longer king, but twenty-first-century Memphis is home of the largest cotton market in the world, as well as North America's Distribution Center, in part because of historical decisions to strengthen the city's comparative advantages in marketing, warehousing, and wholesaling. Some of the early cotton merchandising and distribution companies, and families associated with them, have played significant roles in the city of Memphis and the global economy and are positioned to continue to do so. Significantly, of the four largest privately owned companies in Memphis today, all were established in the late nineteenth or early twentieth century. Three of these companies continue to be involved in cotton merchandising and warehousing. They are Dunavant Enterprises, founded in 1929; Allenberg Cotton, founded in 1921; and Hohenberg Brothers. Hohenberg, founded in Alabama in 1879, moved its operations to Memphis in 1933 and was acquired by Cargill in 1975. The fourth company is Orgill—the world's largest wholesaler of hardware and home improvement goods. Founded in Memphis in 1847, the company's global operations generate annual revenues of $1 billion. Orgill, Inc. operates a modern 600,000-square-foot distribution facility in Memphis.

Dunavant Enterprises, now the largest cotton exporter in the United States, employs agents and conducts business in more than eighty countries in Asia, the Middle East, Australia, South America, and Central America. In 1972, Dunavant participated in the first sale of American cotton to China, after the Nixon administration opened trade between the two nations. In recent years, the three companies have benefited from the booming Chinese textile industry. In 2004, these companies exported a record 14 million bales of cotton, primarily to supply the textile industry in China, and grossed more than $4 billion in revenue.[20] In 2006, a historic meeting took place at the Peabody Hotel between Memphis cotton merchants and an official Chinese delegation that included Vice Premier Wu Yi as well as vice ministers of commerce, agriculture, and finance. At a signing ceremony for contracts to deliver 276,000 tons of U.S. cotton to China, the cotton men and Chinese officials raised champagne glasses as well as expectations for future transactions.[21] The Chinese visitors also met with Fred Smith of Federal Express, the company that operates more flights in and out of China than any other airline. The official meetings in Memphis brought together an interesting combination of government and corporate officials, who share common interests in transportation and commodities, to sign international trade agreements.

The term "Cotton Row" once identified the businesses on Front Street between Jefferson and Beale, but today, the cotton companies are fewer in number and have moved away from downtown and the riverfront. The Cotton Exchange, on the corner of Front Street and Union Avenue, where telegraphs, telephones, and chalkboards once transmitted information between global markets and Memphis brokers, recently reopened as a cotton museum. Cotton warehouses located south of the downtown area stand empty, although some have been converted to residential and commercial space. Modern warehouses, located closer to the Memphis airport, span across the Tennessee-Mississippi state line. Demands from the global economy have brought additional changes to the cotton industry and its business practices.

In 2000, Allenberg, Dunavant, and Hohenberg formed a strategic partnership in an online international trading exchange called "The Seam," also based in Memphis. Growers, merchants, cooperatives, textile mills, cotton ginners, warehouses, and crushers use the system for getting information and trading cotton and cotton-related products. Recently, The Seam expanded operations to include online trading in another commodity—peanuts.[22]

Other local companies have changed in response to the dynamics of modern technology, marketing, and proximity to Federal Express. Patterson Warehouses, the third-largest distribution operation in Memphis, began in 1856 as a stagecoach and transfer operator. It now ships electronics, small appliances, and medical supplies. The Mallory Group, one of the largest warehousing and logistics operations in Memphis, with offices in twenty-seven countries around the world, is the parent company of Mallory Alexander International Logistics. The firm began in 1925 as a cotton warehousing operation known as the Memphis Compress and Storage Company. Eventually, the company diversified into warehousing, forwarding, and trucking. The company's customer base now includes lumber, electronics, chemicals, and consumer goods, as well as cotton. Mallory president W. Neely Mallory Jr.'s explanation of the history of his family business also makes a statement about the Memphis economy: "Cotton was the foundation of this city's economy and it was the foundation of our business. But—like Memphis—we've entered the new, high speed, global economy."[23] Neely Mallory III adds: "We didn't get out of the cotton business. . . . We just stretched and diversified our operations. We simply ship other things now."[24] In twenty-first-century Memphis, shipping cotton and "other things" drives the economy.

ENTREPRENEURIALISM AND GEOGRAPHIC LOCATION

The Memphis business community tends to stress geographic location and an entrepreneurial spirit, rather than ties to an aristocratic Old South or an industrial New South, as their most valuable economic assets. An organization founded in 1991, the Memphis Society of Entrepreneurs, recognizes the city's entrepreneurial past, encourages present-day entrepreneurs, and celebrates the contributions of entrepreneurs to Memphis and the Mid-South region. In many ways, the society's entrepreneurs fit an early-twentieth-century southern ideal type of "commercial-civic elite" that venerated a "newer elite of entrepreneurial spirit" rather than an "older aristocracy at birth."[25] Unlike most early-twentieth-century Memphis organizations, however, the Society of Entrepreneurs includes a few women, African Americans, nonsoutherners, and newly established Memphians, as well as Memphians with deep family ties to the local civic-business elites. The society recognizes companies and entrepreneurs whose activities have made a significant impact on the local and global economy.

The society designates two special groups of entrepreneurs—members of the Hall of Honor and Master Entrepreneurs. The Hall of Honor's eleven exceptional or "legendary" entrepreneurs include two men who ran businesses on Beale Street during times of segregation—Robert R. Church Sr. and Abe Plough. Church, a real-estate investor and founder of Solvent Savings Bank and Trust, was the nation's first African American millionaire. Plough worked his way up in the pharmaceutical business by manufacturing and selling pharmaceutical products, operating local drugstores, and developing an internationally known company that produced a number of well-known products, including St. Joseph's aspirin, Coppertone tanning products, and Maybelline cosmetics. In a 1971 merger, his company became Schering-Plough.

The list of legendary entrepreneurs also includes Fred Smith and J. R. "Pitt" Hyde III, two of the most influential businessmen in the city of Memphis. Interestingly, both men followed business paths established by their families in grocery wholesaling and transportation, but they became innovators creating new internationally recognized companies headquartered in Memphis. Hyde expanded his family business—Malone and Hyde—a grocery wholesale business founded in 1907 by his grandfather. Under Hyde's leadership, Malone and Hyde became the largest wholesale food distributor in the country. In 1979, he created AutoZone as a subsidiary of Malone and Hyde. AutoZone is now the nation's leading retailer of automotive parts and accessories with more than 3,400 stores in the United States and Mexico. Smith's family interests focused on transportation. His grandfather operated a steamboat on the Mississippi River; his father founded the Dixie Greyhound Bus Lines, which became part of Greyhound, and Toddle House restaurants. Fred Smith, who piloted planes, not steamboats, founded Federal Express. Other members of the Hall of Honor include Kemmons Wilson and Wallace E. Johnson, founders of Holiday Inn; Clarence Saunders, who developed the concept of a modern supermarket and founded Piggly Wiggly; and Thomas Briggs, who founded Welcome Wagon.

Similar business patterns associated with real estate, finance, the distribution of groceries and consumer products, transportation, and entertainment appear in the list of eleven Master Entrepreneurs. (Hyde appears on the Masters List as well as the Hall of Honor.) The eleven masters include six men associated with food distribution, transportation, cotton, agriculture, and chemicals. Five masters represent finance, investment, and real-estate development. Two of the five masters in real estate, Jack Belz and Henry Turley, are involved in dramatically changing the built environment in downtown Memphis. The regular members of the organization engage in well-established patterns of commerce, primarily cotton, food, finance, and distribution activities. The names include recognizable Memphis business family names such as Orgill, Dunavant, and Donelson, as well as names associated with newer areas of entertainment, health, and education. The entertainment names include sons of Hall of Honor member Kemmons Wilson, whose business interests expanded beyond Holiday Inns into casinos and entertainment properties. Two entertainment industry names are associated with innovation and popular culture. Sam Phillips, who started Sun Studio and produced records by Elvis Presley, Johnny Cash, Jerry Lee Lewis, Ike Turner, and Rufus Thomas, was inducted. Jack Soden, CEO of Elvis Presley Enterprises, belongs to the society. Representatives of emerging areas of the "new economy" also appear on the membership list. These members include L. D. Beard of Medtronic Sofamor Danek, a manufacturer of biomedical products, and the CEOs of two medical clinics—Shea Ear and West Clinic for Oncology. Two representatives of the region's institutions of higher education have been inducted—the chancellor of the University of Mississippi and a former president of Rhodes College.

SOUTHERN INDUSTRIALIZATION, DEINDUSTRIALIZATION, AND GEOGRAPHIC LOCATION

The membership of the Society of Entrepreneurs does not include names associated with industrial manufacturing concerns such as textiles, steel, and autos. This is not surprising. First, the society recognizes entrepreneurs and the companies they represent with strong ties to the local community—past and present. Second, the society was organized in 1991, following a bruising decade of plant closings and relocations. By the 1980s, several large manufacturing companies abandoned Memphis, leaving the city to bear the costs of unresolved economic, social, and environmental challenges from an era that began with aggressive transregional industrial recruitment and ended with transnational flight.

Memphis, like most southern cities, aggressively pursued industrial recruitment efforts after World War I. Uncertainties about the world cotton market and changes in the agricultural-based regional economy convinced business leaders and the local Chamber of Commerce to pursue economic diversification, that is, to expand the local manufacturing base. Most southern cities and states recruited industry from other more industrialized states by "selling" their communities using business practices commonly found in developing nations in South America, Southeast Asia, the Pacific Rim, and Eastern Europe. One observer described the South as "the most business-oriented region in the Western Hemisphere possibly rivaled only by Brazil and Chile."[26] Typical southern communities competed against each other to create a favorable business climate by offering industrial site development, high tax subsidies, low business regulation, and an abundance of low-wage labor to lure "footloose" companies from industrialized northern states. Consequently, the South became a prime relocation site for "spin-off" industries in advanced stages of the product cycle.[27] But when companies found it more profitable to relocate plants across international borders, the South became a site of deindustrialization.

Prior to the 1980s, most plant relocations involved transregional boundary crossings within the United States; however, by the 1980s, most relocations were transnational. Despite the appeal of still cheaper land and labor in global markets, these were not the only factors driving relocation of capital investment. Cowie suggests that plant location decisions reflect both local and global considerations.[28] "Capital moves" not only when global alternatives undermine existing sites but also when local transformations challenge the use of existing resources. These social, economic, and political transformations arise from many factors, including labor's work experience "within the context of culture and community," that is, within specific places.

Woods relates labor experiences in the Mid-South region to a cultural "pillar of African American identity," which he describes as "the blues epistemology."[29] This worldview, embedded in rural southern communities and their urban diaspora, provided a collective sense of self and laid the groundwork for collective resistance to systems of discrimination and exploitation. Hence, Memphis labor experiences, which include phases of accommodation and resistance and phases of quiescence and rebellion, become a "source of agency and power" for workers.[30] Periodically, despite phases of quiescence, labor actively contradicts elite expectations and disrupts the status quo. In

Memphis, the history of tensions and contradictions between elite expectations and labor experiences and disruptions of the status quo contribute to unique place-specific characteristics of the local economy.

In Memphis and the Mid-South, elite expectations about the availability of low-cost workers for labor-intensive jobs underlie foundations of the local cotton economy, form the basis of industrial recruitment strategies, and affect past investments in public education. Nineteenth-century city founders assumed that slaves would perform the back-breaking labor of clearing delta land for plantations, then planting, chopping, and picking cotton for sale on global markets. They also assumed the willingness of white farmers to migrate into the region in search of economic opportunity. The newly founded city of Memphis benefited from slave labor, not only from agricultural laborers who worked delta fields producing the highest cotton-bale-per-acre averages in the world and laborers who loaded commodities on steamboats and trains but also from the slave trade and from the labor of bondsmen who were hired out for work on buildings and railroad construction. After Emancipation, freed African American workers, as well as white laborers, worked on regional cotton plantations as sharecroppers and tenants. Following the Civil War and the yellow fever epidemics of the 1870s, a steady rural-urban migration brought workers to Memphis. They usually arrived with little formal education but held high expectations for new opportunities to improve circumstances for themselves and their families.

But rigid segregation practices upheld a racial division of labor in the urban labor force. Segregation practices limited employment opportunities for African Americans, confining them to the lowest paid and often the dirtiest jobs in docks, warehouses, lumberyards, hardwood flooring operations, and paper mills. Segregation also limited opportunities for white workers who shared similar economic circumstances with black workers but received a nonmonetary form of compensation that Du Bois described as "a public and psychological wage," or, in other words, the social privileges and status of whiteness.[31] The "wages of whiteness" helped maintain a racially polarized, nonunion work force and a low-wage structure. For early-twentieth-century Memphis, the institutions of slavery, sharecropping and tenancy, segregation, and the "wages of whiteness" had laid the foundation for a low-wage industrial economy, just as it had for a low-wage agricultural economy. Elites expected "a seemingly inexhaustible supply of cheap and racially divided labor" to migrate from rural areas to fill jobs in labor-intensive industries.[32] Counting on an endless supply of energetic newcomers, they made policy decisions that have proved to be costly for economic development, educational attainment, and social equality for the city.

REGION, RACE, AND LABOR

Memphis, like most of the industrializing South before World War II, became a low-wage region in a high-wage country.[33] The city counted on the regional labor cost differential, a racial division of labor, and an absence of unions in a right-to-work state to appeal to outside investors searching for cheap, docile, and "safe" labor. A split labor market occurs when labor costs of comparable workers differ by race. This increases the salience of race and decreases the likelihood of class-based interracial alliances among workers to demand better work conditions or increased wages and benefits.[34] In Memphis, and in other American workplaces, racial identity has proved to be a barrier to class identity and to labor organizing, hence, an economic benefit to employers. These benefits may be obtained passively, that is, by taking advantage of existing local racial divisions, or actively, when employers actively encourage racial divisions.[35] When companies institutionalize the racial hierarchy through unequal treatment of workers, they confer additional psychological privileges as well as better jobs, higher wages, and job security to whites "in an implicit exchange for labor quiescence."[36] Because racially divided workers do not take a common stand, employers are able to gain access to a large labor pool at low costs in terms of wages and benefits. Eventually, the regional labor market, a product of geographic and social isolation as well as the "peculiar institution" of slavery, was undermined by federal labor legislation, the civil rights movement, and labor militancy. Similar factors affected the creation and decline of the segregated, "split-labor" market in the United States.

Place-based economic strategies that include regional and split-labor markets have created problems for Memphis, and other southern communities, by means of increased racial tensions, limited educational attainment, compromised environmental and human resources, and long-term fiscal difficulties for local government.[37] The emphasis on recruiting low-wage, low-skilled jobs not only creates low earnings for workers and families but also limits individual and community expectations in four ways. First, highly subsidized industries deplete resources by reducing state and local capacities to invest in public education, as well as in recreational and health services. Second, these industries tend to generate little tax revenue, further limiting local capacities to invest in public education. Third, the focus on low-wage, low-skill jobs creates low community expectations for educational attainment and achievement that are transmitted from one generation to the next. Fourth, within families, lower income levels and educational attainment negatively affect the hopes and aspirations of future generations. Historically, the most educated workers have been those who are most likely to migrate to higher-wage labor markets. Students who hope to find jobs near families and friends in local communities perceive few benefits to educational attainment. Meanwhile, southern elites who view a high school diploma as a ticket to leave local communities are disinclined to support investment in public education. The legacy of underinvestment in public education and recruitment of low-paying jobs shapes community expectations and perpetuates lower achievement outcomes for generations.[38]

Memphis lured a number of manufacturers during the period from the 1920s through the 1960s but lost most of them through deindustrialization by the 1980s. Several companies, including Firestone, International Harvester, and RCA took advantage of the city's incentives to pursue their own well-established patterns and strategies of capital migration and plant relocation. During this period, the city of Memphis offered a perfect southern recruitment package, including "plenty of underemployed workers at wages below the national average, local elites committed to providing infrastructure and assistance to investors, a controlled and divided local labor movement, and a limited manufacturing base."[39] Outside investors and most local white elites found it appealing to "sell" the city on the basis of low taxes, rich natural resources, an abundance of cheap, docile, and "safe" labor, and an absence of foreigners. Members of both groups hoped to expand the manufacturing base and maximize profits without threatening the regional mechanism of social and political control.[40]

Additional recruitment incentives included assurances from the city's former mayor, E. H. Crump, who dominated city affairs for the first half of the twentieth century by welding "the city's rising business middle class, the rural newcomers, the blacks, the Irish and Italian minorities, and the saloon interests into a potent political force."[41] Alternating between practices of coercion and consensus, unlike most southern politicians who used legal and extralegal means to disenfranchise black voters, Crump enfranchised black voters to support his candidates and maintain white hegemony.[42] Crump believed that "Memphis should be run like a great business corporation."[43] He recruited new companies with assurances that local political authorities would hold unions in check and discipline workers.[44] When new plants located on the outskirts of the city limits, Crump provided city services, such as fire and police, and charged no city taxes. In return for these services, the companies used a check-off system to make sure their employees—black and white—registered and voted for Crump's candidates on Election Day.[45]

Early recruitment successes in the 1920s brought a Ford assembly plant; Fisher Body Works (wooden automobile chassis); Buckeye, Swift, and Humko processing plants; and an eleven-story Sears and Roebuck Mid-South regional center (later expanded to fourteen stories), which included a catalog distribution center and retail sales outlet.[46] More companies followed. Some of the largest employers included Firestone, International Harvester, and RCA. Firestone opened its tire and rubber products manufacturing plant in North Memphis in 1936. Raymond Firestone, son of founder Harvey Firestone, ran the facility, which first operated in a vacant wood-products company building and then expanded to cover nearly forty acres and employ more than three thousand workers. The plant manufactured more than 20,000 car and truck tires per day and marketed them to 25,000 tire dealers from Key West to southern Illinois. During World War II, the Memphis plant produced rubber life rafts, gas masks, and raincoats for military use. By 1963, when the "New Chicago" Memphis plant celebrated production of its 100 millionth tire, it had become the largest Firestone tire plant in the world.

Memphis also recruited International Harvester to North Memphis, outside of Frayser. In 1942, International Harvester purchased 260 acres of land, where it built the largest farm-equipment manufacturing plant in the South. The company transferred most of its Chicago-area operations, primarily those in the North Lawndale[47] community, when the Memphis plant opened in 1958 and employed two thousand local workers to build combines and heavy equipment. In the late 1960s, International Harvester added truck sales and service facilities to the Memphis plant.

RCA's relocation to Memphis occurred somewhat later than Firestone and International Harvester. In 1965, responding to local recruitment initiatives and labor pressure in other U.S. locations, RCA management concluded that the company could not afford *not* to relocate production of color televisions from Bloomington, Indiana, to Memphis. However, by 1965, things had changed—locally and regionally. Coalitions between labor and civil rights organizations strengthened challenges to the status quo. By 1965, the NAACP had filed and won lawsuits to desegregate public facilities in Memphis, including the Memphis Zoo, city parks, public libraries, and public schools. The

Civil Rights Act of 1964 and the Voting Rights Act of 1965 were the law of the land. The Memphis social order had changed dramatically. Former mayor E. H. "Boss" Crump died in 1954, the same year the Supreme Court ruled against segregated public schools in *Brown v. Board of Education* and the year that Elvis recorded "That's Alright, Mama." In January 1956, during the Montgomery, Alabama, bus boycott, African American workers at the Memphis Firestone Tire and Rubber plant sued both the company and their union for maintaining racial segregation at the factory. Citing *Brown*, they won their case against racially segregated facilities.[48]

Before the lawsuit, Firestone divided workers into separate departments. Black men and women performed the hottest, dirtiest, heaviest work at the lowest wages. If blacks tried to move into all-white departments that offered cleaner and higher-paid jobs such as tire-building or machine work, they lost all seniority, which accrued by department. No matter how many years they had worked with the factory, they went to the bottom rung of the advancement ladder and became the first in line to be laid off.[49] The lawsuit challenged the racial division of labor. It changed local work conditions and opportunities for advancement at the Firestone plant and empowered workers at other plants. It took a while, however, for elite expectations to change regarding the value of racially polarized, low-wage labor as a component of industrial recruitment strategies.

By 1965, when RCA decided to move production of color televisions from its Bloomington plant to Memphis, neither workplace segregation nor the rigidities of the old social order of race, class, and gender could be sustained. City officials could subsidize RCA via tax incentives and industrial site development, but they could no longer guarantee employers a rigidly stratified and docile labor market. Unfortunately, however, RCA executives and city leaders overestimated local labor control and underestimated the strength of local union organizing and civil rights activities. They failed to anticipate local resistance to discipline and speed on the assembly line. They also failed to resolve racial tensions on the plant floor. No one could have foreseen the 1968 Sanitation Workers' Strike or the impact of the assassination of Martin Luther King Jr., who came to Memphis to support the rights of poor black workers to join a union and to be treated humanely. The mayor of Memphis failed to anticipate that his efforts to maintain the status quo regarding unions and the racial division of labor, in opposition to the demands of black workers for more equitable wages and humane work conditions, would create a "crisis of inflexibility" that would disrupt the social order. His refusal to negotiate with the union and his denial that black city employees had the right to unionize were consistent with labor positions taken by his predecessors. But Mayor Henry Loeb failed to understand that a major transformation had taken place in Memphis.[50]

In 1971, less than five years after opening, RCA closed its $20 million Memphis plant. Records indicate that Memphis's four thousand RCA workers (90 percent women and more than 60 percent African American) actually surpassed production rates in the Bloomington, Indiana, plant. RCA never faulted the productivity of Memphis workers; however, local observers blamed workers for poor productivity, bad work ethics, and laziness. A few workers blamed management, but the majority of black women workers "more accurately pointed to international competition as the reason for closure."[51] RCA shifted production back to Bloomington, then to Juarez, Mexico, in search of more docile and lower-wage workers.

In Memphis, more layoffs and plant closings followed the departure of RCA. Although International Harvester posted record earnings of $352 million worldwide in 1979, the company suffered a five-month strike and a $222 million quarterly loss the following year. In 1982, International Harvester lost $1.6 billion. The firm cut its local workforce and began restructuring operations around the United States. Despite a concerted effort to keep the plant open and to hold public discussions about plans to manufacture a brand-new kind of cotton picker, in 1983 International Harvester closed its doors for good in Memphis.[52] One month later, Firestone announced closing of its Memphis factory. The largest Firestone plant in the world, which produced bias-ply tires, had lost its market to new radial tires. The combination of changes in demand and production technology, local labor transformations, and the availability of cheaper labor markets overseas dealt a death blow to the Memphis plant and the era of industrialization that began in the 1920s.[53] To make matters worse, in 1983 Sears closed retail operations at its Art Deco–style Crosstown building near Cleveland and North Parkway. The catalog distribution store closed in 1993, leaving 1.4 million square feet of empty space occupying nineteen acres between midtown and downtown.

POSTINDUSTRIAL MEMPHIS: REDEVELOPMENT AND RECOVERY

In the 1970s, Fred Smith's Federal Express, J. R. "Pitt" Hyde's AutoZone, Wright Medical Group, and other innovative companies grew by anticipating and adapting to changes in global markets and technology. Meanwhile, the city of Memphis lost population and struggled with dramatic social and economic changes brought about by suburbanization, deindustrialization, and global economic restructuring, including unemployed and discouraged workers, contaminated industrial sites, economically distressed neighborhoods, community conflict, and a declining tax base. The flight of white and middle-class residents out to newly built suburbs and away from downtown had been under way since World War II; however, the exodus accelerated. Racial tensions escalated. The downtown central business district, on the bluffs of the Mississippi River, lost retail anchors and commercial offices, as well as residents. The Peabody Hotel closed. Most of Beale Street and surrounding neighborhoods were leveled by urban renewal. Weed-infested vacant lots and empty buildings suggested that the city of Memphis had turned its back on the riverfront and its historic downtown, trying to flee from the problems created by deindustrialization and fears of desegregation.[54] Kenneth T. Jackson, an urban historian who grew up in Memphis and later wrote about his boyhood adventures downtown, concluded that the city lost its soul.[55]

Recognizing that downtown was the economic, cultural, and governmental heart of the city, if not its soul, city leaders began to consider ways of facing their problems, developing amenities, and attracting business, residents, and tourists back downtown. Now, thirty years and 2.5 billion development dollars later, downtown has experienced a renaissance. Officially, the transition from a distressed urban wasteland to a "comeback city" began in 1977 when Memphis and Shelby County governments formed the Center City Commission (CCC) to coordinate strategic planning, recruit business tenants, and obtain financing from public and private sources for downtown redevelopment.[56] Today, thirty years later, the CCC promotes downtown Memphis and administers financial incentives for investment, such as the local Payment in Lieu of Taxes (PILOT) program to freeze property taxes (first implemented in 1988) and federal tax credits for community development. The CCC publishes a "Top Ten" list of Center City redevelopment sites in Memphis, which includes buildings that have been vacant for some time. To date, no prospective buyer has been able to close a sale on the Sears Crosstown building, despite marketing efforts supported by incentive packages from state and local governments.[57] Other development projects include commissioning a streetscape master plan and other infrastructure improvements for the central business district. The CCC took out a $5 million bond to start the planned $100 million improvement project. The first phase, renovating Court Square, one of the city's original four squares, was completed in 2005. The current phase includes improving Union Avenue by installing brick pavers for sidewalks, preserving granite curbs, and installing street lights and planters.[58]

A second major economic initiative that played a role in the transition to a "comeback city" was the 1979–80 Memphis Jobs Conference, sponsored by the Governor's Economic and Jobs Conference. Admitting that the local economy "was not as strong as it should be," the organization provided a public forum for diverse Memphis residents to participate in focus group discussions. They weighed local assets and liabilities and set community goals for economic development in a city they criticized for not living up to its potential.[59]

The Memphis Jobs Conference broke with tradition by being "inclusive" regarding racial and gender diversity and by openly discussing racism and community conflict. In many respects, however, conference findings echoed previous discussions about the strengths and weaknesses of the Memphis economy and failed to question underlying assumptions about "selling" cheap labor and natural resources to attract jobs. Like its late-nineteenth- and early-twentieth-century predecessors who focused on agriculture and industrialization, the 1979–80 jobs conference recognized geographic location as the city's greatest asset. It recommended promoting Memphis as North America's Distribution Center. Similarly, it stressed recruiting labor-intensive industry to hire low-skilled laborers. Also keeping with tradition, it viewed Memphis as a city having an identity crisis and a lack of pride, struggling with image problems and a "rural mindset" in conflict with urban realities. The conference seemed to focus on "selling" Memphis but believed problems of image and attitude posed problems.

Although this conference took place twenty-five years after the 1954 *Brown v. Board of Education* decision and following decades of massive social change in the region, conference participants still failed to recognize the structural dimensions of social and racial inequality. They described racism as an attitudinal problem that causes image problems, because racism and intolerance give others a bad impression of Memphis as "an unprogressive, divided city."[60] They viewed the poor state of labor-management relations as an indication of another image problem. The only reported discussion of structural inequality involved criticism of the regressive, inequitable, and antiquated state system of individual and corporate taxation. To date, the state of Tennessee has not adopted a personal income tax; instead, regressive sales taxes have increased at the local and state level.[61] But Memphis state senator Steve Cohen led the successful effort to add a state lottery after tax reform efforts failed in Nashville. In 2006, Cohen was elected to the U.S. House of Representatives.

With a few notable exceptions, including support for expanding the Memphis International Airport and for building the AgriCenter at Shelby Farms, the conference recommendations for improving infrastructure failed to anticipate the demands of the "new economy" and the increasing global demand for research, information, technology, and services. Memphis State University, now named the University of Memphis, was listed among city assets, but no recommendations suggested how to utilize its research potential for future economic development. There was no discussion of the University of Tennessee Health Science Center or St. Jude Children's Research Hospital or the potential for developing a local research industry. No one made references to existing models, such as the Research Triangle Park in North Carolina, established more than twenty years earlier to link research and economic development and improve the lives of ordinary people. At the time the Memphis Jobs Conference took place, Research Triangle Park was planning its Biotechnology Center, which is now recognized as one of the top nine centers in the United States.[62] With regard to environmental matters, the Memphis Jobs Conference listed air pollution as a liability but failed to mention contaminated industrial sites left by Firestone and other companies or the expense of cleaning them up. Most important, discussions about improving city schools seemed limited to vocational-technical education. Meaningful discussions about the connection between K–12 public schooling and higher education and the need to increase support to higher education to improve economic development occurred later with growing interest in recruiting biotechnology to Memphis.

Several strategic economic development planning initiatives have taken place since the Memphis Jobs Conference in 1979–80. The Memphis 2005 project, organized in 1995, and the Memphis Chamber of Commerce's "Partnership for Prosperity," developed in 2002, set goals for raising income, creating new jobs, developing professional sports arenas and downtown entertainment, and making Memphis and Shelby County more globally competitive. These plans stressed the importance of collaboration among state and local organizations, the need to diversify the economy, and the primacy of biotechnology as the means to participate in the "knowledge economy." In 1998, the Governor's Alliance for Regional Excellence asked J. R. "Pitt" Hyde, founder of AutoZone, Pittco, and Hyde Family Foundations, to lead the biotechnology effort. Hyde provided leadership for the Memphis BioWorks

Foundation, a not-for-profit organization formed to establish Memphis as an internationally recognized center for biomedical technology.

Hyde and others began a small strategic planning organization called Memphis Tomorrow, outside of city and county government, consisting of Memphis CEOs. The Memphis Tomorrow organization, like its counterparts in other "comeback cities," relies on a small group of elites who head private and public organizations to target areas for investment of a variety of community resources.[63] The organization's plan for economic growth and prosperity for Memphis and Shelby County, titled "Memphis Fast Forward," addresses four interrelated goals. These goals—good jobs, quality education, safe streets, and efficient government—guide strategic planning for the organization and its public policy recommendations.

To date, this organization counts its successes as the recruitment of an NBA team from Vancouver to Memphis, now the Memphis Grizzlies, and the construction of two sports arenas—the FedEx Forum, home of the Grizzlies and the University of Memphis men's basketball team, and AutoZone Park, home of the Memphis Redbirds AAA baseball team. They also celebrate the successful recruitment of the International Paper headquarters, which relocated from Stamford, Connecticut, to Memphis in 2005.

Plans for the future of the local economy include a number of projects, but efforts to develop a biotechnology industry dominate the others. At first glance, Memphis seems an unlikely place for biotechnology, owing to its late start. Most of the biotechnology industry in the United States is concentrated in nine metropolitan areas, including North Carolina's Research Triangle Park. According to the Brookings Institution, these nine "biotechnology centers," and an additional four "research centers," are way ahead of Memphis and other metropolitan areas competing for growth in the biotechnology industry. But Memphis business leaders see the city as having a number of place-based resources, already available, that will support a thriving biotechnology industry and enhance city growth and development. These resources include the University of Tennessee Health Science Center, the University of Memphis, Baptist Memorial Health Care, Methodist Healthcare, Veterans Hospital, Smith and Nephew biomedical devices, Wright Medical, Medtronic Sofamor Danek, FedEx, a transportation and logistics infrastructure, Le Bonheur, and St. Jude Children's Research Hospital.

St. Jude Children's Research Hospital links the city's research, education, and business economies and affects the course of downtown redevelopment.[64] Located on a fifty-acre campus north of the central business district and visible from I-40 near the Hernando de Soto Bridge, St. Jude opened its doors in 1962 as a philanthropic project to treat catastrophic illnesses in children. Organized by outside forces, St. Jude remained at its Memphis location through the era of plant closings and downtown disinvestment and now participates in city development strategies. Inspired by entertainer Danny Thomas and founded with financial support organized by American Lebanese Syrian Associated Charities, St. Jude has become the third-largest health care charity in the United States. The hospital has treated more than 18,000 children from the United States and sixty other countries without regard for ability to pay. St. Jude also assists with transportation costs and living expenses for patients and their families. At present, St. Jude treats approximately 4,600 active patients, mostly as outpatients. St. Jude trains visiting medical staff from other countries, provides no-cost training via internet technology to registered users in 142 counties, and maintains collaborative agreements with hospitals in sixteen countries. Each year nearly ten thousand children receive treatment through international outreach programs.[65]

In addition to its extraordinary global humanitarian accomplishments, St. Jude is the world's largest pediatric cancer research center. St. Jude's staff of more than 3,000 employees includes 180 M.D. and Ph.D. research scholars from around the world and boasts of having one Nobel Prize winner and three members of the prestigious National Academy of Sciences. Its annual research budget exceeds $370 million. Since St. Jude opened, childhood cancer survival rates have improved dramatically, from 20 percent to more than 80 percent. The research hospital plays a significant role in the treatment of sickle cell anemia and houses one of the nation's most comprehensive programs. St. Jude also houses the Hartwell Center for Bioinformatics and Biotechnology and the St. Jude Influenza Virus Genome Project, an international leader in the study of bird flu viruses.

St. Jude's research connection with the University of Tennessee Health Science Center in Memphis predates the opening of the children's hospital. A sickle cell anemia clinic established by Lemuel Diggs received support from St. Jude and donations from two prominent members of the Memphis Jewish community, Abe Plough and Herbert Herff. Subsequently, the Diggs Clinic at the University of Tennessee and St. Jude, supported by federal research funds and local and national philanthropy, established "a crucial nexus of scholarly activity" that raised the city's reputation as a research center.[66] Supporters came together across racial, ethnic, religious, regional, and national divisions to alleviate the suffering of children from leukemia, sickle cell anemia, and other diseases. Support for St. Jude also helped build powerful coalitions between the business and research economies and undermined local segregation practices. Construction of the St. Jude campus began in the 1950s and was completed in the 1960s, when Memphis hospitals and public accommodations were racially segregated and city residents were ambivalent about the treatment of indigent patients coming to Memphis from the rural countryside.[67] But St. Jude's commitment to medical treatment without regard for race, religion, income, or residence positively influenced local practices and values.

More than forty years later, St. Jude's local influence can be seen in two recent initiatives—uptown residential redevelopment and the city's biosciences initiative. Several years ago, St. Jude expressed dissatisfaction with Memphis city leadership and its failure to address problems of crime and poverty in North Memphis neighborhoods, especially those closest to St. Jude. Hospital officials considered relocating the research and treatment facility to Washington University in St. Louis.[68] The city of Memphis, already involved in massive downtown redevelopment projects, responded with the creation of the Uptown Memphis Community Revitalization Project. The city leveraged a $35 million HUD Hope VI grant into "$142 million of development investment, complemented by $16 million in Community and Supportive Services" and more than $1.3 billion in collateral neighborhood improvements.[69] Uptown's public-private partnership involves developer Henry Turley, the city of Memphis, and the Memphis Housing Authority.[70] The project follows New Urbanism design principles for transforming distressed neighborhoods and public-housing projects into mixed-income, pedestrian-friendly communities.[71] Uptown encompasses 125 city blocks and includes rehabilitation of some of the city's oldest public-housing projects, including Lauderdale Courts, where the teenaged Elvis Presley lived with his parents when they moved to Memphis, as well as some of the city's oldest neighborhoods, including Greenlaw, "the first planned 'suburban' community in Memphis."[72] Also, the project included demolition of Hurt Village, one of the Memphis Housing Authority's largest and most severely distressed public-housing properties.

Deciding to remain in Memphis, St. Jude Children's Research Hospital announced a five-year plan for $1 billion of new investments to expand its Memphis facilities and programs.[73] St. Jude also plays a visible role in the biotechnology initiative. The research hospital partners with organizations supporting the bioscience initiative, such as BioWorks, and its CEO serves on the board of Memphis Tomorrow.

Le Bonheur Children's Medical Center followed St. Jude's lead with plans for a $235 million expansion in the medical district. The Memphis Housing Authority applied for and obtained another Hope VI grant for neighborhood revitalization and improving public housing in the medical district. The $20 million grant was used for redeveloping the Lamar Terrace and Dixie Homes housing projects. The partnership involved the city of Memphis, the Memphis Housing Authority, and developer McCormack Baron Salazar.[74]

RESEARCH, EDUCATION, AND DOWNTOWN:
UT-BAPTIST RESEARCH PARK

The interaction between downtown redevelopment and biotechnology can be seen at the Union Avenue location of the UT-Baptist Research Park. Baptist Memorial Health Care donated the property, which had been vacant since the 1990s, when it moved the Memphis flagship facility away from downtown to what had been its Baptist East campus just outside the I-240 expressway loop. The state of Tennessee provided grants for demolition of the 900,000 square feet of hospital structure. On the site of the old hospital, the Memphis Bio-Works Foundation will build UT-Baptist Research Park, a ten-year, $500 million initiative that will provide 1.4 million square feet of research and laboratory space in the medical center. Like St. Jude, the new research park will have a significant impact on downtown redevelopment.

J. R. "Pitt" Hyde, chair of the Memphis Bioworks Foundation, gave the first $4 million for the project, raised another $8 million in private contributions, and negotiated the donation of the building site from Baptist Memorial Health Care. Hyde views the project as building on the community's strengths, saying: "This creates a great urban-renewal opportunity. . . . It touches all levels of the community." This recruitment and expansion of biotechnology companies is expected to create one thousand jobs and generate royalty revenues for the University of Tennessee.[75]

The BioWorks Foundation also promotes local education programs to address the technical needs of a growing "knowledge economy." It sponsored Tennessee's first charter school—the Memphis Academy of Science and

Engineering—to provide an academically challenging math and science preparatory school in downtown Memphis for students in grades 7–12. Also, the foundation is collaborating with engineering programs in local colleges and universities, including the University of Memphis, Christian Brothers University, and Southwest Tennessee Community College, to enhance degree programs, start new technical programs, and offer seminars. In 2007, the Southern Growth Policies Board honored the Memphis Bioworks Foundation for its support of science education and training at all levels. The Durham, North Carolina–based board was formed by southern governors in 1971 to promote economic development in the South and a better quality of life for all southerners. It now focuses on research and pilot projects in the areas of technology and innovation, globalization, workforce development, community development, civic engagement, and leadership.[76]

The University of Memphis is participating in the growing medical and biotechnology industry not only with undergraduate and graduate degree programs in engineering and sciences but also with creation of a new school of public health and a new graduate program in bioinformatics. New campus facilities are under construction to expand the research and teaching facilities of the Lowenberg School of Nursing and the School of Audiology and Speech–Language Pathology.

EDUCATION, QUALITY OF LIFE, AND THE NEW ECONOMY

Most supporters of biotechnology agree that the push for Memphis to become globally competitive in a high-technology, knowledge-based economy cannot succeed without strengthening local institutions of education, including preschool, K–12, and colleges and universities. The biotechnology industry requires a local research capacity for advanced degrees in science and engineering and laboratory experience in the research park; consequently, the Bioworks Foundation has targeted math and science education at all levels. But work remains to be done across the curriculum, from preschool through postgraduate school, not only to improve city standings in educational attainment and workforce preparedness but also to improve the quality of life for all residents.

A recent study of the "brainpower" of the largest cities in America used census data to analyze the educational attainment of residents of cities larger than 50,000 and assigned a score based on six levels of educational attainment.[77] The levels included not graduating from high school, graduating from high school, attending college but not earning a degree, earning an associate degree, earning a bachelor's degree, and earning a graduate or professional degree. The study identified Seattle, Washington, as the top-ranked city in the United States in terms of educational attainment. Memphis ranked forty-second out of fifty-three communities studied. The only southern city to make the top-ten ranking was Charlotte, North Carolina, ranked sixth. Nashville was ranked twenty-first, and New Orleans was ranked twenty-third (pre-Katrina data).

The low ranking for Memphis is not surprising given the city's low percentage of adults who have completed high school and adults who have obtained a college degree. Table 4.1 compares educational attainment for Memphis and Shelby County to the states of Tennessee, Arkansas, and Mississippi and to the United States. The percentage of people in Memphis who have completed high school is lower than the percentages in Shelby County and the state of Tennessee (which is ranked fortieth in the fifty states and the District of Columbia). The percentage of graduates in Shelby County is higher than the Tennessee average and the U.S. average. (Note: As reported here, Shelby County includes Memphis.)

Table 4.2 compares the percentage of people in Memphis and Shelby County who have completed bachelor's degrees to the percentage of college graduates in the states of Tennessee, Arkansas, and Mississippi and to the United States. The percentage of people in Memphis who have completed a bachelor's degree is lower than the percentage in Shelby County and the state of Tennessee (which is ranked forty-third). The percentage in Shelby County is higher than the Tennessee average and slightly lower than the U.S. average.

The future for educational attainment, economic development, and quality of life in Memphis is threatened by low high school graduation rates for the Memphis city school system,[78] which ranks fortieth in graduation rates among the fifty largest school districts in the United States.[79] Low graduation rates affect the health and well-being of individuals, families, and communities. Communities with low graduation rates spend more resources on crime control, health care, public housing, and public assistance. Low graduation rates also affect potential individual and family income. Recent studies show that the lifetime earnings of individuals who graduate from high school is $260,000 more than the earnings of those who do not graduate. College graduates earn twice as much in lifetime earnings as high school graduates. On average, a person who completes a master's degree earns 2.5 times as much as a high school graduate in lifetime earnings, a person who completes

TABLE 4.1

PERCENTAGE OF PEOPLE TWENTY-FIVE YEARS AND OLDER
WHO HAVE COMPLETED HIGH SCHOOL

Place	Percentage	National Rank
Memphis	79.5	
Shelby County	83.9	
Tennessee	81.1	40
Arkansas	79.7	45
Mississippi	77.4	51
United States	83.6	

Source: U.S. Census Bureau, *American Community Survey*, 2003.

TABLE 4.2

PERCENTAGE OF PEOPLE TWENTY-FIVE YEARS AND OLDER
WHO HAVE RECEIVED A BACHELOR'S DEGREE

Place	Percentage	National Rank
Memphis	21	
Shelby County	25.9	
Tennessee	21.5	43
Arkansas	19	48
Mississippi	18.7	49
United States	26	

Source: U.S. Census Bureau, *American Community Survey*, 2003.

a doctoral degree earns nearly 3.5 times as much, and a person who completes a professional degree earns nearly 4.5 times as much.[80]

A number of studies produced by the Chamber of Commerce and other organizations suggest that Memphis loses more high-income residents than low-income residents through out-migration and gains more low-income residents than high-income residents through in-migration. The Talent Magnet project, sponsored by city and county government and the Chamber of Commerce, targets recruitment and retention of educated workers. The project considers "place" as a factor in improving the quality of life in Memphis and attracting young, talented workers. Its report describes the "real" Memphis as an authentic place that has not lived up to its potential. In some ways, the report echoes the Memphis Jobs Conference 1979–80 report, which also diagnosed a failure to live up to potential. In other ways, however, the Talent Magnet project differs from most previous reports. It commends the city for its recent downtown resurgence, its musical and cultural heritage, and its public parks and recreational amenities, which offer unique and appealing resources to attract talented, educated workers and innovative development. It also acknowledges the limitations of old-style southern recruitment packages. The initial report included this comment from former Shelby County mayor Jim Rout: "Fundamental to what we have already learned is that we must stop selling our community at a discount. Instead, we must sell it for its value. In the old economy, economic development was built on tax breaks, subsidies, cheap land, and cheap labor. But no more. Today, in the new economy, a region's competitive advantage is quality—quality workers, quality of life, and quality innovation."[81]

THE LEGACY OF MEMPHIS DEVELOPMENT
AND UNDERDEVELOPMENT

As Memphis struggles to attract and retain new workers and to meet educational needs of citizens in a high-tech economy, the city faces persistent problems stemming from previous development decisions. First, the city has not resolved the environmental and social costs of the industrial era. New Chicago, a disadvantaged neighborhood in North Memphis, has not recovered from job loss and neighborhood decline associated with deindustrialization. The Firestone plant site, one of a hundred brownfield sites in Memphis, has been designated a National Brownfield Assessment Pilot by the Environmental Protection Agency, but redevelopment efforts are incomplete. Arlington, another North Memphis community, recently opened a park where a former pesticide plant left behind a contaminated waste site. The Environmental Protection Agency spent $5 million to recover the land in its "return-to-use" program, the only environmental recovery program to be completed in the Mid-South region.[82]

Second, questions and criticism plague the city and county's most utilized financial incentive tool for attracting business and job opportunities, the Payment in Lieu of Taxes program. In 1987, the Memphis City Council and the Shelby County commissioners granted the Industrial Development Board (IDB) authority to grant PILOTS to promote development. Because state law does not permit local governments to grant tax abatements for private properties, the PILOT permits ownership of the private property to be conveyed to the IDB, which classifies the property as tax-exempt. The private owner leases the property from the IDB for a specified annual payment and term not to exceed fifteen years. When the term expires, ownership is transferred from the IDB back to the private owner and the property is fully assessed and taxed. The PILOT program uses an economic impact analysis and evaluation matrix to compute the monetary value and time period for extending tax assistance to corporations. Each PILOT applicant receives points for the number of new jobs to be created and jobs retained as well as additional points for capital investment and project location. Special consideration points are awarded to Fortune 500 companies and to corporate headquarters relocations. Currently more than five hundred companies benefit from PILOTS, including FedEx, Thomas Betts, Quebecor, and Medtronic Sofamor Danek.

Confusion about the administration of the program by three separate agencies—the IDB, the Center City Revenue Financial Corporation, and the Memphis Health, Education, and Housing Facilities Board—and oversight by the city council influenced the city-county decision to obtain an external review. Critics of the program object to the amount of deferred taxes and complain about unfairness in the application process. Some view the program as disadvantageous for entrepreneurs and perceive the IDB as serving the interests of the business community, not public interests. Arguing that PILOTS have been good for business, they wonder if the PILOTS have been good for Memphis. Others criticize the proliferation of PILOTS, linking them to local property tax increases for homeowners and businesses who are unfairly burdened with supporting the costs of development in a state that has no income tax.

Consulting firms NexGen Advisors and URS Corporation completed their study of the PILOT program's effectiveness in December 2005. Comparing Memphis to Nashville, Tennessee; Indianapolis, Indiana; Louisville, Kentucky; and De Soto County, Mississippi, they concluded that Memphis is a more expensive place for doing business and needs to offer financial incentives for recruiting employers. The consultants recommended continuing the PILOT program and making changes. First, they cautioned against use of the economic impact analysis and evaluation matrix as the sole measures of granting a PILOT. The study recommended using a "but for" test of true economic need, suggesting a gap analysis or competitive cost analysis for competing sites would provide a more accurate evaluation. Further, they recommended eliminating bonus points for locating businesses in the city of Memphis. Instead, they recommended awarding bonus points for locating in targeted areas of the city, especially areas most affected by deindustrialization and disinvestment as evidenced by declining property taxes. They also recommended restructuring the IDB boards. Most important, the evaluation recommended that Memphis and Shelby County develop additional economic development tools so that they do not rely exclusively on PILOTs.[83]

A separate study conducted at George Mason University's Mercatus Center criticized any use of targeted tax incentives for attracting employers as a means of economic development in distressed communities. The study cited the Memphis / Shelby County PILOT program as a case in point.[84] The Mercatus Center report claims that across-the-board tax cuts actually expand economic growth, whereas targeted incentives do not. Targeted tax incentives are financed at the expense of existing businesses, assuming that employers stay in Memphis when benefits are exhausted. In Memphis, for each year between 1988 and 2000, the PILOT program cost taxpayers an estimated $23 million per year, but the city received few benefits. The city failed to lower unemployment rates and poverty rates. In 1990, the city's unemployment rate equaled the national average. Today, almost twenty years later, the local unemployment rate is higher than the national average and the poverty rate is double the national average.

The Mercatus Center study also criticized failed PILOT agreements. Between 1993 and 2002, the PILOT program terminated twenty-one companies for failure to keep promises they made to receive the incentives. Another nineteen companies stayed for the number of years required to benefit from the PILOTs, then left the city. Most companies that received PILOTs remained in Memphis, but there is no way to know how many of these companies would have come and stayed without the PILOTs.[85]

Two recent examples of PILOT awards have provoked controversy. They involve the relocation of two Fortune 500 company corporate headquarters to Memphis—International Paper and ServiceMaster. International Paper announced its decision to move corporate headquarters to Memphis from Stamford, Connecticut, in 2005. The Memphis–Shelby County IDB granted a fifteen-year property tax abatement that could save the company, and cost the city and county, $15 million. International Paper previously relocated some company operations and employees to Memphis in 1987 but maintained its international headquarters in Purchase, New York. In 2001, International Paper headquarters moved to Stamford and received a $1 million loan from Connecticut's Department of Economic and Community Development. Then, in 2005, company officials announced their decision to relocate to Memphis. International Paper agreed to repay Connecticut the $1 million loan and an additional $75,000 penalty incurred for leaving before 2010. Connecticut officials tried to persuade International Paper to remain in the state by offering $1 million and $2 million loan incentives. These incentives could not compete with the Memphis $15 million PILOT.[86] International Paper's relocation decision drew criticism from Stamford officials, who questioned why Memphis would make such a generous offer in return for relocating ninety-four jobs. In Memphis, local critics also questioned the PILOT agreement, arguing that International Paper would have moved to Memphis without the PILOT to offset the expenses of remaining in Stamford.

The following year, in the fall of 2006, ServiceMaster announced its decision to move its headquarters to Memphis from the Chicago metro area. Like International Paper, ServiceMaster is a Fortune 500 firm that already had employees in Memphis. The move would relocate 165 well-paying jobs and add 335 new ones to the 2,400 jobs already established. ServiceMaster claimed that if a different site had been selected for relocating corporate headquarters, some of its current jobs in Memphis would have been relocated. The company submitted two different PILOT applications. The Memphis–Shelby County Industrial Development Board approved both of them. One application expands ServiceMaster's existing office park in Memphis. The alternate application specifies building a new headquarters on an unspecified greenfield site inside the Memphis city limits. PILOT incentives for ServiceMaster will save the company $8 million over a twelve-year period for expanding its existing site. The PILOT will award $18 million over a twelve-year period for the second site. After the IDB approved the PILOTs, but before the company made its relocation decision, ServiceMaster was purchased by global private equity firm Clayton, Dubilier and Rice for more than $5 billion. Locally, uncertainty was expressed about how the sale would affect Memphis in terms of breaking up the company for resale and creating job loss. But the immediate response of the buyer was that the move to Memphis would continue as scheduled, producing a cost-saving measure for the company. There were no plans to break up the company. The New York–based buyer, Clayton, Dubilier and Rice, is the firm that sold Kinko's to FedEx in 2004.[87]

A third challenge to economic development involves the city's use of public funds for building sports arenas. In 1991, the Pyramid Arena opened to serve Memphis as the home of the University of Memphis men's basketball team, a concert venue, and an exhibition hall. Built at a cost of $65 million, the arena with the stainless steel exterior closed in 2007 with the city owing $25 million in outstanding debt. As part of its recruitment package to attract an NBA team to Memphis—the former Vancouver Grizzlies—the city built a new $250 million sports arena in the Beale Street entertainment district, which opened in 2005. The FedEx Corporation purchased the naming rights. The city named the arena the FedEx Forum. The Memphis Grizzlies' and the University of Memphis men's basketball games, as well as concerts and other sporting events, are held there. From inside the building, visitors can see the Beale Street historic district and the Gibson Guitar factory. The Forum also houses the Rock 'n' Soul Museum, an exhibit created by the Smithsonian. Promoters claim that the arena helped the city attract a new Westin Hotel and retail development, helped convince International Paper to relocate its headquarters to Memphis, and will anchor the redevelopment of another 150 acres adjacent to the Forum. Other cities, such as Sacramento, California, are modeling downtown stadiums after the FedEx Forum, hoping to boost urban redevelopment.[88]

To date, the Memphis Grizzlies have not lived up to city expectations. In 2007, the team had the worst record in the NBA. The team's majority owner, Michael Eisely, offered his 70 percent share for sale. North Carolina developer Brian Davis, former Duke basketball player Christian Laettner, and other investors made an unsuccessful bid to buy the team. A group of local Memphis minority shareholders, including J. R. "Pitt" Hyde III, Barbara Hyde, and others, showed interest in buying Eisely's share after the Davis offer lapsed but were unsuccessful.

Attendance at Grizzly games has decreased, while concerns about the franchise leaving the city are increasing. Initially, critics questioned the use of public funding for a new arena when the Pyramid was operational and $250 million might have been better spent on other essential services. Later, findings that city officials may have misused federal funds in building a private parking garage at the FedEx Forum created additional criticism.

Meanwhile, Memphis and Shelby County governments continue to pay the $25 million debt on the Pyramid while they search for a new tenant. In the fall of 2005, the city and county permitted Memphis film director Craig Brewer to use the building for a sound stage in producing *Black Snake Moan.* Bob Seger and the Silver Bullet Band performed the final concert held there in February 2007.[89] Local governments have considered a number of proposals for reuse of the arena property. Bass Pro Shops proposed a megastore, which includes a hotel and marina, on the site. Memphis developer Greg Ericson proposed an amusement park inside the Pyramid, as well as a hotel and shopping center. Ericson's project would require using private and public funds. Some have suggested renovating the Pyramid and attaching it to the Cook Convention Center, while others have proposed demolishing the structure. A local church, Cummings Street Missionary Baptist Church, offered to buy the Pyramid for $12 million. While the city deliberates the best reuse of the structure, the Pyramid stands empty.

THE FUTURE OF DEVELOPMENT

Local economic activities, embedded in global flows and networks, generate unequal outcomes in the city of Memphis. As twenty-first-century city leaders and policymakers ponder how Memphis might enhance its geographic, economic, and social assets to achieve the goal of becoming a "world-class city," they struggle with the historical legacy of slavery, segregation, smoke-stack chasing, environmental contamination, and underinvestment in education. Recognizing that global competitiveness demands more than "selling" natural resources and low-cost labor to attract investments, Memphis business elites face the challenge of attracting new knowledge workers while trying to enhance employment skills and improve health outcomes for existing city residents. Also, recognizing the desirability of a pristine natural environment, leaders must find solutions to environmental degradation produced by earlier generations. Finally, tax incentive and abatement strategies also need to be analyzed more rigorously to assess the public costs and benefits.

Traditional "place wars" that pit Memphis against other cities, especially southern locations, willing to use tax incentives to "sell" local sites have produced questionable local gains for the majority of residents.[90] As local leaders endorse more public-private partnerships to foster entrepreneurial strategies, support increased investments in workforce development, and make plans for airport expansion, they find new ways to engage in the "production of locality." Recognizing that Memphis—the place—consists of a unique combination of assets such as geographic location and proximity to rich natural resources, as well as a transportation and distribution infrastructure and a heritage of entrepreneurialism, is positive for economic development. But the legacy of underdevelopment in human capital continues to shape inequality and affects efforts to become a "world-class" city.

—— 5 ——

GLOBALIZATION & POPULAR CULTURE

Memphis and the Paradoxes of Innovation

No other city in the South "derives its sustenance and character so completely or from such a large area of farm lands and little towns."[1] Yet this rural-minded city lacking Old South traditions and aristocratic pretensions, as well as New South achievements, repopulated by members of an "impoverished and subjugated rural underclass" after yellow fever epidemics, created the "global popular music of the mid-twentieth century."[2] A unique combination of place-specific cultural resources, technological innovation in recording, the rise of independent radio, and entrepreneurial vision transformed Memphis into an urban center of a global popular culture in the 1950s. But the city's reputation as a cultural center began decades earlier, and global interest in the place where it all began continues long after the deaths of many cultural icons and the demise of early local recording studios. Today, ongoing production of books, films, new releases of old recordings, and new recordings carry on the legacy of the city and its culture for appreciation by mass audiences. But scholars also recognize the city's cultural significance. British scholar Peter Hall identifies Memphis as one of the great "Cities in Civilization" along with Athens,

Florence, Paris, London, Vienna, and Tokyo.[3] Scholarly attention to Memphis as a place of cultural innovation and production is somewhat surprising given the city's fairly recent founding, its racial and class divisions, and its lack of elite support for high culture. Typically, historical and scholarly recognition of cities linked to cultural innovation includes recognition of "old cities dominated by elites . . . or at least bourgeois wealth" and cities committed to "high" cultural pursuits.[4] Memphis, a younger city associated with "low" or populist culture, may not be a typical place of cultural innovation. Nonetheless, Memphis is a significant place. Hall lets us know that "no one kind of city nor any one size of city has a monopoly on creativity or the good life."[5]

Notwithstanding widespread global attention from fans, critics, and scholars, the idea of Memphis as a significant place of cultural innovation and production has not garnered a great deal of local respect until recently. For many years, Memphians really did not like "the idea of being the birthplace of rock & roll."[6] Local appreciation of Memphis as a significant cultural place occurred slowly—decades after Memphis music transformed conventional tastes for popular culture both nationally and globally. Memphis music includes the blues; country; a synthesis of the blues and country, which became rock and roll; and soul music. Originating in the Mississippi Delta and the hills of Appalachia and associated with poor, uneducated migrants or rowdy adolescent rockers, Memphis music, like the blues, preserves "the historical legacy of a people confined to the lowest echelon of the social order" and dramatizes "the cultural vitality and rebelliousness of the participants evoking race and class solidarity."[7] Not surprisingly, Memphis music has a history of rejection by mainstream white Memphians and many middle-class black Memphians, who prefer to distance themselves and their city from what some view as the music's racial and provincial characteristics, as well as the "outsider" status associated with "low-down culture." Late bluesman Willie Dixon wrote about the rejection of blues culture in his autobiography:

> All the blues songs actually related back to Africa or some African heritage things. . . . They've got blues books out there that tell a little about everybody—his name and what songs he sang—but they don't have one of the actual blues experience involved. . . . Ninety-nine percent of the people that wrote stories about the blues gave people phony ideas and this gave the blues a bad reputation. They had people believing the blues was a low-down type of music and underestimating the blues one

hundred percent. The majority of people have been taught to stay away from the blues because the world didn't actually want you to understand what the blues want.[8]

Traditionally, mainstream Memphians have separated themselves from "others" and the culture associated with them. The divide has been marked not only by differences in cultural preferences but also by physical, legal, and social boundaries, especially those associated with the Jim Crow South. But these boundaries have blurred or converged at sites associated with cultural innovation, first on Beale Street, then at Sun Studio and Stax Records. The music and the musicians not only "transgressed the color line and middle-class taste" but also appeared as "a calculated affront to polite white society."[9]

Rock and roll and soul music contributed to "a cultural revolution that recoded music, language, dress, dance, and values."[10] Typically, the city of Memphis, a place associated with that cultural revolution, has not embraced it. At certain historical periods, Memphis city officials acted to demolish Beale Street and surrounding neighborhoods, as if their disruptions of the physical landscapes could "sterilize the very soil" that gave rise to the blues, rock, and soul musical tradition recognized throughout the world. Recently, however, more than fifty years after Beale Street, Sun Studio, Stax Records, and artists such as B. B. King, Otis Redding, Rufus Thomas, Carla Thomas, Johnny Cash, Elvis Presley, Aretha Franklin, Isaac Hayes, Al Green, Steve Cropper, and others captured the imagination of a global audience, some local views have changed. Isaac Hayes said, "It took a whole world outside of Memphis to recognize what a treasure black Memphis had."[11] City leaders and developers, who in earlier times might have distanced themselves from local culture, especially African American cultural contributions, now boast about the global significance of the culture and the *place* associated with it. Consequently, incorporating the legacy of Memphis music, reinvigorating key sites, and reinvesting in downtown are part of rebuilding the urban landscape and developing a relatively new industry—tourism and urban entertainment. Decisions to revalorize Memphis cultural innovation and production and to reposition the city as a site of entertainment and popular culture have been influenced by global cultural and economic trends and local realization that tourism is the fastest-growing sector of the global economy.

Renewed interest in the significance of place and local culture within a global context raises questions about globalization, localization, culture, and place. Most theoretical discussions of the impact of *globalization* focus on the homogenization of culture and the declining significance of place-based local cultural expression as well as the declining significance of place. In other words, the global, which is deemed to be ubiquitous and inauthentic, stifles or suppresses cultural innovation, which is presumed to be both "local" and authentic, and obscures place distinctions.[12] Countertheories of *localization* note the persistence of local culture, explain how "the local resists, absorbs, and ultimately transforms the global," and suggest that new localisms emerge within global flows, which often form resistance.[13] Both perspectives view the global-local nexus as oppositional, but a third perspective views it as relational. In other words, the intermingling of global and local processes fosters hybridization of culture as well as interdependent social, economic, and political relations.[14] Each "place" is uniquely situated in networks of global relations and cultural flows and embedded in its own accumulated local history. When city leaders and cultural innovators find themselves navigating global flows of culture and commerce, local values and practices may change. Some attribute these changing local practices to the intensification of globalization and transnational capitalism. Others suggest, however, that changes in local practices reflect the emergence of new forms of local identity and cultural expression and kindle a progressive sense of place.[15]

Memphis, as a site of innovation and production of popular culture, shows that cultural innovation, when technologically transformed and transmitted through global and iconological processes, can lead to an affirmation of the *local* significance of place and contribute to the transformation of *global* culture. Evidence reveals that for a period of time, local leaders and officials may devalue the significance of cultural innovation and place. But global processes may affect *local* reconsideration of cultural expression as a place-based *local* resource, which leads to repositioning and reimagining place within global and local contexts and changing local practices.[16] Eventually, these global and local processes influence decisions about place building and economic development that affect new cycles of cultural innovation and production but raise new questions about authenticity of place and culture and the future of cultural innovation.

BEALE STREET: THE PLACE WHERE MEMPHIS MUSIC BEGAN

Beale Street, at times revered by African Americans as a center of cultural innovation and commerce but reviled by many straitlaced middle-class Memphians—both black and white—as a haven of sin and vice, has become an object "of cultural consumption for tourists . . . avid for spectacles and the picturesque."[17] Beale Street has become a central component of Memphis development efforts to enhance local urban landscapes as globally branded entertainment. The Beale Street Historic District, part of the city's "theme enhancement" of Memphis music and culture calculated to bring visitors to the "home of the blues" and "the birthplace of rock 'n' roll," attracts more than 4 million visitors per year.[18] And music-related tourism generates an estimated $86 million in state taxes and $12 million in local tax revenues.[19] These tax revenues are extremely significant in a state with a budget that operates without a personal income tax and relies heavily on sales tax revenue.

Some critics discount Beale Street's current transformation as just another theme park in a landscape of consumption. In their view, it has become a central part of a "fantasy city"—a "Disneyfied," sanitized, contrived entertainment district for white tourists in a themed metropolis that is no longer considered a real place.[20] Some supporters view music-related events, especially those associated with the Beale Street Music Festival and Memphis in May, as central to uniting people in the city of Memphis, by developing community pride and creating opportunities for social interaction and economic growth.[21] Some observers may deny the authenticity of today's Beale Street Historic District. Others, however, celebrate the participation of minority investors in twenty-first-century development of Beale Street as a measure of racial and social progress. Others view the current development boom as another incarnation of the famous street that is central to the city's history yet replete with contradictions. Cycles of marginalization, demonization, devastation, and renovation chronicle Beale Street's transformation from a racialized space in a segregated city after the Civil War to a mainstream twenty-first-century tourist attraction. At different times, Beale Street has served the city of Memphis as an urban refuge for poor rural migrants, the center of life in a "separate city," the proud and enterprising Main Street of Black America, the bane of progressive-minded Memphians, a ghost town vacated by urban renewal, and the local center of downtown economic renewal and restoration in a changing global economy.

The white people of Memphis have never understood just what Beale Street really meant
and means to my people.—W. C. HANDY, interview at his home in New York, 1955

Beale Street first appeared on a Memphis city map in 1840. From the beginning, Beale Street—the street, neighborhood, and *place*—assumed a unique identity. The contributions of Beale Street to the city of Memphis began almost immediately, as did contradictions about the place, its people, its commerce, and its culture. From the outset, the people drawn to Beale included many who were segregated and marginalized, including free African Americans who settled Beale before the Civil War, emancipated slaves who moved to Memphis after the Civil War, and streams of rural southern migrants and Italian and Jewish immigrants who arrived after the yellow fever epidemics of the 1870s. During the yellow fever epidemics, when whites who could afford to do so fled the city or moved farther east away from downtown and the riverfront, poor whites and African Americans stayed to care for the sick, bury the dead, and maintain order in the city. Paradoxically, some African Americans became "people of substance" in the Memphis business community. Robert Church Sr., who bought up property on Beale from whites who fled farther east attempting to escape yellow fever, became the dominant property owner in the 1890s. Church, often identified as the first African American millionaire in the United States, transformed Beale Street into a commercial and cultural center and the unofficial capital of Black America. On Beale Street, Church founded the Solvent Savings and Loan in 1906, as well as a privately owned park for African Americans, named Church Park, and an auditorium, Church Auditorium.[22]

At the beginning of the twentieth century, Beale Street was composed of three distinct sections. Cotton warehouses occupied the western end of Beale closest to the Mississippi River. A commercial district spanned from Main to Fourth. A residential section inhabited by affluent whites continued east along Beale to Manassas.[23] Of these three sections, however, only one constituted the "authentic" Beale. Four lively blocks stretched from Main to Fourth Street, where saloons, pool halls, grocery stores, barbecue stands, nightclubs, and bordellos welcomed rural black migrants to an "experiment in urban living for a people who had never known cities."[24] Beale Street, on the margins of white Memphis, permitted black Memphians to enjoy anonymity and freedom from the constraints of segregation and surveillance.

Neil writes: "On Beale, for perhaps the first time in American history, black *was* beautiful."[25] And every night was Saturday night.

Rural African American migrants, as well as Italian and Jewish immigrants, discovered economic and cultural opportunities on Beale Street. They found ways to express creativity, pride, and dignity by creating a meaningful *place* in a racialized space on the borders of a segregated southern city. At first a product of racism and exclusion, Beale Street became a place for black professionals, a black bank, a black newspaper, and a black church, as well as a place for political and cultural expression. Ida B. Wells, former schoolteacher, anti-lynching crusader, and co-owner and editor of the *Free Speech and Headlight* newspaper, lived in the neighborhood before she fled Memphis in exile. In the 1920s, a teenager named Richard Wright boarded with a family on Beale Street while he lived and worked en route from Jackson, Mississippi, to Chicago, Illinois, where he became an eminent author. Black millionaires such as Robert Church and J. E. Walker of the Universal Life Insurance Company lived on Beale. But more colorful street characters lived and worked there, too. Beale Street was home to Mack Harris, cardsharp; Dr. Scissors, the herbal medicine man; Bad Sam and Jimmy Turpri, gamblers; and Louise Cook, an exotic dancer. The street boasted an array of pawn shops and secondhand stores, black doctors' and dentists' offices, and the Memphis Italian Club.[26]

During the first half of the twentieth century, Beale Street and Memphis attracted talented performers from Mississippi, Arkansas, and Tennessee. Some of them, such as W. C. Handy, Robert Johnson, Bessie Smith, Memphis Minnie, and B. B. King, rose to national prominence after playing in Memphis bars and juke joints. In an interview with Robert Palmer, Rufus Thomas reminisced about amateur night on Beale Street, saying, "That's where B. B. King, Bobby Bland, all of them came from, right there. Used to be where they'd give away prizes to the winners. Had three, five, five dollars, three dollars, two dollars . . . at the Palace Theater. It was the only one on Beale Street. The only house, where they did shows on Beale Street."[27]

Beale Street also attracted nationally known performers, including Duke Ellington, Dizzy Gillespie, Lionel Hampton, Count Basie, and others.[28] Because of the color line and class divisions, Duke Ellington and other big bands played for white audiences at the Orpheum and entertained at the Handy Theatre for middle-class black audiences. But after hours, members of big bands—Basie's and Ellington's—came out on Beale Street and jammed with local musicians. Rufus Thomas explained that in the '30s, big bands played in the bigger clubs. The guys who played the blues—harmonica, guitar, and drums—played in the juke joints. But sometimes musicians "started in the rhythm and blues and moved up. Cause some of the players started playing saxophone, getting their basics, and then they'd move up and on occasion they'd go back."[29] These jam sessions sometimes lasted until six or seven o'clock the next morning.

Most white Memphians and many middle-class African Americans, especially religious conservatives of both races, did not share Rufus Thomas's enthusiasm for Beale Street, nor have they embraced its cultural progeny since. City leaders—white and black—obsessed with the need to transform Memphis and its reputation from a raucous riverboat town into a respectable "Middle American Big City" employed various strategies for surveillance and control of Beale and surrounding neighborhoods. Alternately, they patrolled, policed, or demolished the physical place in attempts to "sterilize the very soil" that produced the city's musical and cultural heritage.[30]

Lt. George W. Lee, a local African American business leader and writer who published books and articles celebrating Beale Street and the blues, described Beale Street as "the place where the blues began." He captured the thrill of listening to music on Beale Street during the 1920s and 1930s, which he described as the "breeding place of smoking red-hot syncopation" on "the Main Street of Negro America."[31] Lee, who received the French Croix de Guerre medal for bravery in World War I, returned to Memphis, where he became a "political boss" on Beale Street from the 1920s through the 1950s. By the time of his death in 1976, Lee had written extensively about Beale Street and its people. Lee traced local disapproval of Beale Street to the era of the Crump machine.[32] E. H. Crump, a migrant from Holly Springs, Mississippi, ran a powerful political machine that dominated city and county politics from the time of his own election to the city mayor's office in 1909 until his death in 1954. The Crump machine became famous for ballot stuffing, intimidating voters, recruiting and paying the poll tax to enfranchise "reliable" (that is, promachine) black voters, tolerating vice, and maintaining loyalty files on local residents. Not surprisingly, Crump's machine came under federal scrutiny twice in the 1930s for voter irregularities.[33] But Crump ran for public office as a reformer, and in his mayoral campaign of 1909, he promised voters to rid the city of "easy riders," that is, pimps and gamblers. Interestingly, Crump commissioned W. C. Handy to compose his campaign song, "Mr. Crump," which contained the following words:

Mr. Crump don't 'low no easy riders here
Mr. Crump don't 'low it—ain't goin' have it here
We don't care what Mister Crump don't 'low
We gonna bar'l house anyhow
Mr. Crump can go and catch his-self some air.[34]

Crump won the election but never honored his campaign promise to drive away the "easy riders." In 1916, he found himself ousted from office by the Tennessee Supreme Court for failure to enforce state prohibition laws. The ruling ended Crump's term, but afterward, the former mayor increased his wealth and strengthened his machine's political control in Memphis. He supposedly allowed anything to happen on Beale Street as long as it did not pose a threat to the safety of whites.[35]

W. C. Handy's fortunes changed after Crump's election. Handy changed the title of "Mr. Crump" to "The Memphis Blues," rewrote the lyrics, and published sheet music for the composition in 1912.[36] Handy moved to New York, but after publication of "The Memphis Blues," purportedly written at the bar in Pee Wee's saloon on Beale Street, Handy's career took off. Following publication of "St. Louis Blues" in 1914 and "Beale Street Blues" in 1916, Handy's sheet music and his bands achieved international recognition for the musician and won local respect. The city of Memphis named Handy Park in his honor on Beale Street in 1931.

But early in the twentieth century, Beale Street also won a reputation for having more brothels per square mile than anywhere in the United States except New Orleans. The availability of drugs and prostitution and the frequency of violence and underworld activities in the city gave Memphis the name of the "murder capital" of the United States and an infamous reputation as the most dangerous place in the country.[37] In 1938–39, Crump moved against vice in the city and on Beale Street when it no longer served his political interests to look the other way; subsequently, narcotics, bootleg liquor, gambling, prostitution, and underworld figures expanded their businesses across state lines to West Memphis, Arkansas, and De Soto County, Mississippi.[38] By 1940, the murder rate declined, and in 1960, Memphis reported the lowest homicide rate of any southern city.[39]

Curiously, before the Crump era began, and before Handy wrote "Beale Street Blues," a city ordinance had already changed the official name of Beale Street to Beale Avenue. In 1905, all city streets running north and south were designated as streets, and those running east and west became avenues. For the next fifty years, the street continued to be referred to as Beale Street, but the name Beale Avenue appeared on street signs and city maps. In 1955, when Danny Thomas, the entertainer who founded St. Jude Children's Research Hospital, toured the city, he questioned Mayor Frank Tobey about the absence of the legendary street name, saying: "Hey!! Look. What is this Beale Avenue doing here? This ought to be Beale STREET—the street Handy made famous." At the behest of Thomas, Mayor Tobey, and Frank Ahlgren, editor of the *Memphis Commercial Appeal*, the city replaced the Beale Avenue signs and put Beale Street back on the city map.[40]

A few years earlier, Beale Street's name and reputation had received attention in the September 1950 edition of *Ebony* magazine in a feature article titled "The New Beale Street: New Generation Changing Fabulous Negro Street into Symbol of Business Enterprise."[41] Referring to the name change, *Ebony* commented that "the Beale Street of yesteryear has been no more for years," but everyone still calls it Beale Street.[42] The article went a step further to pronounce the demise of the old Beale Street with its easy riders, gamblers, and pimps to welcome growth of a new generation of businesses on Beale Street in an era of postwar prosperity and racial equality:

> For decades the most colorful, exciting street in all Negro America has been fabulous Beale Street in Memphis—known variously in the past as "the murder capital of the world," "Saturday night heaven" and "the street where the blues began." Today, however, Beale Street is but a ghost of the boisterous thoroughfare of yesterday. Its sweet men and easy riders are gone; its gambling dens and night spots are shut down. . . . But a new generation has come up on Beale Street. . . . Out of the battered, decayed remains of yesterday's glories, a new Beale Street is arising as a symbol of the new, enterprising, forward-looking Southern negro of today. . . . Negroes are now pioneering in new businesses and the Negro cops are walking the beat.[43]

Hopes for a new generation of black businesses on Beale failed to materialize. As noted by the magazine, pawn shops were closing, and new businesses, such as Tri-State Bank, opened doors on Beale and created opportunities for African Americans. But after World War II, the conditions of old buildings worsened and some establishments were forced to leave the area due to high rents, high repair costs, or lost leases.[44] *Ebony* accurately reported that African American policemen walked the beat on Beale Street but failed to mention that black cops wore different uniforms than white police and were not permitted to arrest white citizens. But Ernest Withers, one of the nine African American policemen especially commissioned to patrol Beale Street from 1948 to 1950, credited black policemen with helping to put an end to vice rackets that gave the street a bad reputation.[45] Notwithstanding these improvements in the area, *Ebony*'s prediction of a new era of business prosperity for Beale proved to be inaccurate. Fortunes declined for most downtown businesses, especially Beale Street merchants and musicians, in the second half of the twentieth century due to dramatic urban changes that followed World War II. These changes included rapid increases in private automobile ownership, the expansion of suburban sprawl, the decline of downtown retailing, ascendance of the civil rights movement, and the implementation of urban renewal.

DEVASTATION

Beale Street was the greatest place on earth . . . until they rurnt it.—THOMAS PINKSTON, quoted in Robert Palmer, "Beale Street Redeemed," *Memphis*, April 1978

By all accounts, Beale Street and all of downtown Memphis changed dramatically in the 1950s and 1960s. Karl Diamond, who operated the Green Castle Restaurant on Beale from 1951 to 1956, described the good times: "On the street was like a beehive. It was like Times Square in New York. I mean day and night."[46] But businesses declined and building conditions deteriorated "when suburban shopping drew the whites off Main, and Main then drew the blacks off Beale."[47] The city's small population increases were outpaced by dramatic growth in land area. After World War II, the area of the city expanded to five and a half times its former size. The city of Memphis, which covered 51 square miles in 1945, had sprawled to roughly 280 square miles thirty years later.[48] The rapid expansion of the city over such a large area depleted the historic downtown core of people and capital. Memphis city officials and the Chamber of Commerce sought federal funds to revitalize downtown using the two most powerful federal programs available—interstate highway construction and urban renewal. But these actions exacerbated the problem. Adopting the 1955 Comprehensive Plan prepared by Harland and Bartholomew Associates, the city set in motion a number of significant changes intended to improve streets and parking to accommodate the increasing number of automobiles, make downtown more accessible, improve the urban landscape, and recruit new industry (see chapter 4). By the early

1960s, city planners and the Memphis Housing Authority considered Beale Street to be an ideal site for developing a shopping mall and an entertainment district designed to bring people downtown. But they viewed the dilapidated buildings on Beale Street and low-income people who lived in the area, as well as pawn shops, secondhand stores, and bars, as obstacles to "revitalization." Urban renewal funds seemed to offer a panacea for all problems—the means to remove unwanted businesses and residents and to pave the way for new development. A second planning document claimed that Beale Street had to be destroyed to be saved and to save the center of the city.[49]

Opponents of urban renewal included Lt. George W. Lee and others who worked to preserve Beale Street and recognize its heritage as a valuable part of the city. In 1966, Congress declared Beale Street a national historic landmark and officially recognized it as the birthplace of the blues. Unfortunately, the national designation did not dissuade local leaders from pursuing urban renewal funds for demolition of the area. Paradoxically, most black investors and business leaders, including the Memphis chapter of the National Business League, joined white business leaders to *support* urban renewal plans for Beale Street, whereas local white storeowners on Beale, including a number of Jewish businessmen, *opposed* urban renewal.[50] The Memphis Chapter of the National Urban League supported urban renewal, stating:

> "As a racial group we have been moved and removed in urban renewal programs," the resolution says. "Now for the first time when a Negro group seeks to build and participate in the removal and renewal of an area which will displace a group of white merchants, a loud cry is made against the whole concept of urban renewal. If this concept is fair and legal when Negroes are removed, congruously it is fair when whites are removed. For the sad truth is that if the urban renewal plans were dropped tomorrow, no one would be sadder or more sick than the 'Beale Street merchants' who say they oppose. For they are part of a dying street that vitally needs help from some outside source."[51]

Beale Street musicians and merchants, disagreeing with the dominant views held by black and white members of the business community, opposed urban renewal plans. Blues musician Otto Lee told one interviewer, "I hope they can keep Beale Street like it is. It's going to be a controversial thing. But would it be Beale Street if it was remodeled up?"[52] Alvin Lansky, co-owner of Lansky Brothers, stressed the historical significance of the street and the authenticity of the old buildings. He said: "You're forgetting one thing. If you tear down all these buildings you will no longer have Beale Street, and you will defeat your purpose."[53] In the end, the Beale Street musicians, Lansky, and the owner-merchants failed to convince city officials. Just as they predicted, urban renewal destroyed most of the business district on Beale.[54] Thomas Pinkston, a teenaged violinist with W. C. Handy's band around 1917 who played in the pit band at Beale Street Palace Theater between 1920 and 1930, observed that "Beale Street was the greatest place on earth . . . until they rurnt it."[55] A few businesses survived the hard times, including Schwab's Dry Goods Store, which originally opened in 1876 and continues to operate on Beale.

Lanksy Brothers also fared better than most. On the corner of Beale Street and Second, Lansky Brothers opened for business soon after World War II as an army-surplus store. It evolved into a men's clothing store that specialized in stylish clothes worn primarily by African Americans and then sensationalized by Elvis Presley. On Beale, brothers Alvin and Bernard Lanksy "made a decent living on an indecent street" by selling stylish clothes.[56] Musicians who performed on Beale Street and nearby clubs outfitted themselves at Lansky Brothers in mohair and sharkskin, plaid tuxedo jackets, and peg-leg pants. Customers included Count Basie, Lionel Hampton, Duke Ellington, B. B. King, Jerry Lee Lewis, and Roy Orbison.[57] Elvis Presley purchased his first suit there and shopped for hi-boy collar shirts, pegged pants, and black suits with combinations of pink and black. Lansky Brothers outfitted Elvis for the Louisiana Hayride and for his famous appearance on the *Ed Sullivan Show*. Despite urban renewal, Bernard Lansky remained in business on Beale Street until 1981, when he relocated to the Peabody Hotel two blocks away and leased the building on Beale Street to Elvis Presley Enterprises. Today, Lansky operates four shops in the Peabody Hotel and a website.[58]

Few merchants fared as well as Schwab or Lansky. The city rapidly proceeded with urban renewal and demolished most buildings, not only because business interests prevailed but also because racial tensions and "fear of the other" escalated in a dramatic series of local and national events. Only two years after Beale Street became the city's first landmark to appear on the National Register of Historic Places, local leaders blamed Beale Street and surrounding neighborhoods for city problems ranging from downtown disinvestment to civil unrest, racial conflict, crime, and poverty. The year 1968 was a watershed year in American history with political conflict related to the war in Vietnam, the president's decision not to seek reelection, the assassinations of Senator Robert Kennedy and Martin Luther King Jr., and outbreaks of urban violence. The year marked a critical juncture for Memphis and Beale Street—a period marked by violence, death, and devastation.

One of those significant events that took place in 1968, the fatal shooting of Dr. King on the balcony of the Lorraine Motel in Memphis, occurred in a badly divided city, site of the protracted Sanitation Workers' Strike. In the spring of 1968, city sanitation workers demanded higher wages as well as safer and more humane working conditions following the accidental deaths of two workers. Assisted by the American Federation of State, County, and Municipal Employees and the Southern Christian Leadership Conference, the workers went on strike. Mayor Henry Loeb and the city council refused to negotiate with the strikers or their representatives. A standoff occurred despite pleas of local churches, a black boycott of downtown stores, and peaceful daily marches.

Beale Street and surrounding neighborhoods became central to support for the Sanitation Workers' Strike. Daily marches, involving striking workers and supporters, originated at Clayborn Temple, located on Hernando Street, only a block and a half south of Beale. Each day, beginning on 26 February, two streams of marchers—one in the morning and one in the afternoon—walked fourteen blocks along Main Street to City Hall, then returned along that route to Clayborn Temple. The marchers distributed literature and carried signs, some mounted on sticks, stating simply but eloquently, "I am a Man."[59] Clayborn Temple was surrounded by "an area of rapid deterioration, broken gutters, decrepit houses with dirty yards and a few wilting trees, gas stations, liquor stores, little barbecue places serving the best barbecue in town."[60] The neighborhood also contained offices of the NAACP, Universal Life Insurance Company, and Tri-State Bank, as well as the Foote Homes housing project for poor people. At the time of the strike, little actual demolition had taken place to clear urban renewal sites, except at the corner of Beale Street and Main, where demolition was under way for constructing the Memphis Light Gas and Water administration building.

Responding to invitations from supporters of the strike, Martin Luther King Jr., in the midst of planning for the Poor People's March to be held in Washington, D.C., traveled from Atlanta to Memphis on two occasions to join the peaceful march from Clayborn Temple to City Hall. During Dr. King's first visit on 28 March 1968, violence broke out as marchers approached the corner of Main Street and Beale Street. As young people smashed store windows on Beale Street, the police responded with tear gas and force, and Dr. King's advisers moved him to safety. Looting and rioting followed, and the governor called in the National Guard to seal off the Beale Street area.[61] King returned to Memphis for a second visit with plans to complete the march he had begun earlier. On 4 April, Dr. King was fatally shot on the balcony of the Lorraine Motel, a few blocks from Beale. Rioting broke out once again, the National Guard returned to downtown streets, and the city returned to martial law. However, the march did take place on 8 April 1968 and was delayed for a few minutes at the intersection of Main and Beale for Coretta Scott King, who flew in from Atlanta, to take the lead.[62] On 5 April 1968, the day after King's assassination, the city council met and cast the final vote to expedite approval for interstate construction through Overton Park in midtown and to accelerate the demolition of Beale Street downtown. Beale Street, once tolerated by whites as a boundary between "separate cities"—one black and one white, one perceived as exotic and decadent, the other perceived as conservative and dominant—had become intolerable to white policymakers. Beale Street—a space "inscribed with the politics and ideology" of Jim Crow—had become a place of civil disorder and a symbolic representation of disruption of the social fabric.[63] Consequently, fear of the "other" and fear of "place" associated with the "other" led to devastating material and social consequences for the city.[64]

The link between local (white) perceptions of Beale and city policies had existed for some time. But in the aftermath of 4 April 1968, when fear of "the other" intensified and Memphians struggled to deal with their city's damaged reputation in the eyes of the world, planners felt justified in their conviction that Beale had to be destroyed to be saved and to save the center of the city. Subsequently, the assassination of Dr. King brought about "the assassination of Beale Street."[65] Through urban renewal, the Memphis Housing Authority achieved one aim, "to get rid of what was there: both the houses and their inhabitants."[66] These tragic losses created additional social and cultural costs because they not only failed to restore the city's national reputation but also widened the local racial and class divide.

Despite assertions that urban renewal would restore or revitalize Beale Street, in reality, "revitalizing Beale Street meant tearing most of it down and making what was left into something other than Beale Street had ever been."[67] It would no longer be an authentic community, a mixed-use business district, or a center of cultural innovation. Residents would no longer walk to the historic Beale Street Baptist Church where decades earlier baptisms took place in the bayou out back,[68] visit neighbors, or shop and work nearby. Nor would members of the community organize marches to City Hall. The city spared the two blocks on Beale designated by the National Register, as well as the Beale Street Baptist Church and the Orpheum Theatre. But the Memphis Housing Authority reportedly spent 14 to 20 million federal dollars clearing 27 acres, destroying all but 65 of 625 buildings and displacing an estimated 800 to 1,600 families.[69] By 1970, most of the businesses were gone, but private enterprise had not stepped in to replace the buildings or the businesses as had been expected. The Memphis evening newspaper, the *Press-Scimitar*, editorialized that city actions had "destroyed Beale Street, and with it, a part of Memphis."[70] For the next three decades, Beale Street looked more like a ghost town than the "mainstreet of black America," or a vibrant entertainment district. Buildings located on Beale Street, and at a number of downtown sites, fell to wrecking balls and bulldozers, while others stood vacant and neglected. Few replacements filled the empty lots or occupied the vacant building space. A photo essay titled "The Changing Face of Memphis," published in the 4 November 1970 *Press-Scimitar*, described the Beale Street Urban Renewal Area as "looking like a war zone." Some local residents likened it to scenes from the Vietnam War by referring to it as the "DMZ." During the next few years, subsequent newspaper stories asked, "Where have the people gone?"[71] In Memphis, as in many other American cities where displacement and demolition occurred without replacing homes or residents, urban renewal had become "Negro removal."

By 1973, the city's waiting list for subsidized housing had swelled to more than four thousand people, more than ever before.[72] Memphis Housing Authority board member Ethyl Venson recalled: "Urban renewal from 1966 had dealt with structures more than people, and people are the most important. Where are the people who lived around Beale Street? Out on the fringes of the city. There was no concern for housing, just relocation."[73] Interviews with former residents indicated that they had receded into other black neighborhoods, "where their poor presence does not so obviously challenge the heart of the city, the downtown."[74]

From the dominant perspective, the displaced people of Beale Street and the surrounding area were viewed as "people of little substance." But others believed that these residents, more so than the legends, formed the heart of downtown. According to one newspaper writer:

The people were the warp and woof of the tapestry of Beale. They walked the street and shopped its stores and gave it more than transient character. The legends were not part of the design. They were mere incidents in the whole lot of living that went on. And yet, when the business and political interests began thinking about the rebirth of Beale, they judged that only the legends should endure. Only the myth was marketable; the people would have to go. Perhaps they were right. Perhaps there is power enough in the name of Beale alone to assure profit. But it will never again be the Beale Street that anybody who ever lived there knew.[75]

In the minds of most developers' and many city residents, a new Beale Street entertainment district should not resemble any previous state of existence. One developer's comment reflected general sentiments: "Nobody can truly say he wants Beale to be put back like it was. It was degradation. It was extra-legal. Beale in the early 1900s was what every city fears in its inner ghettos today—an unsafe place to walk at night."[76]

Memphis demolition proceeded in a climate of persistent fear. The Memphis Housing Authority continued to use urban renewal funds for "slum clearance" but not for replacing buildings or relocating people. The magnitude of the project to create, package, and market a controlled, organized urban entertainment and shopping experience for middle-class tourists along Beale Street generated conflict, frustration, and failure among a progression of diverse groups and individuals who seemed eager to develop the property but were unsuccessful in obtaining adequate funding. The city took possession of the Beale Street Historic District but failed to find suitable tenants for demolished or deteriorating space. They learned it costs less to tear down a city than to rebuild it.

Downtown demolition continued under the Memphis Housing Authority. Between 1957 and 1977, a total of eleven urban projects razed three thousand structures covering a total of 560 acres.[77] Cotton traders, and other offices that once dominated downtown, followed residents and retail businesses out of the city core into Shelby County and beyond. As people and capital left downtown, neglect, deterioration, and bankruptcy took their place. In 1975, the historic Peabody Hotel went bankrupt and closed operations. Incredibly, "the South's grand hotel" was sold at auction on the steps of the Shelby County Courthouse for $75,000. That same year, Stax Records closed due to a bitter corporate battle and forced bankruptcy. The studio at the corner of McLemore and College, made famous by Otis Redding, Isaac Hayes, Booker T. and the MGs, Al Green, David Porter, and many others, was sold to the Southside Church of God in Christ for $10 in 1980. The church tore down the

Capitol Theater building in 1988.[78] The Lorraine Motel, site of the assassination of Dr. King, almost met a similar fate.[79] Falling into decline after the King assassination, the Lorraine Motel went into foreclosure in 1982. But prominent Memphians, black and white, formed a foundation to purchase the building and raised funds to build a civil rights memorial and museum, which opened in 1991.

Down the street from the closed Peabody Hotel, at the corner of Beale Street and Main, the deteriorating Orpheum Theatre stood surrounded by vacant lots, crumbling buildings, and closed businesses. The ornate theater, originally built in 1928 for stage productions, had served since the 1940s as a Malco movie theater. Endangered by neglect and surrounded by empty lots vacated by urban renewal, the building was acquired by the nonprofit Memphis Development Foundation and added to its growing list of urban redevelopment and preservation projects. At that time, Jehovah's Witnesses also considered buying the Orpheum and renovating it as a place to hold regional religious meetings. Because Tennessee state law prohibited selling alcoholic beverages within 1,500 feet of a religious building, sale of the Orpheum to any religious group would have drastically altered plans to revitalize the Beale Street entertainment district.

While downtown crumbled, things seemed to get worse for Memphis in August 1977 with the sudden death of Elvis Presley at his home, Graceland. Many Memphians who disliked being identified with a city described as "the cradle of rock and roll" and "the nexus of the blues tradition" found it hard to dislike Elvis, the local boy who had become the most commercially successful entertainer in the world. But few people understood the populist appeal of the mythical Elvis. Thus, most Memphians were shocked by the spontaneous expression "of love and fanatic loyalty that erupted within hours of his death" and the arrival of fans and mourners to the city.[80] One year later, fans returned to commemorate the first anniversary of the death of Elvis and once again strained local resources. Memphis was still unprepared for tourism.[81]

Despite years of local planning and discussion of developing Memphis as a tourist destination and rebuilding a downtown entertainment center around the Beale Street Historic District, city leaders did not fully grasp the cultural significance of Elvis or the lasting appeal of any of the city's musical legends and landmarks. Not only did local leaders fail to recognize the global impact of Memphis music and those who created it, but they did not understand the significance of the city of Memphis itself, as a place. In fact, they did not realize that "the credibility of some musical styles and genres arises from their origins, their sites of production," as is evident by their location in places "off the beaten track" and "their remoteness from hearths of industrial production."[82] The very characteristics of Memphis scorned by city officials and business leaders as evidence of backwardness had fostered cultural innovation that had transformed the city itself into a cultural icon. But the city was unprepared to host tourists, and sites identified with cultural icons suffered from neglect and disrepair. "Graceland was inoperative, the building that housed Sun Records was unrecognizable, and Beale Street was in shambles."[83] Stax Records, located in the old Capitol Theater building at the corner of McLemore and College, had been closed by court order since 1976. Stax, formerly a black music empire, had been forced into bankruptcy. The building would be sold to the Church of God in Christ in 1980 and demolished in 1988.[84]

The death of Elvis drew fans and media attention to Memphis. Gradually, city leaders and residents became convinced not only to honor Elvis but also to reconsider the value of Memphis music and the people who produced it as a catalyst for developing tourism.[85] A spokesman for the Memphis Development Foundation (MDF) stated the obvious: "Elvis fans come to Memphis to see something, and besides Graceland, there's nothing to see."[86] A few years later, Stax recording artist Mavis Staples noticed the growth of Elvis-themed city attractions and the absence of other icons. Staples said: "When I came back to Memphis after Stax closed, maybe five years later, I only saw Elvis. And that's when I said, 'wait a minute.' Something should be out here about Stax. Just because it folded doesn't mean it didn't happen. And the people of Memphis should have remembered all of the music."[87] Since then, Memphians have become more aware of the global appeal of Elvis, and recognition has been extended to other members of the city's pantheon of cultural icons. Organizations, both public and private, have taken steps to develop Memphis as "a repository of people's memories and of the past" and as a "repository of cultural symbols."[88] Today, visitors and residents have more to see in terms of museums and studios and more to do downtown.

In August 1979, during what has become known as Elvis Tribute Week, or what some local residents describe as Elvis Death Week, the Memphis Development Foundation unveiled a nine-foot-tall sculpture of Elvis at the Orpheum Theatre. Commissioned by the MDF with permission from the estate shortly after Presley's death, the project by sculptor Eric Parks captures the energy, character, and mythical quality of Elvis as the young man who became a cultural icon. The sculpture was later installed at the Tennessee

Welcome Center located at the downtown riverfront. In 1982, Graceland opened for public tours and has become the second most visited home in the United States, second only to the White House. Graceland attracts more than 600,000 visitors each year from around the world. Estimates suggest that the economic impact of Graceland on Memphis ranges between $300 and $400 million each year.[89] But rebuilding Beale Street and downtown, recovering the legacy of Memphis music, and honoring the contributions of cultural innovators and political leaders have taken decades. These processes of rebuilding downtown as a tourist destination and promoting a place associated with cultural legends and icons have prompted debates surrounding two issues. The first concerns discussion about whether the redeveloped Beale Street entertainment district, and other landmarks, captures the spirit and heritage of this significant place and its cultural authenticity. The second debate involves questions about the tourism and its constraints on local identity and cultural innovation.

RENEWAL: PUBLIC-PRIVATE PARTNERSHIPS AND THE ECONOMICS OF PLACE BUILDING

> Memphis is a city that hasn't happened yet. There exists an opportunity to make it happen, to be part of it.— Governor's Economic and Jobs Conference, 1979

When the first groups of tourists arrived in Memphis following the death of Elvis, they had nothing to see because the dislocations of urban renewal and white flight had transformed a vibrant city into a virtual ghost town, especially on Beale Street and along the riverfront. Even when Graceland and other "Elvis shrines" began to welcome tourists, it appeared that Beale Street, as well as other landmarks associated with black cultural contributions, including Stax, would be lost forever. But in the wake of tragedy, devastation, death, demoralization, and depopulation of the urban core, two organizations emerged to reinvigorate the city, change the face of downtown, and rediscover the city's cultural contributions.

In 1977, the Center City Commission, formed by Memphis and Shelby County, began to coordinate downtown planning, recruit business tenants, and secure financial commitments from public and private sources for downtown redevelopment.[90] In 1979, the Governor's Economic and Jobs Conference held its first annual meeting in Memphis. The 1979 Jobs Conference, and subsequent meetings, provided a public forum for diverse Memphis residents to discuss common interests, weigh local assets and liabilities, and set community goals for future economic development.

Participants in the 1979 Jobs Conference identified assets and liabilities of the city. Their findings say a great deal about the cultural and social divides in Memphis—past and present. Meeting twenty-five years after the 1954 *Brown v. Board of Education* decision, and after witnessing massive social change in the region, participants identified "new pride in the South" as an asset; but they noted "a lack of citizen pride in Memphis" as a liability.[91] The conference report described "diversity" as an asset but criticized the persistence of "economic, cultural, social and political intolerance" and racism for creating "the impression of an unprogressive, divided city." They listed geographic, material, and cultural assets, including the Mississippi River, big buildings, the Convention Center, and Beale Street. But their liabilities list included negative local perceptions, not material or cultural limitations. The report stated: "Memphis is not perceived by its citizens as being an exciting city in which to live. Citizens do not believe there is adequate entertainment, a thriving downtown nor a variety of things to do in Memphis as compared to other cities." The report quoted a survey of Memphians that found support for developing tourism, downtown, Beale Street, and major-league sports. Among respondents, 84 percent agreed that Memphis should develop tourism; 81 percent agreed that Memphis should have major-league sports; 78 percent agreed that Memphis should revitalize the downtown riverfront area; and 75 percent agreed that Memphis should develop Beale Street.[92]

Recommendations from the conference were instrumental in charting the course of economic development and creating a basis for public-private partnerships. After the initial Jobs Conference, Memphis secured $20 million in state funding, which was matched with local and private funds to redevelop the Beale Street Historic District and to renovate the Orpheum Theatre. The Center City Commission played an important role in two critical projects— the Peabody Hotel and Beale Street. A prominent local developer, Jack Belz, bought the Peabody Hotel at auction in 1975, renovated it, and reopened it in 1981. Belz completed the $25 million renovation with support from the Memphis Center City Commission, which included federal tax credits awarded for the rehabilitation of commercial properties listed in the National Register of Historic Places, a federal Community Development Block Grant, loans from the city's Division of Housing and Community Development, loans involving nine local banks, and a ten-year property-tax freeze from the city.[93]

The reopening of the renovated Peabody Hotel attracted local residents back downtown as well as out-of-town visitors. Restoration of the Orpheum Theatre also played a critical role in renewing interest in Beale Street and downtown. Work to restore the Orpheum began with a fund-raising campaign launched by the Memphis Development Foundation and supported by business and corporate leaders, the Tennessee Historical Commission, and the state of Tennessee. In 1982, the Memphis Development Foundation deeded the Orpheum to the city of Memphis and signed a fifty-year lease agreement to operate it.[94] Since then, Orpheum productions have included special concerts and performances, as well as traveling Broadway musical shows such as *Rent, The Lion King, Phantom of the Opera, Miss Saigon, Evita,* and *The 25th Annual Putnam County Spelling Bee.* The Orpheum, which describes itself as "where Broadway meets Beale," attracts more than 300,000 attendees each year.[95]

Additional entertainment projects followed. The Peabody Place Entertainment Center opened in 2001. It occupies a significant portion of the eight city blocks owned by Jack Belz. Across Union Avenue from the Peabody Hotel, AutoZone Park opened in 2000. Home stadium for the Memphis Redbirds AAA baseball team, AutoZone Park became the first venue outside New Orleans to host the Voodoo Music Experience following Hurricane Katrina. North of the Peabody Hotel, the Cannon Center, a state-of-the-art performing arts and convention center, opened in 2003. The FedEx Forum, one block south of Beale Street, opened in 2004. It is a publicly funded $250 million arena for a newly acquired NBA team. The FedEx Forum is home court for the Memphis Grizzlies, formerly the Vancouver Grizzlies, and the University of Memphis men's basketball team. The building boom continues with construction of new hotels and nightclubs.

BEALE STREET: SELLING TOURISM, FABRICATING AUTHENTICITY

We've seen the city evolve, and this is about looking ahead and what Memphis
can become. It's not about the last 50 years; it's about the next 50 years.— GENE CARLISLE,
Memphis developer, quoted in Amos Maki, "One Beale Sings 'Wow!,' "
Memphis Commercial Appeal, 3 December 2005

Today, Beale Street is part of a $2.3 billion downtown redevelopment project that attracts new businesses, new residents, new investors, and tourists. Tourism is big business globally and locally, and in Memphis, tourism is getting bigger. City and state officials have begun to advertise Beale Street as the number one tourist attraction in the state of Tennessee, and the Center City Commission regularly makes new announcements of multimillion-dollar entertainment projects to be constructed on or near Beale Street. Recent announcements include plans to build a $9.7 million hotel and entertainment complex on Beale near the FedEx Forum and a $150 million hotel and luxury condominium development at the western end of Beale Street facing the Mississippi River. A refurbished Sun Studio welcomes tourists, a newly built Stax Museum and Music Academy operates on the old Stax Records site at the corner of College and McLemore, and the Rock 'n' Soul Museum, a Smithsonian-supported exhibit, has relocated from its space in the Gibson Guitar plant to the FedEx Forum. Plans are under way to open a Memphis satellite of the Cincinnati-based Rock and Roll Museum at the Gibson plant. Memphis International Airport recently completed a $25 million renovation of its passenger terminal to give passengers an introduction to the city. Memphis-themed shops and restaurants sell music and T-shirts from Elvis Presley Enterprises, Stax, and Sun Studios, as well as Memphis barbecue and other local food concessions.[96] "Clearly, music-related tourism and its close ties to the musical heritage of Memphis has a large positive impact on the image and economy of Memphis."[97]

All indicators suggest that the global appeal of tourism and the development of local cultural resources will continue to influence development of downtown Memphis for some time to come. But questions have emerged about the impact of the local tourism industry on Memphis, the *place* of cultural heritage and innovation. Has revitalization of Beale Street and a downtown renaissance contributed to a better local understanding of the city's interdependent cultural, social, economic, and political relations? Does commercialization and pursuit of tourism exploit local resources and obscure place distinctions while constructing an idealized representation of place by means of a symbolic economy of authenticity?[98] Other questions emerge concerning commercialization and suppression of cultural innovation associated with populist culture. Will established patterns involving cycles of cultural innovation, local rejection, global recognition, and local revaluation continue?

In many cities, as the tourist industry grows, "the city becomes increasingly dependent upon the construction and maintenance of its place image."[99] It becomes not only a place to be seen and heard but also a product to be sold. Tensions emerge between commercialization and authenticity as developers promote a sanitized, idealized version of downtown for tourist consumption. A paradox of tourism is that it supposedly promotes opportunities for visitors to see something different; yet cities that re-create themselves to attract tourism seem to become more alike. City boosters and developers lose sight of the distinctive traits and cultural heritage that made the city an attractive, unique place to visit.[100]

Downtown redevelopment, when undertaken with tourism in mind, leads to creation of a sealed-off, bounded, artificial, "urbanoid environment," which purports to be a public area. In reality, this controlled, policed, and Disneyfied environment becomes a separate and "private city." Focused on commercialization, this private city becomes an idealized version or representation of reality that replaces the disorganized reality of older streets, neighborhoods, and urban spaces that are unique to each particular place with "standard" attractions. Tourists seek this "measured, controlled and organized kind of experience which is intimately linked to a fusion of consumerism, entertainment and popular culture" and supports the "brand" image of the city.[101] Subsequently, promoters of the commercialized environment rely on cultural symbols and simulated cultural experiences to *fabricate authenticity* within this idealized and contrived environment.[102] Organizers and investors try to provide the energy and thrill of the real thing in an artificial setting that conceals evidence of urban problems, such as unemployment, poverty, crime, and homelessness.

Because of the emphasis on tourism and consumption, redevelopment for consumption suppresses elements of "roughness, serendipity and creativity" and conceals the complexity of real-life problems facing cities and neighborhoods. In addition, it may impose "constraints on local identity and creative initiative,"[103] hence producing perhaps the greatest paradox. Ultimately, selling the legacy of former artists and musical genres as a consumer product, and packaging the city as a theme park for consumption, changes environmental and cultural conditions associated with cultural innovation. By obscuring place distinctions and obstructing creative initiative, these developments reduce the likelihood that city residents will be producers of innovation and alternative forms of music in the future. As Goldberger explains, all places consume culture, but only a few special places create culture:

> Those places that manage to create culture in a more than incidental way tend, almost always, to be great cities: New York and Los Angeles rank above all others in this country in this regard, and it is no accident that

they are both complicated, rough, difficult cities, profoundly original in their physical makeup and highly diverse in their population. . . . New York and Los Angeles may be as different in their physical form as they are in their climate, but they share an intensity and a power, not to mention a certain sense of disorder—even, if this is not too extreme a word, anarchy.[104]

In Memphis today, the easy riders have disappeared from Beale Street, along with the pawn shops and secondhand stores. Order prevails in the primarily city-owned and -leased Beale Street "historic district," where police officers on horseback, bicycles, and motorcycles patrol the beat. Schwab's store still displays and sells goods ranging from overalls to voodoo dolls in its historic building that has been preserved for more than a century. Across the street, W. C. Handy Park, once a vacant lot, is now occupied by a modern amphitheater. A Pepsi-Cola Pavilion sign dominates the park entrance and replaces an earlier sign that identified the area as the Budweiser Pavilion. B. B. King's Restaurant and Blues Club, the Blues City Café, and a few local establishments also welcome visitors. But most of the old saloons and shops, as well as more recent arrivals such as the nonprofit Center for Southern Folklore, have been replaced by juke joint façades, frozen daiquiri bars, franchises such as Pat O'Brien's and Hard Rock Café, and the FedEx Forum sports arena for basketball games and concerts.

The FedEx Forum sports arena, built with 250 million taxpayer dollars to attract the former Vancouver Grizzlies to Memphis, stands one block south of Beale and looms over the Beale Street entertainment district. The city sold the naming rights to FedEx Corporation, headquartered in Memphis. When the newly completed Forum opened in 2004, a press release announced: "FedEx Forum offers something for everyone. . . . From family shows and concerts, to sporting events and special events, every Memphian will be able to enjoy the amenities and atmosphere of FedEx Forum. 'The Thrill Is On' and you don't want to be left out of the fun."[105]

The phrase "The Thrill Is On" covers billboards around Memphis and dominates the Grizzlies' website. An adaptation of the title from B. B. King's famous song "The Thrill Is Gone," the phrase uses a cultural symbol to sell a product—the Grizzlies—and fabricate feelings of excitement and authenticity for visitors as well as residents in the "home of the blues."[106] Family fun and "thrills" at the Forum also include home games for the University of Memphis men's basketball team. But the Forum does not host acts associated with thrills from Beale Street entertainment from the past. Ten Dollar Jimmy, Cousin Hog, Black Carrie, River George, Dr. Scissors, and Memphis Minnie have been replaced by Usher, Alan Jackson, Martina McBride, Nora Jones, Bill Gaither, Kenny Chesney, Elton John, the Rolling Stones, Hannah Montana, Cirque du Soleil, and the Ringling Brothers Circus.

The Blues Foundation, based in Memphis, hosts events to keep the blues alive, but some might argue that the "thrill is gone" from Beale Street. A writer for the *Chicago Sun-Times* who attended a Blues First international talent contest reported that "real blues" has disappeared from Beale Street. He described the "former cultural mecca" as "a blues Disneyland that offers few authentic experiences."[107] Further, he quoted a "connoisseur of authentic music" who disparaged Beale Street musicians, saying, "Those bands couldn't get work in Chicago."

The use of cultural symbols to "sell" Beale Street enterprises is not limited to the appropriation of song titles to promote the Grizzlies and the FedEx Forum. Promoters of new business ventures on Beale Street position themselves and their enterprises, both globally and locally, by using a *symbolic economy of authenticity*. In other words, they announce and market new projects using "a specific network of commodified signs, social relations, and meanings" with popular appeal.[108] For example, on 17 January 2006, the holiday honoring Martin Luther King's birthday, city officials and investors attended a groundbreaking ceremony for Lee's Landing, a $9.7 million entertainment and retail complex built on Beale Street that includes a parking garage, retail stores, and a nightclub next to a $30 million Westin Hotel. John Elkington, chairman of Performa Entertainment, which develops Beale Street, specifically chose to break ground on the King holiday. In his view, the Lee's Landing project, which is 73 percent minority-owned, honors Dr. King's life, demonstrates African American participation in the economic system, and shows the progress the city of Memphis has made since the death of Dr. King. The project name itself is laden with symbolism. Lee's Landing is named for Lt. George W. Lee, a black Memphian who received the French Croix de Guerre for bravery in World War I, served as a "political boss" on Beale during the Crump years, chronicled the history of Beale, and played a significant role in establishing the Beale Street Historic District on the National Register of Historic Places. The millionaire investor-owners of Lee's Landing include Steve A. Sallion, a partner in Carthage Capital Group of New York and principal stakeholder in local Captain D's restaurants; Elvin W. Moon, a commissioner on the West Los Angeles Area Planning Commission and owner of E. W. Moon Inc. Infrastructure Group, a construction management firm; P. J. Benton, who owns Outback Steak Houses in Memphis; and Dr. Kenneth Williams, who owns Alliance Health Care System in Holly Springs, Mississippi.

Lee's Landing contains a Ground Zero Blues Club, a second location for the Clarksdale, Mississippi, juke joint and restaurant owned by a partnership that involves Academy Award–winning actor Morgan Freeman, who was born in Memphis, and attorney Bill Luckett.[109] The original club opened in Clarksdale in 2001, and Memphis is the site of the second and possibly last. Luckett said that the owners have declined offers from around the world to launch new Ground Zero clubs. They selected Memphis because it is a "natural." In other words, in Memphis, there is an authentic association with the Mississippi Delta and the blues. In Luckett's words, "Memphis was the first stop many of the blues artists made on the northern pilgrimages. The Delta blues ended up on Beale and, frankly, we're probably not going to open up other locations."[110]

NEW DIRECTIONS FOR A SOUTHERN PLACE

To the world, we seem like this place that killed Martin Luther King, when really we were a city that needed Martin Luther King. And then he was killed. . . .

So we're a city that has a little bit of a scar on us. Now, a lot of us, especially in the rap community, we're feeling less and less apologetic for being who we are. We want to claim our heritage and at the same time we want to build something new.

— CRAIG BREWER, quoted in Sandy Cohen, "Southern Sensibilities Inspire 'Hustle and Flow' Writer-Director Craig Brewer," *International News*, 5 January 2006

At the beginning of the twenty-first century, Memphis may once again achieve global recognition as a significant place of cultural innovation and production but provoke local tensions. Fifty years after Memphis became the birthplace of rock and roll, the city is associated with cultural productions involving music and filmmaking. One of the innovators is Memphis writer-director Craig Brewer, who combines new technology, his own originality, his appreciation for local blues and rap, and his knowledge of "people of little substance" to create internationally acclaimed films about local subjects. But others have taken note of Memphis as a site of cultural production. The city has become the subject of and film location for several popular movies, including *Walk the Line*, a biopic about Johnny Cash, who began his career at Sun Studio in Memphis, and June Carter Cash.[111]

Brewer, who has been compared to the late Sam Phillips of Sun Studio, dedicated his second film to Phillips. In the 1950s, at the beginning of the rock and roll era, Phillips innovated using radio and recording technology, his own creativity and entrepreneurialism, and an uncanny ability to identify talented performers. B. B. King, Elvis Presley, Johnny Cash, Carl Perkins, Jerry Lee Lewis, Howlin' Wolf, and Ike Turner are a few of the artists he recorded on the Sun label. Brewer, whose musical interests range from blues to rap, began his filmmaking career with digital video technology, his own creative ability and entrepreneurialism, and a deep appreciation and understanding for Memphis culture and people. Brewer's movies tell sympathetic stories about "low-down" Memphis characters, including car thieves who work for automobile chop shops, drug dealers, pimps, prostitutes, strippers, rappers, and other "people of little substance," some of whom have big dreams. His movies, like rap music, express a strong "place-based concept of 'the real'" and are "grounded in the immediate environments of personal experience," including the home, the neighborhood, the city, and the South.[112]

Brewer wrote and directed his first film, which he produced independently in 1999, with $20,000. The film, *The Poor and Hungry*, named for a midtown Memphis restaurant and bar, won the Hollywood Movie Award for Best Digital Feature in 2000. Brewer returned from the festival not only with the award but also with an agent and producers for his next film. The second film, *Hustle and Flow*, was also filmed at sites in Memphis that included a poor neighborhood located near Stax Records and the birthplace of Aretha Franklin. Produced for $2.8 million, *Hustle and Flow* won the Audience Award at the 2005 Sundance Festival. Paramount won a bidding war with other companies to purchase the film for $9 million. In 2005–6, the film's lead actor, Terrence Howard, won best actor nominations from the Golden Globe and the Oscars, as well as the Independent Spirit Award, for his performance as Djay, a pimp who wants to rap. And one of the film's songs—"It's Hard Out Here for a Pimp"—won the Academy Award for best original song. It was written by Memphis rappers—Jordan Houston (Juicy J), Paul Beauregard (DJ Paul), and Cedric Coleman (Frayser Boy)—all members of rap crew Three 6 Mafia.[113] Brewer's third film, *Black Snake Moan*, debuted in 2007.

The release of *Hustle and Flow*, with performances by Memphis rapper Al Kapone and soundtrack compositions by Scott Bomar, attracted international attention, as well as local criticism. Concerned Memphians wrote letters to the editor of the *Commercial Appeal* and called radio talk shows to express concerns that the rest of the world might get the wrong image of Memphis and its people from the film. They expressed discomfort, and in some cases outrage, with a movie that portrayed a pimp who wanted to rap as heroic and featured rap songs titled "Whoop That Trick" and "It's Hard Out Here for a Pimp." A local radio personality who disliked *Hustle and Flow* described it as "yet another black exploitation type of film that we saw so many times . . . during the sixties. . . . People already think Memphis is a backwater river town. It will just further their perceptions."[114]

Brewer, who is white and comes from a modest socioeconomic background, claims the film is about redemption and the desire for a better life—familiar themes about the South. He explains: "We have a history of sin and salvation, and one really can't exist without the other. With 'Hustle,' . . . I don't feel like I was trying to make a quote-unquote black movie, even though it had a predominantly black cast and it dealt with rap, the iconography of pimping and the blaxploitation-type of theme. I really felt like I was making a Southern movie."[115]

Brewer acknowledges that Memphis—the place—plays a significant role in his films and is an important site for filmmaking. He views local tensions about race and morality as part of Memphis history: "When I look at the history of Memphis that I love most, from the musical to the truly heroic, it's always been about some force going against what most people seemed to feel was in everybody's moral interest. . . . Whether the issue was whether Elvis Presley should be gyrating his pelvis or whether sanitation workers should be paid a fair wage, there's always been this wrestling match in Memphis between what we ultimately really respond to and what we may feel like we're supposed to respond to."[116]

Three 6 Mafia performed "It's Hard Out Here for a Pimp" at the seventy-eighth annual Academy Awards, the first time a rap song was performed at the event. They took home the Oscar for best song. But local reactions to the international attention followed a predictable pattern. The *Memphis Commercial Appeal*'s metro columnist, Wendi Thomas, wrote: "If the gods are merciful, Memphis won't be mentioned on the Oscars Sunday. That way no one outside the River City will be reminded that a homegrown threesome wrote the first rap song to be performed at the Academy Awards."[117] After the awards ceremonies, Thomas, who is African American, wrote that she was mortified at the Oscar performance and the acceptance "ramble." Still worse than glamorizing pimps, flashing metallic grills, and speaking improper English, one of the rappers shouted out, "Memphis, Tennessee."[118] Thomas disagrees with those who claim that the Oscar win is good for the city of Memphis. She is not proud and shudders about a remark made by actor Terrence Howard in an interview about the film. He explained that while making the film he learned that Memphis stands for "Makin' Easy Money Pimpin' Hos In Style."

Thomas despaired over the song giving a "bad rap"[119] to Memphis. But she and others noted the negative social impact of a musical genre, song, and film that glorify the pimp life. A local minister, Stacy L. Spencer, a longtime critic of hip-hop music, warned his congregation against celebrating the Oscar. In his view, the young performers are pawns of the devil. The violent and misogynistic lyrics of gangsta rap undo the strides made by African Americans. Dr. Spencer says: "We've come a long way from slavery and Jim Crow, but this is pushing our image back down."[120] Others expressed concern about the image of African Americans. A Washington, D.C., resident mourned that "this country is experiencing an influx of people coming over here from all over the world, and the only thing they see of black America through the media is . . . pimps and gangsters and all of that. It's always some low-down brother or some welfare mother."[121] And Beverly Hunt, in the *Albany (N.Y.) Times Union*, wondered "what was going through members' minds when they voted for a song with every vile, derogatory word for women and blacks sprinkled liberally throughout."[122] Hunt did not blame the devil. Instead, she faulted corporate America, since rap is a $1.2 billion industry. But *Daily Variety* wrote: "Once the eminent domain of Disney Cartoons, the nod to the Memphis hip-hop group for best song also seemed like Oscar's nod to the contemporary musical culture."[123]

Brewer's third film, *Black Snake Moan*, shares its title with a 1920s blues song by Blind Lemon Jefferson and features blues music from local artists such as R. L. Burnside and Jessie Mae Hemphill. The cast included not only Samuel Jackson, Christina Ricci, and Epatha Merkerson but also Justin Timberlake, a native-born Memphian. Timberlake, now an internationally recognized celebrity, rose to fame as a cast member of the 1990s revival of the Mickey Mouse Club and a former member of the boy band *NSYNC. He performed at the 2004 Super Bowl with Janet Jackson and won a Grammy Award for his first solo album, *Justified*. While making Brewer's film in Memphis, Timberlake connected with authentic musical roots at a downtown gala sponsored by the Memphis chapter of the Grammy-awarding academy. Timberlake received an award from Morgan Freeman and warm praise from notable Memphis musicians such as Isaac Hayes. David Porter, of Stax songwriting fame, compared Timberlake to local legends Otis Redding and Elvis Presley, praising him as being "in that league. He is the real stuff."[124] Timberlake responded to gestures of acceptance and recognition by saying, "I forgot about Memphis. . . . I realized where my heart was. I realize where my soul came from."[125] Paradoxically, Timberlake's association with local Memphis soul music legends, and the daughter of Elvis Presley, at the event conferred a mantle of authenticity on Timberlake that contradicted his Disney and *NSYNC image.

A different version of Memphis soul can be found in the film *Walk the Line*. Made in Memphis at key downtown and midtown locations, the movie captures Memphis in the 1950s and tells the story of musician and cultural icon Johnny Cash. At the 2005–6 Golden Globe Awards, it won the best picture award and best actor and actress awards for Joaquin Phoenix and Nashville native Reese Witherspoon, who play Johnny Cash and June Carter Cash. The film received five Oscar nominations from the Academy Awards, including best actor, best actress, best costume design, film editing, and sound mixing. Reese Witherspoon won the Academy Award for best actress.

The global success of *Walk the Line* and *Hustle and Flow* has attracted attention from the Tennessee Film, Entertainment, and Music Commission, who want more movies to be made in Tennessee. The commission and the governor urged the state legislature to enhance state incentives to make Tennessee more competitive with other states, especially Louisiana and Georgia, to attract filmmakers. Because film production is a high-wage, labor-intensive business that hires local workers and relies heavily on the hospitality industry, it is viewed as a desirable boost to local economies.[126] But in recent years, Memphis and the state of Tennessee lost eight film projects to other locations in the United States and abroad, which cost the state an estimated $69 million. In 2006, the Tennessee legislature funded the Tennessee Motion Picture and Television Grant to make the state more competitive with national and international markets. The state funded $10 million to support any production that spends 50 percent of its total costs and shoots 50 percent of its principal photography in the state.[127] Film companies receive bonuses for spending at least $500,000 in Tennessee, using Tennessee music, and hiring Tennessee crews.

Most of the feature films made in Tennessee have been shot in Memphis and recruited by the Memphis and Shelby County Film Commission. In 2007, the commission recruited Robert L. Johnson, the African American billionaire who founded the Black Entertainment Television network, to locate his new movie production company in Memphis. The company plans to produce relatively modestly budgeted films with African American themes and casts aimed at African American family audiences. Representatives of the movie company viewed Memphis as a potential location not only because of state incentives, local artists, and a promising local movie industry but also because of the presence of a large and influential African American community.[128]

GLOBAL CULTURE, LOCAL INNOVATION

Memphis music—the blues, gospel, country, rock and roll, soul, and rap—gives voice to a disadvantaged class whose cultural expressions are rooted in a southern, rural, oral tradition. Since the mid-twentieth century, global flows of technology and communication have carried Memphis music from its "place" of origin to a receptive global audience, even during times when local members of polite society devalued the music, the musicians, and the place. Ironically, the global flows that took the music away from Memphis brought back admiration and recognition for the place where it began. Tourism in Memphis, which boomed as the result of spontaneous expressions of grief and affection for Elvis Presley following his death, has developed into a major industry, bringing millions of visitors and hundreds of millions of dollars to the city.

Because of flows of culture and transportation, visits by global tourists to local sites now influence the production of locality in Memphis in ways that were not anticipated by cultural innovators or place-building decision makers. Musical purists caution that when local cultural innovation and the sites associated with it are perceived as valued resources that can be "sold" to boost economic development, these strategies may compromise the authenticity of those resources and affect creative processes. Consequently, the "tourist gaze"[129] may become disruptive to local processes of cultural innovation. Interestingly, however, the music of a disadvantaged rural population has proved to be resilient throughout many disruptions. The culture was not destroyed by flows of rural-urban migration; instead, it was transformed by urban life experiences, entrepreneurialism, and technology. Demolition of Beale Street also failed to destroy the local impulse for cultural innovation or weaken its legacy. Today's marketing aimed at attracting tourists to "landscapes of consumption" on Beale Street and Graceland may be promoting experiences that satisfy tourist expectations but do not nurture local cultural innovation. However, all of these processes of cultural innovation and commodification, past and present, contribute to the production of locality and the unique characteristics of place.

You know, I guess it is in my blood since I had a mom who was queen in '73, my dad was king in '94, my great-grandfather was king in '37, my grandfather was king in '56, so as far as I can think back, there's a king and queen almost every couple of years.— CAMILLA BRINNER, 2000 queen of Carnival Memphis, quoted in Lance Murphey, "The Land of Cotton— The Carnival Queen Camilla Brinner," *Memphis Commercial Appeal*, 4 December 2005

----- 6 -----

GENDER, RACE, RITUAL, & SOCIAL POWER

Memphis and the Paradoxes of Tradition

Carnival Memphis, sponsor of an annual festival involving the coronation of a king and queen, presentation of a royal court, a salute to business and industry, and support for local charities, celebrated its seventy-fifth anniversary in June 2006. Members of the original Carnival association organized in 1931 during the throes of the Great Depression. They intended to showcase Memphis to the region and the world as a modern, progressive city capable of hosting a festival promoting commerce, community, and celebration. Carnival founders included the presidents of the Retail Clothiers Association, the Cotton Exchange, and the Junior League. Supported by the directors of the Cotton Exchange, they tapped into the city's nineteenth-century commercial and social roots to find business sponsors and festival themes. Cotton Carnival founders succeeded in fostering civic participation, boosting community identity, attracting spectators and media attention, and promoting the region's most vital economic product at the time—cotton. Today, cotton no longer dominates the local economy, but Carnival Memphis continues to promote commerce and civic engagement. In 1931, the founders established a collective ritual and a form of local associational life that helped identify

Memphis as a unique place. Today, the rituals and symbols of Carnival Memphis, conducted within a historically generated social space, perpetuate place distinctiveness and reproduce the social order.

Initially, Cotton Carnival enlisted volunteer support and promoted civic engagement but restricted African American participation. The founders' vision of civic pride, despite claims of providing a festival for *all* people, actually established racially segregated events. Cotton Carnival reproduced forms of exclusion and otherness associated with patriarchy, namely, racial and gender subordination, which characterized Memphis and other racially divided communities in the Jim Crow South. Hence, racialized representations of community pride and honor, in the region described by organizers as the Cotton Kingdom, naturalized whiteness, incorporated traditional gender roles, and produced degrading images of blacks. Paradoxically, however, the racially exclusive organizational framework challenged African Americans to contest racism and Jim Crow, to actively engage in civic participation, and to rearticulate racial identity through their own "embedded agency."[1] Black Memphians, working within constraints and privileges of the local context, created a parallel civic organization and festival that became known as Cotton Maker's Jubilee. This organization's reinterpretation of Cotton Carnival used local material and symbolic resources, and incorporated conventional gender representations, to portray blacks as people of substance and to work for community change. These actions of Cotton Maker's Jubilee founders not only helped preserve the dignity of the African American community during the Jim Crow era but also helped build social capital networks that linked the "separate city" to the region, the nation, and the world. Today, Cotton Maker's Jubilee, renamed Kemet Jubilee, focuses on promoting civic engagement and racial identity. Jubilee organizers publicize their festival as "the party with a mission."

Today, following decades of change, a racially integrated and organizationally restructured Cotton Carnival, renamed Carnival Memphis, promotes its June festival as "the party with a purpose." By scaling back the public spectacle associated with the original Carnival, continuing an emphasis on the three C's—commerce, community, and celebration—and stressing the importance of doing "good deeds," primarily fund-raising for charitable organizations, Carnival Memphis actively promotes civic engagement and commerce. Some Carnival traditions, especially formal rituals presided over by kings and queens wearing ceremonial regalia and following scripted gender roles, seem anachronistic, irrelevant, or incomprehensible to many twenty-first-century observers, especially non-Memphians. Yet Carnival Memphis, headed by an executive director, supported by a small office staff, and funded by individual and corporate sponsors, remains a viable part of contemporary city life. The rituals of Carnival Memphis are meaningful for local participants, who share many things, including membership in an active civic organization, a publicly recognizable collective social identity, and a common purpose.

The success of Carnival Memphis as a revitalized twenty-first-century civic association, following a period of late-twentieth-century decline, is based on its ability to accept some changes that promote civic engagement while maintaining continuity with certain local traditions and rearticulating Carnival's place-based identity. The recent seventy-fifth-anniversary celebration of Carnival Memphis suggests that claiming a local and regional identity and promoting civic involvement through participation in a ritual tradition have become increasingly important, not less important, with the intensification of globalization processes.[2] Today's Carnival Memphis organization and members of its Twelve Grand Krewes not only continue repetitive and conservative aspects of a local ritual tradition but also adapt to global changes that have weakened some old social boundaries and strengthened others.[3] Carnival Memphis furnishes a formal context for the display and transmission of place-specific cultural and social values; networks for enhancing social capital; an institutional framework for maintaining and reproducing class, race, and gender boundaries; and a showcase for the world to see how the transformation and reconstruction of local culture fits changing social, economic, and political realties.[4] Although most theories of globalization predict the liberation of "social relations from local contexts of interaction"[5] by weakening local culture, in fact, the opposite sometimes occurs. The connection between social relations and local contexts of interaction may strengthen in response to global change. Carnival Memphis and Memphis Kemet Jubilee show that processes of globalization may invade local contexts of action without destroying local culture.[6] Paradoxically, the Carnival tradition intertwines seemingly incompatible aspects of local and global processes related to the perpetuation and contestation of social power with the reproduction and transformation of the social order. These interpersonal rituals sustain family, communities of meaning, and civic engagement.[7] These rituals also show how local and global processes shape the social construction of race, class, and gender.

Decades ago, the rituals of Carnival's segregated predecessors, Memphis Cotton Carnival and Cotton Maker's Jubilee, created a public spectacle that attracted hundreds of thousands of people to Memphis. Photographers from *Life* magazine; newsreel cameramen from Hollywood studios, including Fox, Paramount, and Universal; national network radio broadcasters from NBC and CBS; and onlookers from Memphis and the Mid-South region watched the festivities. Barge landings of the royal court on the Mississippi riverfront, parade floats rolling down city streets lined with cotton bales, and other public displays of pageantry, including segregated beauty contests for the Maid of Cotton (white) and the Spirit of Cotton (black), left no doubts about the economic and cultural dominance of cotton. The *spectacle* of Cotton Carnival festivities provided a "symbolic context" for enacting and communicating traditional beliefs, cultural values, economic concerns, and self-understandings shared by local commercial elites.[8] Carnival traditions "reflected the priorities, attitudes, and histories of most of the individuals producing the festivals, but not the majority of those attending it."[9] The symbolic universe created by Cotton Carnival did not invert social hierarchies or temporarily relieve participants of the routines associated with the dominant social order. Carnival did not establish rituals of reversal to provide a few days of merriment as might have been expected in a pre-Lenten Carnival tradition.[10] Instead, the symbols of Carnival, embedded in a culture of inequality, incorporated the social hierarchy and delineated local race, class, and gender boundaries.[11]

Today, the parades, cotton bales, crowds of onlookers, beauty contestants, and national media attention have vanished. Participation in Carnival events is no longer racially segregated, and the word "cotton" no longer appears in the name of the sponsoring organization or its events. The spectacle of Carnival Memphis as a *public* festival has diminished in response to changing times, but the continuation of Carnival Memphis as a civic association, the participation of local elites, and the organization's sponsorship of annual civic events remain distinctive characteristics of place.

By the time of its seventy-fifth-anniversary celebration in 2006, Carnival Memphis exhibited a significantly lower public profile than Cotton Carnival enjoyed in 1931 or in 1956. Now, local media coverage of Carnival Memphis has shifted from the front page of the local newspaper to the social page. Meanwhile, Memphis in May, a month-long spring celebration established in the 1970s, which includes the International Barbecue Contest and the Beale Street

Music Festival and salutes a different country each year, attracts thousands of people downtown to Tom Lee Park on the Mississippi River. Attendance for Beale Street Music Festival weekend usually exceeds more than 100,000 people. Because Memphis in May attracts crowds to public events and generates international media attention during the month preceding Carnival Memphis, many current and former Memphians mistakenly believe that Carnival Memphis no longer exists, or no longer matters. Despite these perceptions, however, Carnival Memphis continues to operate and significantly affect local culture. Members of krewes with mysterious Egyptian-sounding names like Memphi, Osiris, Sphinx, and Ptolemy annually select adult dukes and duchesses and kings and queens, as well as junior royalty. Carnival activities include attending private balls at hotels and country clubs; visiting hospitals, senior centers, nursing homes, and schools; sponsoring a children's festival; and donating to charitable organizations. The continuation of these rituals and the practices of their *private* supporters reveal a great deal about globalization processes, place attachment, and perpetuation of the structure of social power in Memphis.

Through the years, organizational changes have increased racial inclusiveness and decreased the number of public spectacles. Despite changes, however, continuation of old practices such as a secret selection process for naming the queen and king, gendered activities that include Arkansas duck-hunting trips for men and fashion shows for women, and formal presentations of royalty at the Crown and Scepter Ball reproduce traditional patterns of race, class, and gender. These practices, established when "King Cotton" dominated the Memphis economy and structured its social hierarchy, continue to reflect and reinforce dominant local values. These traditional practices counter theoretical predictions that global processes somehow liberate "social relations from local contexts of interaction" and eliminate territoriality as an organizing principle for social and cultural life.[12] The history of Carnival Memphis demonstrates that processes of globalization and social change have brought new people, new industries, and new social arrangements to Memphis, but global flows have not restructured the city's "power geometry," especially in terms of class and gender, nor have they severed the ties between social power and place.[13] Indeed, globalization has produced an intensification of stratification processes and an amplification of local contexts of interaction for elites. The weakening of some status-group boundaries permits relative newcomers to participate. Carnival Memphis now welcomes prominent African Americans who were once excluded, Memphians whose families have achieved corporate

status or entrepreneurial wealth more recently, and new arrivals with noteworthy corporate, community, or professional connections. The participation of
relative newcomers who adopt local cultural practices and the continuing
interest of members of "established" families, especially those who proudly
claim Carnival and cotton factor genealogies, strengthen other status-group
boundaries, sustain place-based identities, reproduce upper-class privilege, and
link local elites to transnational networks.

Carnival rituals, embedded in social hierarchies and regulated by traditional boundary-maintenance activities, not only help socialize the next generation for maintaining distinctions of wealth, power, and status but also
reproduce local culture, place distinctiveness, and attachment to place. Consequently, despite changing times, the most crucial Carnival traditions have
changed very little. The original Cotton Carnival committee organized the
first event to improve commerce during the lean years of the Depression, to
promote cotton, to promote civic pride, and to have fun. For decades, Carnival successfully combined elite private rituals and public displays. Free
public pageants, parades, and fireworks provided mass (albeit racially segregated) public entertainment when most people had little disposable income.
Today, professional sports arenas and other commodified public spectacles
such as Memphis in May, as well as television and electronic media, provide
mass entertainment. In continuity with tradition, however, the expressed
goals to promote commerce and civic pride, and to have a good time, remain
at the forefront of Carnival activities. Also following traditional patterns,
Carnival Memphis continues to receive support from social and economic
elites who recognize each other at events that enable them to interact in
ballrooms as well as boardrooms. Carnival-sanctioned events bring together
prominent Memphians, such as descendants of city founders and cotton factors, with newcomers of similar social standing for them to get to know each
other, to feel solidarity with each other, and to experience a socially derived
moral energy. While enhancing the city's commercial prospects and making
contributions to charities, diverse participants become allies as twenty-first-
century practitioners of the Carnival tradition. While relative newcomers and
"old-timers" engage in charitable causes to preserve an "authentic" local
tradition, they help perpetuate "distinctions."[14] These distinctions form symbolic boundaries that separate people into social groups and maintain place
uniqueness. Consequently, participants enhance social, cultural, economic,
and social capital and pass along these advantages to their children and grandchildren. Subsequently, those who participate in Carnival Memphis, and are

socialized into membership of this community of meaning, maintain a mechanism for the intergenerational transfer of cultural meaning and tradition, or symbolic capital.

Social boundaries are somewhat more relaxed, given that events are no longer racially segregated. For twenty-five years (1981–2006), Carnival Memphis included a krewe sponsored by Memphis Kemet Jubilee, formerly the Cotton Maker's Jubilee organization. Many events are open to the public, and anyone who pays the minimum $75 membership fee can join Carnival Memphis; however, each individual krewe maintains separate membership criteria, organizes its own social events, and charges its own membership fees. Some krewes are more exclusive than others, even within the Carnival Memphis organization. Local residents who can afford to pay basic membership fees to join may not be able to pay additional costs of participation by purchasing formal evening attire and tickets to coronation balls. Lack of krewe membership, and an absence of occupational, educational, or residential connections to members, may exclude them from social capital networks and limit their access to cultural and economic capital. Also, continuation of secret selection processes, the operation of secret organizations such as the Secret Order of the Boll Weevils, and a legacy of secret party invitations and initiation ceremonies separate insiders from regular members and nonmembers. These practices maintain traditional class, race, and gender boundaries within the organizational structure and between the organization and outsiders.

One secret organization polices the boundaries and ridicules the ceremonies of Cotton Carnival. This nonprofit group, not a krewe, known as the Secret Order of the Boll Weevils, first appeared in the 1965 Cotton Carnival parade. For more than forty years, the Boll Weevils have been an integral part of Carnival Memphis rituals, despite the ending of parade festivities. Men cloaked in green caped costumes and wearing large gold snouts attached to fencing masks participate in Carnival events and make public appearances throughout the year at children's hospitals and charity events. Police motorcycle escorts accompany the Boll Weevils who travel around the city, waving at passersby, riding in a variety of green vehicles. These include an ambulance, a 1941 Ford fire truck, and old school buses painted green and turned into customized convertibles. The leader is called the Evil Eminence. Their identities are kept secret, but each year one weevil is unmasked during Carnival events.

Carnival's Boll Weevils have a reputation for disrupting ritual events. They wear costumes representing the beetle (*Anthonomus grandis*), a cotton pest known for infesting southern and southwestern cotton crops and producing billions of dollars of devastation to the regional economy and disrupting the "production of locality." For decades, the boll weevil's disruption of life in the Cotton Kingdom has been a subject of blues and folk songs and a target of USDA eradication programs. But "boll weevil" has also been used as a political term. Conservative southern white Democrats in Congress who supported some Democratic social legislation, such as Roosevelt's New Deal, but resisted desegregation and civil rights initiatives, such as Lyndon Johnson's Civil Rights Act of 1964, also became known as boll weevils. Political use of the term continued into the Reagan administration. In all three cases—economic, political, and social—the boll weevil has served as a symbol of disruption in southern cultural tradition.

RITUAL: PLACE AND SPACE

Change and progress are the essence of civic duty. Parades are yesterday's ball of leftover twine. . . . Talk about old habit. The Cotton Carnival is just a minor social event. Even after the merger with the Cotton Maker's Jubilee, there weren't any national TV cameras on the parade route. No publicity. No pizzazz. A few young families and nostalgia buffs may be willing to put up with pigeons and panhandlers and risk tired arches to boot. But is it really worth the extra expense of policing and cleanup?

— *Memphis Commercial Appeal*, cited in Perre Magness, *Carnival Memphis*

Some Carnival traditions have changed, but they are no less compelling.[15] Most obviously, the physical *space* for holding formal Carnival rituals has changed with the passage of time. The civil rights movement, the King assassination, and decades of downtown disinvestment and devaluation of the urban core dramatically changed the city of Memphis in many ways and affected local perceptions of the physical space and symbolic context associated with Cotton Carnival. In April 1968, Cotton Carnival and Cotton Maker's Jubilee cancelled events following the assassination of Martin Luther King Jr.[16] Both festivals resumed in 1969 but were never the same.[17] Lavish public civic displays and pageants on the riverfront never fully regained an appreciative audience. Instead, many city residents expressed negative views of Carnival as "the embodiment of the divisions—social, economic, and racial—that prevented the city from developing."[18] In 1981, bystanders greeted the Cotton Carnival's royal barge landing at the riverfront with booing; subsequently, the barge landing was discontinued. Public parades featuring marching bands strutting down streets lined with cotton bales also ground to a halt.

Despite difficulties, the Carnival Memphis organization has survived and continues sponsoring royal visits to charities and hospitals and hosting private parties in clubs and hotel ballrooms. Few events are held downtown. Formal social events include private coronation ceremonies for the king and queen, princesses, scarabs, and royal courts of krewes, as well as other balls and performances.[19] These formal ceremonies, consistent with the past rituals, involve grand entrances by the king and queen, who sit on gold and burgundy thrones, surrounded by women wearing formal gowns and men in tuxedos, as well as Boll Weevils in costume. Carnival participants wear traditional regalia and accoutrements, including royal crowns, tiaras, scepters, medallions, collars, and sashes. A presidential mace, inscribed with the names of each president, is transferred from one reign to the next.

Importantly, however, the shift from open public space downtown to closed private space in other parts of the city did not weaken Carnival's close relation to place. The significance of Memphis as a symbolic, material, and geographic location for Carnival has not diminished, despite waning enthusiasm for public spectacles. In the 1980s, Cotton Carnival integrated membership and events. Recognizing that cotton no longer dominated the local economy, the organization eliminated "cotton" from its name. At first, the name was changed to Great River Carnival. Then, it became just Carnival. Finally, organizers settled on Carnival Memphis. After struggling to rename Carnival and recapture its social significance in a period of declining public interest, organizers realized that *place matters* to members of this community of meaning. The identity of Carnival, and social bonds and attachments associated with it, relates more to the city of Memphis as a place than to cotton or the Mississippi River. In other words, *place* continues to be a repository of distinctive local resources, "a privileged locus of culture,"[20] and a crucible of social and economic interactions. It is *place*, not cotton, that gives shape and boundaries to social stratification processes and rituals that celebrate them, including Carnival Memphis.[21] Place provides physical, material, geographic, cultural, and symbolic resources (including cotton) for identity formation, social recognition, and boundary maintenance. Participation in a ritual tradition identified with place confirms and sustains individual and family connections. The level of participation also reveals one's individual status, one's family status, as well as race, class, and gender status within local and regional networks. Social distinctions and aspirations are displayed and contested in rituals that produce and reproduce the structure of social power.

GENDER, RITUAL, AND SOCIAL POWER

The Flynns never had a thing in this world but money and they lost that, they were nothing at all but fairly successful climbers. . . . Why, y' know ole Papa Flynn, he barely escaped doing time . . . for shady manipulations on th' stock market when his chain stores crashed, and as for Mae having been a cotton carnival queen, as they remind us so often, . . . well, that's one honor that I don't envy her for!—Sit on a brass throne on a tacky float an' ride down Main Street, smilin,' bowin,' and blowin' kisses to all the trash on the street.

—MAGGIE, *Cat on a Hot Tin Roof*, in *Tennessee Williams: Plays 1937–1955*

Maggie's disparagement of Cotton Carnival queens appeared in a Tennessee Williams play written more than fifty years ago, at least one decade before most Memphians publicly expressed negative sentiments about the festival.[22] Yet the familial honor of a daughter's "being almost royalty, a paragon of good taste and elegance, a name to be reckoned with" continues to be valued in elite circles.[23] Despite many changes, one ritual that has changed very little in the last seventy-five years is the practice of selecting a queen and king, and a royal court, to preside over Carnival Memphis events. Royalty—past and present—embody dominant social values and traditional gender expectations. They also serve as reminders of the meaning of place. Annually, a young unmarried (white) woman from a prominent family, typically a second- or third-year student at a prestigious university, receives an invitation to accept the title and wear the crown of queen. An older,[24] married (white) man whose established professional reputation is based on distinguished family or business connections becomes king. Both titleholders emerge from a ritualized secret selection process. The honorific status of king or queen, especially queen, is valued by families and individuals, not only during the year of the queen's reign but also throughout her lifetime. Her reign affects future generations of her family. One former Carnival queen, interviewed fifty years after her own coronation, fondly recalled a lavish Carnival presentation in 1935 when she donned a Hollywood movie costume, wore a borrowed Comus[25] crown from New Orleans, and rode through Memphis in a golden bejeweled horse-drawn carriage. Her wedding to a member of one of the city's most prominent families, a cousin of the 1935 Carnival king, followed a couple of years later. She proudly noted that in 1977, their son became Carnival president.[26]

Seventy-five years after the founding of Cotton Carnival, a local newspaper obituary for a woman related by birth and marriage to prominent city families reported the deceased's status as a former queen of Memphi, a krewe that traces its origins to the 1870s Mardi Gras era and maintains its high status within the Carnival Memphis hierarchy. The obituary, published in the *Memphis Commercial Appeal* on 18 September 2006, also published the names of her husband and children and accounts of her social connections and her educational and professional accomplishments.

> MAY SNOWDEN TODD died Saturday, September 16, 2006 in Memphis. She graduated from Lausanne Collegiate School and from Ogontz Junior College in Rydal PA and attended Barnard College in New York City. May was past president of the Women of Calvary Church where she was a member of the altar guild, St. Elizabeth's guild, and the flower committee. A published poet, she was also a past president of the Junior League of Memphis and the Board of the Old Crippled Children's Hospital. She was on the Board of Directors of Special Kids and the Children's Foundation of Memphis. She was queen of the Mystic Society of Memphi in 1967. She was a member of the Memphis Rose Society, the Memphis Garden Club, Ikebana, the Antiquarians, the Poetry Society of Tennessee, the Colonial Dames of America, and the Memphis Woman's Club. In 2000, May and her brother, Robert G. Snowden, donated the land and the family's farm house for the establishment of Snowden Grove Park in Southaven, MS. She is survived by her husband of 59 years, Thomas Hardy Todd, Jr.; her children, Thomas Hardy Todd, III (Ainslie), Bayard Snowden Todd (Nancy), Robert Carroll Todd (Christine), Roberta Todd Anderson (Steve); her grandchildren, May and Caroline Todd, Gray and Bayard Anderson, Isabelle and McLean Todd; and her brother, Robert Galloway Snowden. Services will be at 10:30 A.M. Tuesday, September 19 at Calvary Episcopal Church with burial in Elmwood Cemetery.

Recently selected queens have proudly traced their family lineage of kings and queens back through generations of Carnival Memphis royalty. For example, 2000 queen Camilla Fisher Carr traces her Carnival genealogy through both parents. Her mother, Mary White Leatherman, became queen in 1973. Her maternal great-grandfather was 1937 king Samuel Richard Leatherman. Camilla Carr's father, 1994 king Oscar C. Carr III, is the son of 1956 king Oscar C. Carr Jr. In addition to the 2000 and 1973 queens, Samuel Richard Leatherman's descendants include 1953 queen Mary Abbay Joyner, 1958 queen Irene Leatherman Orgill, and 2004 queen Abbay Leatherman Brownlow.[27]

In many ways, the selection of festival queens and kings is an American tradition that is neither uniquely southern nor exclusively white. Despite the contradictory images posed by symbolic aristocrats in a democratic society, royal pageantry has become part of an American tradition of community festivals organized to invoke civic pride and affirm community values. These festivals and pageants would be incomplete without queens and kings who embody local values and conform to culturally specific, gender-based social expectations, especially with the selection of queens. But some southern communities assign special significance to selecting festival queens who represent nineteenth-century images of idealized traditional womanhood and carry those ideals into the twenty-first century.

In Memphis, the Carnival queen is neither a beauty queen nor a debutante. But a queen's personal appearance conforms to attractiveness norms, her family tree withstands local genealogical scrutiny, and she may be a debutante. Symbolically, the Carnival queen is the embodiment of southern womanhood, an ideology combining two nineteenth-century ideals—the British Victorian lady and the American cult of true womanhood. She also represents the "idealized role of the patriarchally protected Southern [white] woman."[28] Consequently, she is a representation of "emphasized femininity" in a system of "patriarchy and womanly subordination."[29] The Carnival Memphis queen is young, feminine, attractive, sociable, and single. As a young woman who is still a daughter but not yet a wife, she is recognized for her accomplishments in academics and community service, respected for her own good character, and identified by her family reputation. She is selected by a secret committee whose members anticipate that eventually she will marry and have children who also will participate in Carnival Memphis. These characteristics, along with membership in and loyalty to a prominent local family, meet standards for selection by the secret committee. They also represent standards for how young southern women are expected to look and act. For official portraits, the queen wears an elaborate ball gown, usually white, with her crown and regalia.

Kings also embody community values and conform to a model of "hegemonic masculinity." In other words, these practices institutionalize men's dominance over women and other subordinates.[30] The Carnival Memphis king is older, married, and well established in business or professional life. He is the embodiment of masculine cultural capital. For official portraits, the king wears a tuxedo or tails, sometimes adorned with military-looking sashes and stripes. The king's wife, who may be a former queen, also represents "emphasized femininity" in a patriarchal system. Carnival publicity often refers to her as the "forgotten woman," but various rituals recognize her for helping carry out the king's Carnival responsibilities. The king is recognized for his business and professional accomplishments, not only locally but also nationally and internationally. Usually, he represents a prominent family. For example, the 2008 king is described as Carnival's first third-generation king who continues a tradition established by his grandfather and his father. His wife was Carnival queen in 1993. The king's children participate in Carnival Memphis activities in age-appropriate roles that prepare them to assume future leadership roles in the organization and in the community. The list of former Carnival queens and kings includes representatives of Memphis cotton broker families, Mississippi cotton plantation families, and modern industries, including hotels, transportation, the music industry, and investment banking. In recent years, efforts to racially integrate Carnival Memphis krewes and events have created racial diversity among princesses and krewe royalty; however, to date, all queens, kings, and presidents have been selected from white, privileged families.

Family ancestry, an important basis for social prestige, also plays an important role in sustaining Carnival Memphis. The 2006 president of Carnival Memphis, Neely Mallory III, traces his family origins to two local cotton factor families, Neely and Mallory, two of the most prominent families in Memphis history with ties to national and international economic and social elites.[31] His grandmother, Noreen Cathey Mallory, president of the Junior League, served as one of the original incorporators of Carnival Memphis in 1931. His grandfather, W. Neely Mallory, served as president in 1934 and became king in 1935. His father, William Neely Mallory Jr., was selected king in 1970. His uncle, B. Lee Mallory III, served as king in 1983. This Memphis family's ties to business and Carnival maintain continuity between the past and present. Their connections to the global economy span from nineteenth-century cotton factoring and warehousing to twenty-first-century international warehousing and logistics. Neely Mallory III, the president of Mallory Alexander International Logistics, served as the 2006 president of Carnival Memphis, continuing the cultural and economic legacy of Memphis and his family's place in the city.

Patriarchy also continues to sustain Carnival Memphis. It is not uncommon for prominent local men to serve terms of president and king of Carnival

Memphis, but not simultaneously. The 2006 king of Carnival Memphis, Giles Coors III, also served a stint as president in 2000. Coors's father preceded him as king in 1972, and two uncles also served as king. Coors's sister, wife, and three cousins have reigned as queen. No woman has ever served as president, but several queens have married men who became king and / or president. Coors, for example, married Suzette Turner, the 1984 Carnival queen. A few years ago, women who served in supportive roles, that is, subordinate roles traditionally held by women—including mothers of queens and wives of kings and presidents—formed their own service group within the organization and named it the Queen Bees.[32] The Queen Bees, like Carnival queens, are the embodiment of feminine cultural capital. Former kings and presidents embody masculine cultural capital.

Festival queens, an important part of American civic life throughout the United States, probably originated with medieval European "Queens of the May" and similar festivals. Harvest queens, winter or spring festival queens, and football queens reign throughout the United States. In Pasadena, California, a rose queen has reigned over the Tournament of Roses since the early 1900s.[33] St. Paul, Minnesota, selects a Winter Carnival queen and king. Kansas City selects a Renaissance Festival queen, and Orange City, Iowa, selects its Tulip Festival queen. But festival queens seem imperative for southern communities who select queens for festivals honoring daffodils, azaleas, oranges, pecans, strawberries, mushrooms, apples, watermelons, catfish, stock car races, and pirogue races. Some trace the southern propensity to crown festival queens and beauty queens back to white southern fascination with nineteenth-century romanticism. The appeal of Sir Walter Scott's novel *Ivanhoe* and a regional culture that valued horses and military display fueled interest in sponsoring elaborate re-creations of medieval jousting tournaments, including pageants, coronations, and balls, both before and after the Civil War.[34] Others see a connection between these festivals and Mardi Gras, a staple of New Orleans culture dating from 1699, that influenced many community celebrations, including Carnival Memphis. During the 1870s, the city of Memphis sponsored its own lavish Mardi Gras festivals with royal courts; however, yellow fever epidemics and a mounting public debt crisis ended Mardi Gras in the 1880s. When Memphis commercial interests planned the first Cotton Carnival in 1931, the selection of a king and queen assumed great importance for the embodiment of civic pride and community values and for demonstrating continuity with the city's (pre–yellow fever epidemic) past, both socially and economically.

Today, the rituals associated with selection of a queen and king show greater continuity with the past than most aspects of Carnival Memphis. The secret selection process, the individual characteristics of king and queen, and the ceremony for introducing the newly selected king and queen to each other are among the most enduring and exclusive traditions. Each year, the first meeting of the king and queen occurs when Carnival officials appear at the home of the king and his wife, blindfold them, and drive them along a roundabout route to the queen's (parents') house. Formal introductions occur, followed by a working dinner where the royal couple makes plans for their reign, including a schedule of visits to charitable organizations and appearances at formal balls.[35] Each of the twelve krewes of Carnival Memphis holds its own ritual parties and dinners for announcing queens and other members of the royal courts, starting in January each year.

The continuation of these elaborate gendered traditions, and the willingness of women to participate in them, especially young women, seems quite remarkable to twenty-first-century observers. Outsiders may view these traditions as archaic and meaningless. Modern-day feminists may find it incomprehensible that young adult women agree to take the passive role of waiting and allowing themselves to be chosen. Even in the South, today's young women have greater opportunities for actively pursuing equal educational and occupational goals and attaining economic power. Indeed, some Carnival queens have expressed aspirations to pursue graduate and professional school in male-dominated areas such as finance and law. Yet by being chosen and agreeing to enact the role of Carnival queen, the young woman becomes an embodiment of the "body social"—the prime symbol of the self and the society.[36] Like the idealized "southern lady," the Carnival queen is a symbol of submission to social obligations of family, community, and patriarchal authority, as well as a symbol of ideal and normative femininity. Following tradition, today's Carnival queen does not question dominant social expectations about the role of women. Selection of a Carnival queen does not threaten dominant power arrangements in the local or global sphere. She is the embodiment of traditional authority and social power. The source of that social power comes from economic and social power shared within families, and power derived from social connections and affiliations with prestigious organizations, including Carnival Memphis.[37] These social circles, grounded in local and regional organizations, overlap with national and international networks.[38]

The rituals of Carnival Memphis, especially the selection of queen, are important for maintaining and reproducing traditional social power for generating all forms of capital—human, social, and cultural—which have value, symbolically and materially, at local, regional, national, and international levels. These resources also contribute to class formation. Locally and region-ally, the symbols of Carnival are more recognizable and make a stronger contribution to elite group cohesiveness. But families and businesses with national and international prominence who participate in Carnival Memphis also enhance the organization's social power. Consequently, members from es-tablished families, prominent African American families, and newcomer cor-porate elites find participation to be beneficial for acquiring cultural and social capital to enhance their participation in social life and pass on these social and cultural advances to their children. Cultural capital—consisting of ideas, knowledge, attitudes, and shared culture—begins with early socialization in families.[39] It can be invested locally to yield "social profits" in the form of sym-bolic goods, such as titles, honors, recognition, and membership in exclusive groups with connections to regional, national, and international networks.

Volunteer work plays an important role in sustaining Carnival Memphis and in generating social and cultural capital. Traditionally, the volunteer activities of elite women's organizations have enabled women to perpetuate and enhance class-based privileges for themselves and their families in the name of performing "good deeds."[40] Volunteer work for Carnival Memphis includes organizing formal social events for members as well as participating in charitable events on behalf of the community. The work involves invest-ments of human, social, and cultural capital that yield "social profits."[41] At the level of individual investment, human capital involves a combination of "work-relevant skills and material resources."[42] Members use their individual know-how within social networks, often via membership in krewes, to assist each other in fund-raising for charities and in supporting other activities. At the relational level, reciprocity among members builds social capital within social networks. Social capital networks strengthen social power, the ability to influence others to get things done in the community and in the greater society. Traditionally, elite white women have attained capital—human, so-cial, and cultural—and wielded social power through these kinds of social activities. As women enter professional and business positions and gain access to other forms of power, traditional volunteer organizations do not decline in importance. In fact, having the "good taste" to participate in appropriate activities that produce good deeds and generate additional social capital has become increasingly important to twenty-first-century professional and busi-ness women.[43]

For more than twenty-five years Carnival Memphis has operated as a racially integrated organization, but no African American members have been selected as Carnival king, queen, or president. In 1981, an African American krewe, Kemet Jubilee, joined Carnival Memphis, but its sponsoring organization—Cotton Maker's Jubilee, renamed Kemet Jubilee—continued operations as an autonomous organization. In 2007, after twenty-five years of participation, Kemet Jubilee withdrew its krewe from Carnival Memphis. But Carnival Memphis royalty attended Kemet Jubilee's Crook and Flail Tableaux Ball for the coronation of the Kemet king and queen, and relations between the two organizations remained amicable.

Kemet Jubilee carries on its tradition of celebrating racial pride and promoting African American culture and achievements in ways that challenge the prevailing social order. Family members of founders Dr. and Mrs. R. Q. Venson play leadership roles in the organization, which is based in Memphis but has expanded activities to include two more cities—Nashville and Detroit. Clyde Venson, a retired law enforcement professional and nephew of the late Dr. Venson, who first attended Jubilee festivals in the 1940s, serves as general chairman of Kemet Jubilee's board of directors.

Community interest in an organization committed to promoting racial pride and challenging the prevailing social order may seem misplaced in the post–civil rights era, especially in twenty-first-century Memphis. The city, where African Americans now constitute a majority of the population, has elected African Americans to the city mayor's office, the county mayor's office, the city council, the county commission, the state house and senate, and the U.S. Congress. In Memphis, African Americans have occupied highly visible professional and administrative positions at the University of Memphis, the UT Memphis Health Science Center, St. Jude Children's Research Hospital, and Memphis city schools and also fill numerous business and professional positions throughout the city. Today, African Americans have greater opportunities to join Carnival Memphis and other civic organizations that once excluded them. But racial inequalities continue to exist. Despite significant social, political, and economic gains since the civil rights era, the African American community in Memphis, and in most American cities, has a bifurcated class structure with extremes of poverty and wealth, and Memphis school and neighborhood segregation has intensified along race and class divisions. Consequently, Kemet Jubilee, an established identity-based local cultural tradition, continues to appeal to a predominantly African American audience and works to provide scholarships and adult mentors for children, especially children from lower-income families. Its public festival remained downtown throughout decades of disinvestment and decline and still carries on a tradition of family fun and entertainment established by the Vensons in the 1930s. Jubilee parades, talent shows, and other public events maintained the interest of an appreciative public audience long after declining public interest in Carnival Memphis events. Members of Kemet Jubilee feel the need to continue with these traditions because of increased disparities between rich and poor and because of disparaging and misogynistic representations of African Americans in rap music and popular culture. The Kemet Jubilee organization works to promote dignity and to celebrate racial identity in a manner befitting the tradition established by the founders of Cotton Maker's Jubilee in the 1930s. But the organization also struggles to adapt to changing times and maintain relevance to meet the needs of a diverse African American community.[44]

A TRADITION OF RACIAL PRIDE AND POSITIVE PROTEST

O Southland, dear Southland!
Then why do you still cling
To an idle age and a musty page,
To a dead and useless thing.
— WELDON JOHNSON, "O Southland"[45]

In the 1930s, public expression of Memphis "community values" included support for the cotton industry, respect for traditional gender norms, an acceptance of racial segregation, and nostalgia for an imagined Old South. Because the Cotton Carnival founders represented the prevailing social order, it is not surprising that they selected "The Old South" for Cotton Carnival's first year's theme. Parade floats depicted subjects such as "Romance and Chivalry" and "Southern Hospitality." A fortune-teller rode a float titled "Mammy."[46] A float titled "Worth Its Weight in Gold" carried cotton being weighed on a scale.[47] A similar theme, "King Cotton's Dream of Fair Women," announced the festivities for the 1935 Carnival. The public and highly visible process of announcing Carnival themes, constructing parade floats, and presenting kings and queens and members of royal courts produced admiration among some observers and attracted a cadre of volunteer workers needed to sustain Carnival activities. However, Carnival's representations of "community values," including strategically placed black men on parade floats or seated on cotton bales stacked on city street corners, picking banjos and eating watermelon, also provoked intense scrutiny and criticism that increased over time.

These "community" values did not go undisputed or unchallenged in the 1930s. From the outset, Cotton Carnival provoked disturbing questions about elitism and racism and prompted accusations of insensitivity to widespread human suffering during the Depression.[48] A surge in labor militancy and advances in the civil rights movement in the region demonstrated that the status quo—the division of labor and concentration of wealth and power associated with King Cotton, as well as stereotypical representations of race—were not causes for celebration among black and white workers. Times were especially hard for displaced agricultural workers and factory workers, who experienced difficult lives under ordinary circumstances given the structure of the southern economy, but they found themselves facing staggering adversity magnified by the Depression.[49] The 1936 Carnival inspired John Handcox, poet laureate of the Southern Tenant Farmers' Union, to write a poem criticizing King Cotton. He countered Cotton Carnival's nostalgic references to a mythical and romanticized "Old South" tradition with images of planters, slavery, starvation, and death:

The planters celebrated King Cotton in Memphis, May fifteen.
It was the largest gathering you most ever seen.
People came from far and near—to celebrate King Cotton
Whom the planters love so dear.
Thousands of flags was hung in the street,
But they left thousands of sharecroppers on their farms with nothing to eat.
Why do they celebrate Cotton? Here, I'll make it clear,
Because they cheat, beat and take it away from labor every year.
Cotton is King, and will always be,
Until labor in the South is set free.
The money spent for decorations and flags,
Would sure have helped poor sharecroppers who are hungry and in rags.
Oh! King Cotton, today you have millions of slaves
And have caused many poor workers to be in lonesome graves.
When Cotton is King of any nation,
It means wealth to the planter—to the laborer starvation.[50]

Handcox's images of slavery and planters not only addressed the treatment of impoverished delta sharecroppers, black and white, who could not afford a trip to Memphis to watch a free parade, but also extended to the systematic misrepresentation and exclusion of African Americans. Cotton Carnival denied membership to African Americans and limited black participation in public festivities to standing along the parade route, posing as stereotypical characters for street performances, providing labor power for moving floats in the parade, and spending money for entertainment in segregated midway activities.

Handcox was not alone in voicing his objections. In 1934, an African American dentist on Beale Street, Dr. R. Q. Venson, his fiancée Ethyl Horton (the couple married soon afterward), and her five-year-old nephew, Quincy Johnson, stood along the parade watching Cotton Carnival festivities. Afterward, the child commented to the adults that he did not enjoy the parade "because all the Negroes were horses." In those days, parade floats were mounted on old ice wagons drawn by horses and mules led by black men wearing white coats. Walking home after the parade, the Vensons passed a large sign hanging across Beale Street that identified the entrance to the segregated black midway as the "Gates of Ham."[51] The Vensons, local black middle-class professionals, experienced feelings of frustration and anger in response to these representations of African Americans. They expressed feelings Du Bois had described as a "double consciousness": "It is a peculiar sensation, this double consciousness, this sense of always looking at one's self through the eyes of others, of measuring one's soul by the tape of a world that looks on in amused contempt and pity. One ever feels his twoness—An American, a Negro; two warring souls, two thoughts, two unreconciled strivings; two warring ideals in one dark body, whose dogged strength alone keeps it from being torn asunder."[52]

Interviewed fifty years later, Mrs. Venson still vigorously recalled the anger and humiliation she and her husband felt in 1935 and their reaction to Quincy's comments: "The only parts that Blacks had in the Carnival was that they did set up a midway where they could go and spend their money. And then they had called that the 'Gates of Ham.' Well, all that had become very distasteful as we watched it. . . . My husband decided that he would go the next day to see if we could not have some kind of dignified role in the Cotton Carnival."[53]

A segregated midway on Beale Street—the business and cultural center of black Memphis—which admitted African Americans through the Gates of

Ham,[54] and took their hard-earned cash, offended the Vensons. The couple felt their nephew's humiliation at watching black men who worked alongside animals moving floats representing "Old South" nostalgia and featuring white Carnival royalty. The next day Dr. Venson appealed to officials for a more dignified role for African Americans in Cotton Carnival. The committee rejected Dr. Venson's request. Their decision not only denied access to this avenue of civic participation to African Americans but also refused to reconsider their festival's misrepresentations of African Americans. The committee's response to Venson, a familiar one in the Jim Crow era, confirmed a reaction that Du Bois had found in 1899: "In all walks of life the Negro is liable to meet some objection to his presence or some discourteous treatment; and the ties of friendship or memory seldom are strong enough to hold across the color line."[55] No doubt, the Vensons anticipated rejection and were prepared to accept a challenge from one founder, Arthur Halle, to start a black celebration. Immediately, the Vensons started an organization that not only reinterpreted Cotton Carnival in the 1930s but also continues to play a civic role in twenty-first-century Memphis.

Initially named Cotton Maker's Fiesta, then renamed Cotton Maker's Jubilee, the first celebration took place in 1936. The Vensons adopted a strategy used by many leaders to gain social honor for African Americans "by incorporating conventional representations of gender into newly articulated representations of the race."[56] Mrs. Venson appointed herself the first queen. Eddie F. Hayes, director of Hayes Funeral Home, became the first king. Although Mrs. Venson privately contributed to the work of the organization, her public role was that of queen.

The first Cotton Maker's festival honored the blues. W. C. Handy, the father of the blues, returned to Memphis from New York to serve as grand marshal. He led the first Cotton Maker's parade down Beale Street, where he had written "The Beale Street Blues," the music that brought international acclaim to Handy, himself, and the city. Handy returned to Memphis many times to participate in Jubilee and Cotton Carnival. The first parade theme was "Rebirth of the Blues." The blues, like cotton, symbolized local cultural values and represented the region. Subsequent Jubilee themes and honorees also celebrated the region's musical contributions to the world. During the decades that followed, celebrities such as B. B. King, Rufus Thomas, Danny Thomas (the founder of St. Jude), Ethel Waters, and others participated in Jubilee festivities. Parades featured high school marching bands and drill teams; beauty contests selected the Spirit of Cotton; and talent shows entertained black and white audiences. The festivities attracted national attention, as well as local critics and admirers.

> Beale Street's Hero. A centre of celebration last week was Memphis' Beale Street, the garish Negro thoroughfare with its assortment of poolrooms and pawnshops, its gin parlors and its hot-fish restaurants. While Memphis whites were celebrating the annual Cotton Carnival, Beale Street was having its own fiesta, crowning its own king and queen, parading its own elaborate floats. The king was Undertaker Eddie Hayes. Queen was Ethyl Venson, pretty young wife of a Negro dentist. Highest honors throughout the fiesta were paid to a portly old Negro who had motored from his home in Manhattan for the occasion. A great hero in Beale Street is William Christopher Handy, 62.
>
> On every possible occasion last week bands played his music—Memphis Blues, Beale Street Blues, St. Louis Blues. Whenever he sauntered down the street there was a clamor for his autograph, a crowd of pickaninnies with hands out for pennies. Paul Whiteman brought Handy to the stage of Municipal Auditorium when he played there for the big Floral Ball. Beale Street made him the leader of its grand parade. He stood in the first automobile, doffing his hat to left & right. At small Handy Park, named in his honor, he mounted a reviewing stand, settled down in an old-fashioned rocking chair, solemnly bowed as the marchers saluted him.[57]

Cotton Maker's Jubilee has continued operations for more than seventy years with themes that reflect the changing social and political status of African Americans. Themes in the early years focused on music and cultural contributions. After World War II, Jubilee focused on African American patriotism with such themes as "I Am an American" in 1950. Themes of the 1960s such as "Moving Forward" suggested social change. Jubilee, like Cotton Carnival, suspended festivities in 1968, but in 1969 the theme selected was "Black America Moving Forward." In 1970, the theme was "Where Do We Go from Here?" Later, themes focused on the future, faith, peace, and international celebrations.[58]

In 1999, the board of directors changed the name of Cotton Maker's Jubilee to Memphis Kemet Jubilee. Adopting "Kemet," an Egyptian word meaning "black," to replace "Cotton Maker's" denotes a symbolic shift in the organization's racial identity. No longer identifying its members as the descendants of sharecroppers and slaves, or emulating European-style royal courts, the organization chooses to identify with the descendants of an ancient African culture. When the board of directors changed the name to Kemet Jubilee, it also eliminated its crowns and regalia patterned after European royalty, as well as its logo, and replaced them with Egyptian-themed, African-centered symbols. Paradoxically, however, the name of the organization and its regalia not only recognize symbolic ties between twenty-first-century African Americans in Memphis, Tennessee, and the ancient African city of Memphis but also refer to the nineteenth-century founding of the city based on the cotton economy. City founders identified the new city as Memphis on the Mississippi River, dubbed the "American Nile." Nineteenth-century efforts by white leaders to identify the new city with an ancient Egyptian city influenced the Memphis Mardi Gras festivals of the 1870s and the naming of Cotton Carnival krewes in the 1930s. All of these city founders and city festivals excluded African Americans.

Memphis Kemet Jubilee, like its predecessor Cotton Maker's Jubilee, still sponsors an annual parade on Beale Street, a midway, and other festivities. Whereas more privileged members of the African American community may have improved their social position vis-à-vis krewes associated with the Carnival Memphis organization, all members of the African American community celebrate their community heritage and racial identity with Memphis Kemet Jubilee. Yet the contributions of this organization, like those of many African American urban associations in the history of the United States, have been questioned, contested, critiqued, and redefined over the years. The work of African American civic organizations has not always been valued or treated with respect by the white community, nor has it always been taken seriously by academics. Some critics stereotype the activities of African American fraternal and civic organizations as parodies of white organizations and scorn them as symbols of disablement and disempowerment.[59] Others ridicule these organizations as "flights into fantasy"[60] and diminish them as "crude, unconscious parodies of white societies, with pretentious names for organizations and offices and extravagant regalia and parades" that offer few benefits to most members of the community or "exaggerated" versions of white civic associations.[61]

More recently, scholars have given serious attention to reassessing the meaning and value of historical African American urban associations and their impact on building networks of social capital and trust. These associations also receive more favorable attention from African American scholars. Maxine Craig, who describes African American bodies as "marked" by race, explains: "Only the unmarked can trivialize the fleeting joyous, cultural victory experienced when dominant meaning is subverted and what was formerly ridiculed is finally celebrated."[62]

At times, Cotton Maker's Jubilee has been treated as an object of ridicule and derision, but, when viewed from the perspective of some African Americans in the 1930s, the Jubilee association can be seen as a form of protest and a means of empowerment worthy of celebration. The Vensons resisted the exclusion of African Americans from Cotton Carnival because they understood exclusion to be one of the most pervasive forms of power. It produces "dehumanization, frustration, disruption, anguish, revolt, humiliation, resentment, disgust, despair, alienation, apathy, fatalist resignation, dependence, and aggressiveness."[63] Exclusion from Cotton Carnival meant not only being kept out of an all-white civic organization but also being excluded from idealized representations of southern womanhood and manhood. So, for the Vensons, the authorized organization of a parallel association was an act of resistance, not a parody.[64] Intended to promote positive images of African American men and women and to create community empowerment, Cotton Maker's Jubilee provided interorganizational links to Cotton Carnival and other white associations, which helped bridge the racial divide. White Carnival members served as members of the Jubilee board, but board membership was not reciprocal. Blacks were not permitted to serve on white Carnival committees, but efforts to reach across the racial divide still helped create social capital within the African American community.

Black participation in a separate Carnival organization allowed members to respond to the misrepresentation of African Americans without risking further humiliation or incurring negative sanctions. Taking the initiative to start a separate organization to express alternate community values and counter negative racial images seemed to offer the best means available to dignify African Americans and to contest their public humiliation. A more defiant challenge to inequities in the socioeconomic system, and direct criticism of negative representations of African Americans produced by Cotton Carnival, would have been unthinkable in the Jim Crow South, a time when "the structure of coercion and of socialization was so formidable that defiance simply could not be contemplated."[65] It was too risky—personally and politically. Mrs. Venson "knew that we could not just get out and protest." The Vensons understood that openly expressing anger was one way to challenge white supremacy. But less overt expressions of protest, muted for safety's sake, allowed the Vensons to resist accepting the white world's portrayal of

African Americans and to create effective alternative images.[66] Acting on the basis of this situated knowledge, they created an alternative celebration as a positive "protest" of the all-white Carnival and as a way to "dignify" black people by portraying them as queens and kings, as people of substance.[67] But they also celebrated African Americans as the creators of a powerful folk culture. On one level, Cotton Maker's Jubilee sought dignity and recognition by reinterpreting symbols of the dominant culture such as cotton and royalty. On another level, however, Jubilee created a social space for calling attention to symbols of African American culture. By honoring the contributions of black workers, that is, cotton makers, and providing a showcase for regional music and performers, as well as imaginary black royalty, the Jubilee organization brought national and international attention to Memphis as a place at the center of African American culture.

The theme "The Rebirth of the Blues" selected for the first Cotton Maker's Jubilee introduced an African American cultural aesthetic to Carnival festivities and underscored the element of protest. The blues, a musical genre described as "the voice of those who are dedicated to the preservation of their humanity, focuses on a range of everyday experiences of working class African American life."[68] These everyday experiences include love, work conditions, imprisonment, travel, pain, and ecstasy. By celebrating the blues and inviting blues performers, Jubilee leadership reached out across racial and class divisions to create a broad-based, inclusive Jubilee. They proved that resistance to racism and protest of dehumanizing treatment came from the ground up as well as from the top down.

A "positive" protest against degrading images usually meant taking collective social action to advance alternatives to racist representations of blacks. Constrained by local political and cultural contexts, a positive protest typically involved reinterpreting the dominant ideology and promoting atypical images drawn from ideals of black, middle-class life.[69] A positive protest of these images in Memphis, circa the 1930s, meant resisting the images of black men and women in the dominant ideology. Cotton Carnival's portrayal of privileged young white women as queens riding along the streets of Memphis on floats drawn by horses, mules, and black men who averted their gaze from those women seemed "natural" to most whites. The symbolic degradation and assignment of brutish or animal qualities to blacks, the exclusion of black women, and the elevation and praise of white women were naturalized and made invisible in the minds of most whites and supported an ideology of white male dominance.[70]

Blacks not only were excluded from Carnival participation but also were excluded from ideals of honor and beauty and from access to practices that generated cultural and social capital. Consequently, the Vensons' efforts to organize the African American community, to change their roles from passive spectators to active organizers, and to change images of African Americans from brutalized beasts of burden to idealized queens and kings mattered. The all-white Cotton Carnival reciprocated by sharing the use of floats and donating dress-making materials for many years before finally extending Carnival krewe membership to Cotton Maker's Jubilee in 1981. The actions of participants in the Jubilee organization challenged the racial order and the dominant racial ideology. Acting on the basis of situated knowledge and life experience, they redefined familiar, local, cultural, and political symbols to produce a rearticulation of racial meaning that pushed racial boundaries at the time.[71] In Depression-era Memphis, the rearticulation of racial meaning was based on the adaptation of local material and symbolic resources and the adoption of conventional gender representations, as embodied in Cotton Carnival. Cotton Maker's Jubilee was one of many black civic organizations in the United States that actively challenged the dominant ideology. Subsequently, these organizations won the right to everyday dignity for individual persons and generated cultural and social capital for African American communities.

The Vensons were motivated not only to change the image of blacks in the white imagination but also to change the image of blacks in the black imagination, as demonstrated by their concern for their young nephew, Quincy Johnson. Social scientists have long recognized that those negative images, products of institutionalized racism, a legacy of slavery and segregation, "actively coerce black folks to internalize negative perceptions of blackness, to be self-hating."[72] Throughout U.S. history African Americans have contested and revised the meanings of "black racial identity through spectacles, protests, and daily acts" of self-preservation.[73] Members of the African American community never have completely agreed about what positive images or symbols should replace negative ones; however, many people have agreed on the need for positive images. The Vensons may have been familiar with Alain Locke's 1925 essay, "The New Negro." Locke declared that the day of "aunties, uncles, and mammies," as well as Uncle Tom and Sambo, had passed.[74] He rejected these minstrel images of blacks from nineteenth-century popular culture and called for new images that reflected middle-class achievement and self-determination within the African American community, which he identified as "the New Negro."[75] Locke and others intended to transform white racist images of blacks and to overcome internalized oppression by restructuring the *race's* image of *itself*. Henry Louis Gates describes this trope of "the New Negro" as an attempt to transform "a white racist image of the black," then an effort "to restructure the race's image of itself," a call to "progress" and "respectability."[76]

In the 1930s, when the Vensons appealed to the African American community to support their efforts to create a positive and dignified image of "the New Negro" through emulation of Cotton Carnival, they encountered differences of opinion. Many people agreed with John Handcox, poet laureate of the Southern Tenant Farmers' Union, who rejected the images of cotton kings and queens, finding them to be unacceptable. They rejected any identification with cotton, a symbol of poverty, oppression, and slavery.[77] For them, the image of cotton makers was not consistent with personal dignity or idealized symbols of community progress and middle-class respectability. Local schoolteachers rejected overtures from the Vensons, complaining that cotton had done nothing for African Americans except put them at the bottom of the social hierarchy. Twenty years later, the local NAACP voiced similar criticism. In 1960, the NAACP organized a boycott of Cotton Maker's Jubilee.

Mrs. Venson responded to criticism with the African American community in a 1984 interview: "They had not been at that parade. . . . We had heard this, we had seen it and to us it was a different story."[78] For the Vensons, it was a battle for winning honor and fighting self-hatred. In their view, the battle for honor needed to be waged locally by revising and reinterpreting the symbols used by the dominant culture on their own turf. The best way to combat stereotypes of African American men and women and revise social meanings of black identity was to hold a parallel festival with its own kings and queens, parades and pageants. Participation would call attention to the contributions made by African Americans in producing the region's greatest source of wealth and in producing a folk culture.

Although initially, the Vensons failed to persuade local teachers, that is, one group of middle-class black professionals, they succeeded in gaining support from members of Post 27 of the American Legion, whose commander was Dr. Venson. These World War I veterans had received a bonus that year, and most of them were willing to use their own money to sponsor the first Cotton Maker's Jubilee. Mrs. Venson noted that many of the Legionnaires were illiterate. But because of their military service, their life experience included international travel and meaningful work "beyond the veil." From their position in the local status hierarchy, black veterans who had not found recognition for their military service in their own country to be equal to the treatment they had enjoyed in Europe, and who had not shared some of the benefits of education and middle-class respectability within their own community, found emulation of Cotton Carnival appealing. The veterans financed Cotton Maker's Jubilee with their bonus money and supported it with their participation. Gradually, the Vensons and their festival obtained support from some prominent leaders in the African American community. Over the years their supporters included Robert R. Church Jr., son of the first black millionaire, and Nat D. Williams, a history teacher and radio disc jockey on WDIA. At one time, Benjamin L. Hooks, who later became the national executive director of the NAACP, served as legal counsel for the Jubilee organization.

RACE, GENDER, AND SOCIAL POWER

So queen just popped into my head one day, and I was like, "Me, Queen Latifah." It felt
good saying it, and I felt like a queen. And you know, I am a queen. And every
Black woman is a queen.— QUEEN LATIFAH, quoted in Cheryl Keyes, "Empowering Self,
Making Choices, Creating Spaces: Black Female Identity via Rap Music Performance,"
in *That's the Joint! The Hip-Hop Studies Reader*, edited by
Murray Forman and Mark Anthony Neal

The actions taken by the Vensons, and Jubilee supporters, not only addressed the dignity of the African American community but also challenged racialized gender images. Watching black men working alongside horses and mules to pull parade floats and hearing Quincy's remark that "all the Negroes were horses" struck a nerve with the Vensons. For them, the symbol of cotton was subject to differing interpretations, but a comparison of African Americans to horses and mules was not.

Black workers still labored in cotton fields alongside mules in the 1930s, just as they had done for generations. Images of black workers, cotton, and mules have long been viewed as symbols of southern agriculture.[79] In McIlwaine's 1948 book on Memphis, his account of Carnival includes the statement that "Negroes, mules, and cotton are an old Southern Trinity."[80] Mules represented hard work and difficult labor relations in many blues songs, such as Blind Lemon Jefferson's "Balky Mule Blues." In recent years, playwright August Wilson used mules as symbols of work relations and racial tensions in the rural South. But mules also symbolize racialized gender representations. One 1930s era African American writer, Zora Neale Hurston, used the imagery of mules throughout her book *Their Eyes Were Watching God*. In one memorable scene, the main character's grandmother describes black women as the mules of the world. She explains a cycle of white men giving work to black men, who pass it on to black women. Her reference to mules suggests not only that black women suffer the burdens of arduous physical labor but also that they bear the brunt of racist and sexist attitudes in the minds of blacks as well as whites.[81]

The stigmatization of black women, their exclusion from generally accepted cultural ideals of womanhood, and their invisibility in the politics of gender equality occurred during slavery and continued long afterward.[82] In 1851, Sojourner Truth argued for including black women in political discussions of gender equality during her "Ain't I a Woman" speech given at the Ohio Women's Rights Convention. In the patriarchal Jim Crow South, white women had exclusive rights to be called "Lady" and served as idealized symbols of beauty and chastity. The term "Lady" referred to a dignified and supposedly "protected" social status that excluded all men, women presumed to lack sexual virtue, and all black women. Typically, throughout the dominant culture, black women were portrayed as hypersexualized Jezebels, desexualized Mammies, masculinized laborers, and beasts of burden. These dehumanizing images of black women lingered in the dominant culture long after slavery ended, supporting old stereotypes and newly minted ones, such as welfare queen and video ho.[83] Some critical scholars believe that these images negatively affect self-esteem as well as educational and occupational opportunities for African American women. Indeed, disparaging and misogynistic representations of black women that deny them their humanity have become institutionalized as part of twenty-first-century popular culture. The hip-hop music and video industry capitalizes on "a new black gender politics."[84] Rappers denigrate women as "bitches," "hos," and "chickenheads," while comedians such as Eddie Murphy make films that portray black women characters as vulgar and unfeminine. In 2007, radio host Don Imus provoked a national controversy, and lost his job, over a comment he made referring to members of the number-two-ranked women's basketball team at Rutgers University as "nappy-headed hos."

The response of African American women to sexist and racist images varies with historical time and local context. In the early twentieth century, some middle-class African American women embraced the cult of "true womanhood," which stressed piety, purity, submissiveness, and domesticity for native-born white women. Seeking validation and equality, middle-class black women also wanted "to prove that they were women whose lives were firmly rooted in the family."[85] Not surprisingly, Mrs. Venson, wife of an educated professional African American man, endorsed a traditional model of gender while challenging racial subordination. As the first Jubilee queen, Ethyl Venson became the embodiment of conventional representations of gender as a part of a newly articulated, and unconventional, representation of race.[86] She remained active in the Jubilee organization until her death in 1996, serving as a queen mother for generations of young women she helped groom to represent Cotton Maker's Jubilee locally and on national and international tours. Ideals of "true womanhood" influenced creation of the "Spirit of Cotton" contest and the selection of young African American women, either high school students or students from historically black colleges and universities, for "Spirit." Seeking conventional respectability for black women became a means to racial "progress."

For the era of the 1930s, Jubilee's recognition of the dignity and beauty of black women was an expression of nonconformity and resistance to the prevailing view of black women held by most Americans. Consequently, Memphis Jubilee queens attracted media attention from international news media outlets such as *Time* magazine. Yet nearly fifty years passed between the time when the first Jubilee queen paraded down the streets of Memphis and when the first African American woman strolled down an Atlantic City runway as Miss America. But dynamic tensions between racial and gender equality and popular culture are complex. In 1968, the NAACP protested the racial exclusionary practices of the Miss America pageant and staged its first Miss Black America pageant to publicly recognize Afrocentric standards of beauty for women. Many white feminists, who protested both sexism and racism in the Miss America pageant, also criticized the objectification of women in the Miss Black America pageant. And some African American feminists found themselves facing contradictions between and within these separate struggles against sexism and racism. Contradictions about representations of beauty and divisions concerning racial and gender equality still exist. But Craig argues that many African American women found "the call to queendom was hard to resist, when the alternative was the wider culture's disparagement."[87]

In Memphis, the first call to Jubilee queendom echoed the call for white Cotton Carnival queens. Historically, however, the selection process differs. Candidates for Jubilee queen do not conform to the age limits and marital status requirements of Carnival Memphis queens, but they do conform to normative expectations for appearance, personal integrity, and community status. Ethyl Venson, a young married woman, became the first queen in 1936. Memphis blues diva Ruby Wilson, sometimes billed as the Queen of Beale Street, became the queen of Jubilee in 1985. Over the years, African American women from diverse backgrounds have served as queen, including members of the Ford family—a prominent local African American family—as well as teachers, models, and others. Wives, mothers, and single women have been represented. Kings also come from diverse backgrounds but are more likely to be members of the small business community and hold positions in public service than to hold corporate CEO status. Except for the continuing organizational influence of members of the Venson family, passed on from generation to generation, genealogy does not appear to play a significant role in the selection process for kings and queens.

Ironically, in the post–civil rights era, the call to queendom has been answered by a few female performers who appropriate rap for constructing positive racial and gender identities. Their representations of black culture use symbols adopted by Kemet Jubilee as symbols of empowerment. Rappers described as queen mothers, like Jubilee queens, wear African headdresses and ankh-stylized jewelry. Moreover, their performances give voice to women and demand respect. Their music embraces "black female empowerment and spirituality, making clear their self-identification as African woman, warrior, priestess, and Queen."[88] Queen Latifah, Nefertiti, Isis, Queen Kenya, and others present a very different image of black women than many rappers. Their images and their messages have greater appeal to young people—the target of Kemet Jubilee's ongoing efforts to rearticulate racial identity.

CONTEMPORARY CHALLENGES

Kemet Jubilee, in more than seventy years of existence, has worked to contest racism, promote civic engagement, and rearticulate African American racial identity. While adapting to dramatic change and staying focused on racial identity and community, the group still hosts public celebrations to promote dignity. Historically, Jubilee challenged the exclusion and misrepresentation of African Americans not only in the original Cotton Carnival but also in the dominant society. The founders gave rise to a separate festival that honored African Americans and eventually led to integration and sponsorship of an African American krewe. But the twenty-first-century Kemet Jubilee organization faces new challenges. First, the images of African Americans in Carnival

Memphis have changed, but cultural representations of African Americans—locally, nationally, and globally—continue to dehumanize and disparage African Americans, especially women. Members stress the need to counter the influence of rappers, such as the Memphis group Three Six Mafia, and offset the global popularity of entertainers who make derogatory statements and create negative images of the black community. Faced with media portrayals of what critic Stanley Couch has described as "neo-Sambos," Jubilee supporters want to take a stand for what is good and decent for young people.[89] Interestingly, like some twenty-first-century female rappers and some nineteenth-century white city founders, they have adopted African-centered symbols to promote their vision of racial dignity.

Second, the social and economic costs of inclusion in Carnival Memphis have created a different set of problems for Jubilee than the costs of exclusion they experienced decades ago. Director Clyde Venson explains that Kemet Jubilee decided to withdraw its krewe from Carnival Memphis because "the more we tried to get in step with Carnival Memphis, the more we got out of step with the black community."[90] In his view, adult participation in year-round Carnival Memphis social events depleted Kemet Jubilee's valuable resources of time and money that could have been invested in promoting activities for disadvantaged African American youth. But withdrawing the Kemet Jubilee krewe from Carnival Memphis raises questions about the polarization of race and class divisions in Memphis. Elite and upper-middle-class African American residents may choose to participate in Carnival Memphis without assistance from an African American krewe. They also have options to belong to "Jack and Jill" chapters and participate in black debutante organizations. Consequently, members of the lower-income African American community experience exclusion and alienation—socially, economically, and politically—from more affluent blacks and whites, becoming what William Julius Wilson described as "the truly disadvantaged."[91]

Third, the revitalization and resurgence of downtown Memphis, especially in spaces formerly identified with a segregated African American community, may pose a formidable challenge to continuing the Jubilee tradition. Kemet Jubilee now encounters bureaucratic obstacles from city officials in obtaining access to downtown spaces traditionally used for setting up midway rides and reviewing stands. The redevelopment of historic spaces in and around Beale Street, Church Park, and Tom Lee Park—once part of black neighborhoods but now part of a commercialized tourist space—and the city's restrictive use of those spaces, especially during Memphis in May, limits access. Also, the public calendar now overflows with downtown civic events held in May. These events include commencement ceremonies for UT Memphis and the University of Memphis held at the FedEx Forum adjacent to Beale Street, as well as Memphis Redbirds baseball games at AutoZone Park. In 2007, Jubilee held its parade in March rather than May because, in the words of Clyde Venson, they were "forced" to choose between moving to a different space away from downtown, such as Overton Park, and rescheduling events for another time. Presumably, because of a lack of effective communication about the schedule change from May to March, attendance numbers for Kemet Jubilee declined in 2007. It remains to be seen whether new growth and reinvestment downtown, as well as new tourist attractions and expanding entertainment venues, will force Kemet Jubilee to relocate or reschedule on a permanent basis and how these changes will affect attendance and participation.

Fourth, the greatest challenge to Kemet Jubilee may be generational relevancy.[92] In the 1930s, a young couple started the original Cotton Maker's Jubilee organization and nurtured it throughout their own lifetimes. Dr. Venson chaired the organization until his death in 1970. Subsequently, Mrs. Venson took charge and served as chair until she stepped down in 1985. Since 1986, Dr. Venson's nephew, Clyde Venson, has held the leadership position. Venson, and many supporters of today's organization, grew up during the 1940s and 1950s when Jubilee enjoyed its golden age, raising hopes and aspirations within the segregated black community in the pre–civil rights South. Today's organizers express nostalgia for the world imagined by the Vensons and feelings of loss for the traditional parade route, reviewing stands, and midways. Jubilee members say they recognize the needs of disadvantaged youth and want to formulize an antidote to dehumanizing trends in popular culture. But the hopes, dreams, and fond memories of a conservative black middle class may be out of step with today's black urban youth, who see their life chances affected by widening disparities between rich and poor, high incarceration rates for black males, and increasing rates of poverty, violence, and addiction.

TRADITION, INEQUALITY, AND THE PRODUCTION OF LOCALITY

Today the rituals and symbols of Carnival Memphis and Memphis Kemet Jubilee perpetuate place distinctiveness and reproduce the social order. Despite the weakening of some social boundaries, primarily racial exclusion, however, the race, class, and gender distinctions that defined the two organizations in the 1930s have grown more intense. Subsequently, these ritual traditions remain embedded in a culture of inequality. Elite white families with strong local economic and genealogical ties still reign over Carnival Memphis, while Kemet Jubilee continues its struggle for dignity and respect. In recent years, Jubilee has renewed and redefined its emphasis on racial identity, whereas Carnival Memphis has emphasized the obligations of an elite social class to do good deeds in the community. Carnival Memphis has proven, at least for the time being, that place matters more than physical space or public spectacles in maintaining its ritual tradition. Meanwhile, Kemet Jubilee wrestles with the city to maintain access and meaningful ties to historic physical spaces. Still positioned in opposition to the dominant culture, that is, a culture that glamorizes pimps and hos, Kemet Jubilee must find generational relevance, as well as appropriate urban spaces, to sustain its place-based rituals. Following its own years of struggle with public space and generational relevance, Carnival Memphis has found new private spaces and reinvented itself to attract newcomers, as well as young, affluent, partygoers, to support a place-based ritual tradition.

The continuation of both ritual traditions seems to rely on the willingness of its members to enact and idealize conventional understandings of masculinity, femininity, and heterosexuality and efforts to pass these understandings along to future generations. Women must agree to perform traditional roles of queen mother, supportive wife, community organizer, member of a royal court, and queen. In Memphis, the call to queendom provides avenues for women to attain recognition within two separate communities of meaning. The processes of globalization and social change have brought new people, new industries, new social arrangements, and new opportunities to Memphis, but they have not severed the ties between race, class, gender, and place.

No man can know where he is going unless he knows exactly where he has

been and exactly how he arrived at his present place.—MAYA ANGELOU,

quoted in Ester Hill, "Maya Angelou: Resolving the Past, Embracing the Future,"

in *Conversations with Maya Angelou*, edited by Jeffrey M. Elliot

—— 7 ——

PLACE MATTERS

Continuity and Discontinuity

Many studies of globalization and cities focus on the "flattening" of the world, the homogenization of culture, and the demise of place distinctiveness. This book, however, analyzes qualities that make "place" distinctive, cumulative, durable, and meaningful. The overarching concern of this project is to show that place matters by presenting a narrative case-study analysis of one resilient southern city. Memphis, anchored in global flows of technology, culture, people, and goods, reveals the complexity of local and global processes intertwined in the production of locality and in urban transformations.

A city created by nearly two hundred years of investment, labor, conscious design, and rural migration, Memphis has faced periodic disruptions in the ongoing production of locality. Some disruptions, such as the yellow fever epidemics, have threatened the physical and material existence of the city, as well as its power relations. At some times, organized responses to these disruptions led to institutional practices that created a more restrictive social order and increased racial exclusion. But at other times, disruptions challenged the prevailing racial and social hierarchy and the dominant ideology—for example, the Overton Park Supreme Court case and the Sanitation Workers'

Strike. In Memphis, local responses to environmental and social disruptions sometimes exacerbated conflicts, and at other times, responses have helped the city take important steps for coming to terms with the past and advancing a progressive sense of place.

Despite ongoing local tensions about what kind of place Memphis *ought to be*, rooted in past conflicts and disruptions as well as undervalued achievements, Memphis *is* a distinctive place that matters. This sociological narrative about globalization and the paradoxes of place reveals much about the formation of local identity, the configuration of urban space, the structure of economic power, the legacy of cultural innovation, and the persistence of tradition. Reminders of these processes exist in musical and literary expression, as well as in parks, statues, rituals, downtown buildings, transportation infrastructure, and status hierarchies. These physical and symbolic manifestations of past failures and achievements are cumulative, transmissible, and subject to reinterpretation and re-presentation by members of different groups in different times and places.

PERSPECTIVE MATTERS

Key to advancing and informing interdisciplinary discussions of place is finding theoretical and methodological approaches that not only are "general enough to be worth speaking about" but also can provide means for describing particular cases.[1] This study uses a narrative, historical-sociological, case-study approach as one way to view place from "points in between" the general and the particular, creating a work "with narrative power and human interest."[2] This perspective, and the selection of Memphis as a particular case, permits us to begin developing a richer understanding of the *urban* South within a global context. By reframing the discussion of place, it reframes the discussion of Memphis and assessments of the city's global significance.

This approach offers an alternative to a southern-exceptionalism perspective, which emphasizes internal regional explanations within a national context for place distinctiveness. It also challenges global perspectives that reduce complex global-local processes to binary opposites. Subsequently, place can be seen as a crucible of cultural, social, and political interactions that occur within global flows of trade, migration, and epidemics and not as a space of stasis. These interdependent processes connect real people and places to the past, present, and future while integrating the global and local, as well as the urban and rural, in positive and negative ways.

These processes are observable in Memphis, in part because the city itself occupies a position of "betweenness," and "otherness," rather than a position of dominance in the United States or in the world. Since its inception as an American city, Memphis has served as a crossroads for rural-urban and urban-suburban migration and an entrepôt for imports and exports, ranging from groceries and cotton to athletic shoes and medical devices. As a regional "other," Memphis has been neither Old South nor New South but has been both rural and urban and simultaneously center and margin. As a musical crossroads, Memphis became a place of cultural innovation where new musical forms emerged from oral traditions of a rural underclass. The music expressed feelings of "otherness" and alienation but also gave dignity and meaning to the lives of the performers and their audiences. First recorded and widely disseminated using media technologies of the 1950s and 1960s, Memphis music reached diverse listeners and brought Memphis to the center of global popular culture. Decades later, "Memphis music has refused to disappear," and the city has become an "iconic" American place.[3] Defining how the city's complex positions of betweenness and otherness, center and margin, affect the production of locality helps explain how place remains distinctive and enduring within global flows of commerce and culture. Despite critics who claim that Memphis is a provincial, backwater town, however, quiescence has never been an apt descriptor. Memphis is a dynamic site of entrepreneurialism, economic productivity, cultural innovation, and social tensions where global and local products and signifiers are reworked into a particular production of locality.[4]

POVERTY AND POWER IN MEMPHIS

Memphis is a place where patterns of inequality, produced and reproduced throughout city history, affect the present and future life chances of people who live there. Deeply rooted in the city's economic structure and historic ties to the global economy, inequality has been sustained by slavery, segregation, smokestack chasing, and patriarchy. Historically, the civic "ethos" of most leaders in Memphis, as well as those in other southern cities, has produced "an aversion to investment in human capital and city services" and a fondness for publicly supported economic development plans.[5] Subsequently, southern development strategies designed to "sell" local resources for attracting industry, such as low wages, low tax rates, and cheap natural resources, have benefited private investors, often at the expense of investments in public services and human capital. The costs of these strategies can be seen in local health and educational disparities, concentrations of poverty, environmental contamination, the prevalence of crime, and capital flight. In Memphis, generations of low expectations and decades of low investments in human capital have created cumulative disadvantages for people and place. These difficulties hinder local efforts to educate workers for full participation in the knowledge economy and pose many challenges for the city "to fashion a progressive politics of well-being and emancipation out of multiplicity and difference and from the particularities of the urban experience."[6]

Yet many twenty-first-century city officials and residents pursue place building primarily through top-down strategies to make Memphis a more appealing "place" to outsiders. The desire to make the city more cosmopolitan, or at least more appealing to cosmopolites, and more salable to outside investors has been reproduced from one administration to the next, as well as from one generation to the next. Strategies, often described as boosterism or branding, reflect local and global pressures to redefine the city, reinvent the past, adopt more (or less) relevant symbols to shape identity, change the built environment, and reorganize local political structures. Physical evidence of many past strategies to redefine the city and capture national or international attention fills the urban landscape. These objects include Civil War statues and reliquaries placed in public parks more than one century ago, as well as two publicly funded sports arenas built only a few city blocks and a couple of decades apart from each other. The accumulation of relics on the urban landscape, as well as the circulation of stories and feelings about them, reminds generations of Memphians of past follies and misdirection and shapes future hopes and aspirations. Stories and tensions represented by these material and symbolic resources sometimes spur efforts to make changes in place building and the production of locality but sometimes impede them. Together they capture "complex interactions between structure, agency, and contingency"[7] and contribute to the unique characteristics of place.

GLOBAL COMPETITION / LOCAL GOVERNANCE

Memphis, like many urban areas in the United States, has struggled to maintain its fiscal base and its population despite decades of suburbanization, deindustrialization, shrinking federal revenues, periods of recession, and global restructuring. The local costs of public services include not only maintaining parks, schools, and libraries but also supporting strategies intended to make the city more competitive. Redefining the city's image to attract new residents and tourists and recruiting businesses also place demands on local resources. Since World War II, typical solutions to increase revenues in the city of Memphis and Shelby County have involved annexing suburban areas into the city and raising property taxes. Recent proposals to meet budgetary demands by increasing property taxes *and* reducing public services, such as park maintenance and public library operations, have provoked city residents.

Given the current system of dual government, residents of the city of Memphis pay property taxes in the city and in the county, whereas county residents pay only county taxes. Most urban and suburban dwellers believe their taxes are too high. Hence, the city mayor and the county mayor, as well as the Chamber of Commerce and local media, have given new life to old debates about consolidation of city and county governments.[8] Twenty-first-century support for consolidation blends old themes of progress and efficiency with new themes of globalization to make state, regional, and national comparisons between Memphis and other cities. In the view of advocates, consolidation provides regional solutions for cutting government costs, improving public services, and reducing inequalities between urban and suburban communities.[9]

Proposed consolidation is not a new idea in Memphis. City-county merger has been an option since Tennessee's Constitutional Convention of 1953, and subsequent ratification created the legal framework for a popular vote to end dual administrations. The constitutional process for a popular vote on consolidation originates with a local petition to the state legislature, signed by 30,000 legal residents who request a vote on consolidation. When elections are held, a simple majority approval in both the city and the county is required for passage. Two previous attempts to form a metropolitan government have failed. Memphis and Shelby County voters rejected merger in 1962. Later, in 1971, Memphis voters narrowly approved consolidation, but Shelby County voters rejected it by a two-to-one margin. Nashville, Memphis's neighbor and in-state rival, was consolidated as Nashville–Davidson County in 1962 after a 1958 consolidation referendum failed.

Consolidation proponents describe a metropolitan form of government as more progressive than dual city and county governments and stress that consolidation will improve government efficiency, eliminate redundancies, and increase accountability. Advocates also compare Memphis (unfavorably) with cities that already have consolidated local governments, such as Indianapolis and Nashville. Former Nashville mayor Bill Purcell spoke to a Rotary

Club audience in Memphis, saying, "The decision to become a metropolitan government was the single smartest thing that Nashville has ever done."[10] According to Purcell, Nashville's growth has outpaced that of Memphis and Knoxville because of Nashville's comparative efficiency and lower property taxes, which he attributed to consolidation. Former state legislator Cecil Branstetter, considered one of the founding fathers of metropolitan government in Tennessee more than half a century ago, agreed: "Nashville could never have grown like it has if it did not have metropolitan government."[11]

One local writer suggests a new argument in favor of consolidation that calls attention to globalization and place. In her view, metropolitan government can be a unifying form of community organization that bridges social divides. She writes: "But I've long argued for consolidation because I think the artificial boundaries of 'the city and the county' pit the community—neighbors even—against each other. In a global economy, 20 miles apart is barely a hop. We act as if it's a world away."[12]

One reason that twenty-first-century scholars and residents find "city-county consolidation back on the urban agenda" is the recent successful merger of the city of Louisville and Jefferson County, Kentucky.[13] Louisville, the first successful consolidation in a major metropolis in more than thirty years, defied "conventional wisdom that merger is politically infeasible" and subsequently became a "harbinger for metropolitan reorganization."[14]

Although consolidation is portrayed as a unifying process that reduces inequality, empirical evidence suggests that "consolidations are divisive and confer both privileges and penalties."[15] As is the case with any form of organizational change, consolidations can be expected "to magnify the influence of some groups and diminish the presence of others."[16] Critics add that consolidation is a radical change that can be difficult to reverse.[17] Because consolidations have disruptive effects that may have long-term consequences, a thorough study of the costs and benefits of consolidation based on empirical evidence would be advisable to inform public discussions before initiating a referendum.

As a caveat to reorganization, city leaders might review the consequences of the 1879 decision to surrender the city charter and the subsequent 1891 restoration of home rule. At the time, Memphis lost the momentum for development, as well as the human and capital resources needed to sustain it, because of a lack of support for public services (health and sanitation), disease, and debt repudiation. Politically, these actions to reorganize government further concentrated power in the hands of upper-class white males during commission government and limited the civic participation of African American and minority voters. These exclusions lasted until the 1960s.[18] Also, following restoration of the city charter, leaders established an official monument to honor a Confederate general as a symbol of unification among whites and of the dominant racial ideology. The monument still stands as testimony to lingering and perhaps irreconcilable differences regarding place, power, and racial identity. A review of decisions made more than a century ago shows that changes in local organization can create divisions, confer privileges, and leave lasting effects on place.

CULTURAL INNOVATION, CONSUMPTION, AND TOURISM

The music originating in Memphis and the Mid-South that became global popular music—blues, rock and roll, soul, and hip-hop—has not always been welcome in the place that produced it. Now, however, more than fifty years after the birth of rock and roll, global investors are partnering with local officials and developers to expand and improve significant sites as part of the city's "theme enhancement" of Memphis music and cultural heritage. Recognizing that tourism contributes more than $2 billion to the local economy each year and constitutes the fastest-growing sector of the global economy has fueled interest among local and global developers interested in developing tourist sites for the *consumption* of popular culture. Public and private partnerships support development of the Beale Street entertainment district, as well as a tourism development zone at Graceland and in the Whitehaven suburb, characterized by shabby souvenir shops, used car lots, and fast-food vendors on the commercial strip that built up around the home of Elvis Presley.

Until recently, Elvis Presley Enterprises (EPE) was a privately owned local company belonging to Lisa Marie Presley, Presley's daughter and heir. Now EPE is a subsidiary of a global conglomerate owned by CKX, Inc. Robert F. X. Sillerman is chairman and CEO of CKX, which owns the *American Idol* and *British Idol* television properties. In 2004, Lisa Marie Presley sold an 85 percent interest in EPE to CKX for more than $100 million. Priscilla Presley, Lisa Marie's mother, was appointed to the CKX board of directors.[19] Although Lisa Marie Presley retains ownership of the house, CKX owns the rights to the image and likeness of Elvis Presley and the operations at Graceland, as well as the rights to the name, image, and likeness of another icon of popular culture, Muhammad Ali. According to Sillerman: "We have come to realize there is a substantial opportunity to capitalize on the Elvis Presley and Muhammad Ali asset in real estate and location-based attractions."[20] Sillerman plans to invest $250 million in a new visitor's center, a convention hotel, and hi-tech digitalized entertainment exhibits on one hundred acres adjacent to Graceland acquired by EPE. Investors hope to double the number of tourists who visit Graceland and increase the amount of time and money they spend. Jack Soden, CEO of EPE, and Robert Sillerman expect government funding at all levels—city, county, state, and federal—to support infrastructure improvements for Whitehaven's redevelopment. Plans to expand Graceland and enhance Whitehaven as a location-based (place-based) attraction won support from Tennessee legislators in June 2007, when they passed legislation authorizing a tourism development ment zone (TDZ) at Graceland. Subject to city council approval and some rezoning, the TDZ will allow tax abatements and incentives to support cleaning up the neighborhood and building the new hotel and entertainment facilities. Proponents of the TDZ suggest that targeting Whitehaven for redevelopment not only benefits tourism but also supports other industries in the area near the airport, including transportation and logistics and biotechnology.[21] Local subsidies for attracting global tourism and foreign investment may be beneficial for some, but they do "little to alter the traditional southern pattern of financing economic development at the expense of human development."[22]

Critics wonder if the local emphasis on tourism and cultural consumption, which constitutes an intensification of global capitalism, and some would say an intensification of cultural appropriation, will suppress future local cultural innovation. If so, it will create yet another paradox of place. Even Graceland, which once distanced itself from Elvis Presley impersonators, now invites them to Graceland in an *American Idol* type of competition. Questions about commercialization, appropriation, and authenticity are unlikely to attract much discussion on Beale Street or at Graceland given that both properties have been "sold" to promote economic development and consumption.

The production of cultural innovation may continue at other Memphis locations. The successes of young hip-hop musicians in North Memphis and young filmmakers such as Craig Brewer seem likely to carry on the legacy of cultural innovation linked to global flows. Their music and films seem to express a strong "place-based concept of 'the real' . . . grounded in personal experience."[23] Like their predecessors from earlier times on Beale Street and at Sun Studio and Stax, these contemporary artists display characteristics of creativity and entrepreneurialism. Their work, also like that of many of their predecessors in cultural innovation, expresses the feelings of marginalized outsiders and sometimes poses an affront to polite society.

Cotton is no longer king, but the cotton and logistic industries drive economic growth and connect Memphis to the past, present, and future. In May 2007, a ceremonial meeting took place in downtown Memphis at the historic Peabody Hotel involving Memphis cotton merchants, Chinese textile executives and trade ministers, and Tennessee state officials. Representatives of Memphis families who have traded cotton on world markets for generations, executives of the world's largest transportation company (FedEx), and government officials from the world's largest developing economy endorsed the sale of $500 million of cotton to China. While cotton men and Chinese officials raised champagne glasses and trade expectations, Governor Phil Bredesen announced plans to locate a Tennessee economic development office in Beijing, commenting that "Memphis and the cotton industry have always viewed trade as a global venture."[24]

Global ventures involving Memphis, Beijing, and other Chinese cities are expanding rapidly. FedEx, headquartered in Memphis, operates more flights in and out of China than any other airline. In 2003, the company transported two giant pandas from Beijing to the Memphis Zoo on a ten-year loan from the Chinese government to reside in the zoo's $16 million China Center. To date, the partnership of Ya Ya and Le Le has not produced a single offspring in Memphis; however, trade and cultural partnerships are proliferating. Tennessee is the fastest-growing state in the United States in terms of trade with China. Since 2000, Tennessee exports to China have grown more than 1,000 percent. With exports to China valued at approximately $2 billion annually, China is the state's third-largest export partner behind Canada ($7 billion) and Mexico ($2.3 billion). Agricultural and agricultural-related products account for half of the state's exports to China.

The cotton industries led the way for Memphis trade with China in 1972 when Dunavant participated in the first sale of American cotton to China. FedEx became the first express air carrier in China in 1984. Now FedEx employs six thousand workers in China and offers direct flights from China to Europe, India, and most major Asian airports to connect two hundred Chinese cities to international networks. In 2006, FedEx paid $400 million to buy out Datian Group, obtaining full control over Datian's truck fleet and its eighty-nine distribution hubs. In 2008, FedEx opened a new $150 million hub in Guangzhou, China. FedEx also became the first American customer for Airbus A380 cargo haulers, accepting delivery of twenty in 2008 intended for nonstop flights from Asia to American hubs.[25]

Meanwhile, in Memphis, the local transportation infrastructure continues to expand to provide faster and cheaper transportation access to Asia. Canadian National Railway has spent more than $100 million in Memphis at Frank C. Pidgeon Industrial Park constructing an intermodal container facility. Cargo ships from Asia unload containers at Prince Rupert in Canada, where they are shipped to Memphis via Canadian National Railway. Prince Rupert, the deepest warm-water harbor on the North American west coast, is 1,200 nautical miles closer to Shanghai than Los Angeles. Containers of consumer goods can be unloaded directly from ship to train for more efficient and cost-effective transportation. Shipping containers are expected to go through Memphis for storage and distribution, further enhancing the local distribution and logistics industry.[26]

Global flows connect Memphis and China through cultural exchange as well as commercial trade. A cultural partnership between the University of Memphis and China's Hubei University led to establishment of a Confucius Institute, which opened in Memphis in August 2007. Dr. Hsiang-te Kung, professor of earth sciences at the University of Memphis and a seventy-fifth-generation descendant of Confucius, heads the institute. In September 2007, University of Memphis provost Dr. Ralph Faudree and Memphis men's basketball head coach John Calipari visited Beijing to formalize a five-year agreement with the Chinese Basketball Association. The University of Memphis and Hubei University now exchange coaching staff and players as well as faculty and students. The University of Memphis operates exchange programs with several Chinese universities, including Huazhong Normal University, East China Normal University, Xinjiang University, and Shanghai University.[27]

The following month, Governor Phil Bredesen traveled to China to open the Tennessee-China Development Center, intended to serve as a clearinghouse for information about economic opportunities in China for Tennessee companies and to raise Tennessee's profile to attract potential Asian investors. The governor's trade mission to China involved representatives of higher education in Tennessee, including the state's Doctoral/Research Universities–Extensive (Vanderbilt, the University of Tennessee, and the University of Memphis), which emphasized the importance of the knowledge economy.

Memphis representatives on the trip included Dr. Shirley Raines, president of the University of Memphis, as well as representatives of the cotton, logistics, and health industries.[28] St. Jude Children's Research Hospital already has established partnerships with children's hospitals in Beijing and Shanghai.

MEMPHIS, PLACE, AND THE FUTURE

Place, anchored in global flows, gives shape and boundary to social inequalities, cultural traditions, personal identity, family ties and history, interpersonal relations, economic development, and social change. Place affects our quality of life, economic security, self-esteem, employment opportunities, leisure activities, the availability of public services (especially education), access to health care, and the quality of our air and water. In other words, "place mediates social life" and contributes to our understanding of global processes, social practices, and historical change.[29]

Place, and feelings about place, can form the basis of community cooperation as well as conflict. In any place, especially an urban one, deciding what best serves the public good can be a contentious process when various individuals and groups hold conflicting feelings about place, disagree on the importance of place, and assign different values to place-based assets—physical and symbolic ones. But decisions, consciousness, and actions contribute to the ongoing physical and symbolic "production of locality."[30]

As Memphis competes with other cities to create high-paying jobs, improve educational attainment, make local government more accountable, and improve the quality of life for residents, the city also struggles with its legacy of identity crises, social inequality, and conflict. At times residents and city leaders need to be reminded that social struggles, political battles, cultural icons, and the area's human and natural resources comprise authentic place-specific resources that cannot be digitized or duplicated in any other location. Changes in local practices regarding the value of these resources, especially its human resources, will foster a progressive sense of place. Subsequently, new forms of local identity, cultural expression, and economic development, integrated with old ones and mediated by processes of globalization, will sustain the *genius loci*, or the spirit of place, that makes Memphis distinctive.

NOTES

INTRODUCTION

1 Odum cited in Hall, *Cities in Civilization*, 556–57.
2 Moe and Wilkie, *Changing Places*, 86.
3 Kuhn, *Structure of Scientific Revolutions*.
4 U.S. Census Bureau, *County and City Data Book: 2007*, table C-1, 728; table D-2, 844.
5 U.S. Census Bureau, *State and Metropolitan Area Data Book: 2006*, table C-1, 197; table B-1, 123; table E-14, E-19.
6 Memphis Regional Chamber of Commerce, *Memphis Region Sourcebook*, 8.
7 Moe and Wilkie, *Changing Places*, 77.
8 DeCell, "In the Beginning."
9 Cohn, *God Shakes Creation*, 14.
10 Childers, "Memphis," 100.
11 DeCell, "In the Beginning"; Peter Taylor, *Summons to Memphis*, 1.
12 Peter Taylor, *Summons to Memphis*, 3.
13 Ibid., 1–3.

CHAPTER ONE

1 Appadurai, "Production of Locality."
2 Welty, *Eye of the Story*, 128–29.
3 Foucault, *Discipline and Punish*, uses the term "people of little substance."
4 Richard Wright, *12 Million Black Voices*, 93.
5 Gladney, *How Am I to Be Heard?*, 38.
6 Brownell, *Urban Ethos*; Scherzer, "Southern Cities."
7 Portes and Stepick, *City on the Edge*.
8 Feagin, *Free Enterprise City*, 2.
9 Biles, *Memphis in the Great Depression*, 6–7.

10 Woods, *Development Arrested*, 91.

11 Crosby, *American Plague*.

12 Capers, *Biography of a River Town*, 162.

13 Ibid., 163–64.

14 Rousey, "Yellow Fever and Black Policemen," 373.

15 Ibid., 364.

16 Ibid., 367; Bond and Sherman, *Memphis in Black and White*, 64.

17 Wrenn, *Crisis and Commission Government*; Goings and Page, "African Americans versus the Memphis Street Railway Company," 133.

18 Sigafoos, *Cotton Row to Beale Street*, 58.

19 Wrenn, *Crisis and Commission Government*; Capers, *Biography of a River Town*; Woodward, *Origins of the New South*.

20 Ibid., 28.

21 In 2005, Memphis rights to the water aquifer were challenged by the Mississippi attorney general, who filed for $1 billion in damages. The lawsuit claims that the Memphis municipal water supply drains a critical aquifer of water belonging to the state of Mississippi.

22 Sigafoos, *Cotton Row to Beale Street*, 58.

23 M. Warner, "Local Control versus National Interest."

24 Ibid., 421.

25 Goffman, *Stigma*, 3–5.

26 M. Warner, "Local Control versus National Interest," 421.

27 Ayers, "Portraying Power."

28 Orum and Chen, *World of Cities*.

29 Massey, "Power Geometry"; Griswold and Wright, "Cowbirds, Locals, and the Dynamic Endurance of Regionalism"; Gotham, "Tourism from Above and Below"; Rushing, "Globalization and the Paradoxes of Place"; Rofe, " 'I Want to Be Global.' "

30 Gieryn, "A Space for Place," 466.

31 Dreier, Mollenkopf, and Swanstrom, *Place Matters*, 2–3.

32 Gieryn, "A Space for Place," 467.

33 Griswold and Wright, "Cowbirds, Locals, and the Dynamic Endurance of Regionalism," 1414–15.

34 Massey, "Power Geometry," 64.

35 Woodward, *Burden of Southern History*.

36 Ayers, *What Caused the Civil War*, 46.

37 Key, *Southern Politics*; Grantham, *Life and Death of the Solid South*; Black and Black, *Rise of Southern Republicans*.

38 Reed, *Enduring South*; Reed, *Southern Folk Plain and Fancy*.

39 Cobb, *Most Southern Place on Earth*; Reed, *One South*; Reed, *My Tears Spoiled My Aim*.

40 Lichter, "Race, Employment Hardship, and Inequality"; Goldfield, *Region, Race, and Cities*.

41 Goldfield, *Cotton Fields and Skyscrapers*.

42 Odum, *Southern Regions*; Cash, *Mind of the South*.

43 Falk, *Rooted in Place*; Twelve Southerners, *I'll Take My Stand*.

44 Woods, *Development Arrested*, 28.

45 Reed, *Enduring South*, 12.

46 Dirlik, *Postcolonial Aura*, 86.

47 Chacko, "Understanding the Geography of Pellagra," 201; Griffin and Doyle, *The South As an American Problem*.

48 Billings, *Planters and the Making of a "New South"*; Wood, *Southern Capitalism*; Wallerstein, "What Can One Mean by Southern Culture?"; Woods, *Development Arrested*.

49 Omi and Winant, *Racial Formation*; Harrison, "Persistent Power of 'Race' "; Roediger, *Wages of Whiteness*.

50 Persky, "The South"; Wallerstein, "American Slavery "; Dunaway, *First American Frontier*; Woods, *Development Arrested*.

51 Wallerstein, "What Can One Mean by Southern Culture?," 11.

52 Samir Amin, *Accumulation*, 27.

53 Peacock et al., *American South*; Cobb and Stueck, *Globalization and the American South*; Fink, *Maya of Morganton*.

54 Peacock, *Grounded Globalism*.

55 Smith and Cohn, "Introduction: Uncanny Hybridities," 9.

56 Mills, *Sociological Imagination*.

57 Paulsen, "Making Character Concrete," 244.

58 Massey, "Power Geometry," 66.

59 Hodos, "Globalization, Regionalism, and Urban Restructuring"; Rushing, "Rural Empowerment Zones"; Cowie, *Capital Moves*; Gustafson, "Meanings of Place," 7.

60 Allen J. Scott, "Cultural Economy of Cities," 324–25.

61 Urry, "Sociology of Space and Place"; Massey, "Power Geometry"; Zukin, *Landscapes of Power*; Allen J. Scott, "Cultural Economy of Cities."

62 Giddens, *Consequences of Modernity*, 2.

63 Griswold and Wright, "Cowbirds, Locals, and the Dynamic Endurance of Regionalism."

64 Brown-Saracino, "Social Preservationists."

65 Friedman, *The World Is Flat*; Harvey, *Condition of Postmodernity*; Arrighi, *Adam Smith in Beijing*; Sassen, *Global Cities, Linked Cities*; Lughod, *New York, Chicago, Los Angeles*; Taylor and Lang, "U.S. Cities in the 'World City Network.' "

66 Foucault and Miscowiec, "Of Other Spaces," 22–23.

67 Gotham, "Tourism from Above and Below"; Harvey, "From Managerialism to Entrepreneurialism."

68 Waters, *Globalization*, 3; Rofe, " 'I Want to Be Global,' " 2515; Smith and Timberlake, "World City Networks."

69 Abbott, *Discipline and Department*, 196.

70 Hannerz, *Cultural Complexity*.

71 Weinbaum, *To Move a Mountain*.

72 Molotch, Freudenburg, and Paulsen, "History Repeats Itself, but How?"

73 Appadurai, " Production of Locality," 207

74 Hannerz, "Flows, Boundaries and Hybrids," 5.

75 Hannerz, *Cultural Complexity*.

76 Hall, *Cities in Civilization*.

77   Ibid., 7.

78   Ibid.

79   Ibid., 519

80   Hannerz, *Cultural Complexity*, 192.

81   Gordon, *It Came from Memphis*, 6.

82   Ibid.; Hall, *Cities in Civilization*, 602.

83   Capers, *Biography of a River Town*, 206.

84   Biles, "Memphis," 1460.

85   The term is used in contrast with Foucault's "people of little substance" in *Discipline and Punish*.

86   "Visions of Plenty" is a song written and performed by Kate Campbell.

87   Childers, "Memphis," 100; Woods, *Development Arrested*, 30.

88   "Identity Crisis," *Memphis*, 4.

89   Geertz, *Interpretation of Cultures*; Feagin et al., *Case for the Case Study*, 1991; Abbott, *Discipline and Department*; Ragin, *Comparative Method*; Reed, "On Narrative and Sociology."

90   Reed, "On Narrative and Sociology," 2.

91   Reed, *One South*, 57.

92   Reed, "On Narrative and Sociology"; Reed, *One South*.

93   Smith and Timberlake, "World City Networks," 2.

94   Sjoberg et al., "Case Study Approach," 28; Bradshaw and Wallace, "Informing Generality."

95   Adams and Gorton, "Southern Trauma."

96   Feagin et al., *Case for the Case Study*, 6.

97   Sjoberg et al., "Case Study Approach," 39.

98   Bahr and Caplow, "Middletown As an Urban Case Study," 85.

99   Sjoberg et al., "Case Study Approach," 39.

100   Gotham and Staples, "Narrative Analysis," 482.

101   Feagin et al., *Case for the Case Study*, 20.

102   R. Stephen Warner, "Oenology," 189.

103   Gotham and Staples, "Narrative Analysis," 491.

104   Feagin et al., *Case for the Case Study*, 13.

105   Griffin, "Temporality, Events, and Explanation," 405.

106   Abbott, "History and Sociology," 227; Gotham and Staples, "Narrative Analysis," 483.

107   Ibid.

108   Ibid.

109   Duvall cited in Busbee, "Mississippi's Man of Letters."

110   Ibid.

CHAPTER TWO

1   Harkins, *Metropolis of the American Nile*.

2   Wailoo, *Dying in the City of the Blues*, 11.

3   Olick and Robbins, "Social Memory Studies," 122.

4 Schudson, "How Culture Works," 108; Schwartz, "Social Change and Collective Memory," 232; Saito, "Reiterated Commemoration," 354–55.

5 Saito, "Reiterated Commemoration," 355.

6 Share, *Union*, 5.

7 Schwartz and Schuman, "History, Commemoration, and Belief," 185.

8 Bishir, "Landmarks of Power."

9 Mumford, *City in History*; Jacobs, "Symbolic Urban Spaces."

10 Bond and Sherman, *Memphis in Black and White*, 66–76.

11 Schein, "Place of Landscape," 666; Jacobs, "Symbolic Urban Spaces," 257.

12 Bond and Sherman, *Memphis in Black and White*, 77.

13 Tilly and Faudree, *Yesterday's Evergreen*; McFarland, *Memoirs and Addresses*; Wrenn, *Crisis and Commission Government*.

14 Boyer, *Urban Masses and Moral Order*, 265.

15 Coski, *Confederate Battle Flag*, 59.

16 Savage, "Politics of Memory," 132.

17 Forrest Monument Association, *Forrest Monument*.

18 Dwyer, "Location, Politics, and the Production of Civil Rights Memorial Landscapes," 31.

19 Schein, "Place of Landscape," 669.

20 McFarland, *Memoirs and Addresses*.

21 Kessler, "Forrest Park."

22 Osborne, "Landscapes, Memory, Monuments, and Commemoration."

23 Savage, "Politics of Memory"; Osborne, "Landscapes, Memory, Monuments, and Commemoration."

24 Forrest Monument Association, *Forrest Monument*.

25 Dwyer, "Location, Politics, and the Production of Civil Rights Memorial Landscapes," 32.

26 Hobsbawm and Ranger, *Invention of Tradition*, 1f.

27 Jedlowski, "Memory and Sociology," 41.

28 Savage, "Politics of Memory," 133.

29 Ibid., 132.

30 Du Bois, *Black Reconstruction*; Roediger, *Wages of Whiteness*.

31 R. W. Connell, *Masculinities*, 77.

32 Savage, "Politics of Memory," 133.

33 Gramsci, *Selections from the Prison Notebooks*; Foucault, *Discipline and Punish*; R. W. Connell, *Masculinities*.

34 Brundage, "White Women," 2–3.

35 Cox, *Dixie's Daughters*.

36 Bishir, "Landmarks of Power," 141.

37 Appadurai, "Past As a Scarce Resource," 203.

38 Brundage, "White Women," 3.

39 Ibid., 16–17.

40 Capers, *Biography of a River Town*, 206.

41 Ibid.

42 Ibid.

43 Biles, "Memphis."

44 Foucault, *Discipline and Punish.*

45 Logan, *Negro in American Life and Thought.*

46 Williamson, *Crucible of Race.*

47 Bond and Sherman, *Memphis in Black and White*, 65.

48 "Black" Thursdays were reserved for "colored" admission to the Memphis Zoo at Overton Park during the 1950s.

49 Wells, who was orphaned by the yellow fever epidemics, lost her job as a public school teacher for writing a newspaper article criticizing "separate but equal" schools.

50 Franklin, *Living Our Stories, Telling Our Truths*, 67.

51 Fred Hutchins cited in Decosta-Willis, *Memphis Diary of Ida B. Wells*, 2.

52 Wrenn, *Crisis and Commission Government*, 131.

53 Foucault, *Discipline and Punish.*

54 Gramsci, *Selections from the Prison Notebooks*; Centre for Contemporary Cultural Studies, *Unpopular Education.*

55 Boggs, *Two Revolutions*, 158–61; Robinson, *Promoting Polyarchy*, 20–25; Rushing, " 'Sin, Sex, and Segregation,' " 168.

56 Rossiter, *American Presidency*, 8, describes Lincoln as "the richest symbol in the American experience."

57 Coski, *Confederate Battle Flag*, 65.

58 McLaurin, "Commemorating Wilmington's Racial Violence," 37.

59 Yolanda Jones, "Freedom Rings."

60 Fontenay, "Another Battleground"; Branston, "In a City on the Move, a Civil War Issue Refuses to Die."

61 These websites are located at <www.scv.org>; <www.mortonsbattery.org>; <www.dixierising.com>.

62 Mitchell, "Confederate Parks."

63 Branston, "Man on Horseback."

64 Jacintha Jones, "It's Not a War."

65 Mitchell, "Confederate Parks," 3A.

66 The subtitle comes from an article by Wagner-Pacifici and Schwartz, "Vietnam Veterans Memorial."

67 Sigafoos, *Cotton Row to Beale Street*, 337.

68 Joan Beifuss, *At the River I Stand*, 455.

69 "Assassination," 18.

70 Rushing, "Cold War Racial Politics," 55.

71 Moe and Wilkie, *Changing Places*, 84.

72 Cowie, *Capital Moves.*

73 *Memphis Commercial Appeal*, 21 May 1979, A7, cited in Adderley, "Monument on the Mississippi," 31.

74 Later, the name of the foundation was changed in response to a request from Coretta

Scott King and the King Foundation in Atlanta. It is now the Lorraine Civil Rights Museum Foundation.

75 Wagner-Pacifici and Schwartz, "Vietnam Veterans Memorial."

76 Jacqueline Smith, who resided in the Lorraine Motel from 1973 to 1988, has maintained a protest vigil in front of the museum since 1988.

77 Adderley, "Monument on the Mississippi," 48.

78 Dwyer, "Location, Politics, and the Production of Civil Rights Memorial Landscapes," 46.

79 Adderley, "Monument on the Mississippi," 46; Chambers, "This Dreamer Cometh."

80 Dwyer, "Location, Politics, and the Production of Civil Rights Memorial Landscapes."

81 Risher, "Civil Rights Museum Opens Eyes to History."

82 Kane, "Mourning the Promised Land," 563.

83 Ibid., 558.

84 Haynes, "Civil Rights Museum Grows into Second Decade."

85 Burch, "Expanding the Legacy."

86 <www.sitesofconscience.org>.

87 Eden, " 'Sites of Conscience' Get Boost from Libeskind, Parley."

88 The National Civil Rights Museum website is located at <www.civilrightsmuseum.com>.

89 Yolanda Jones, "Freedom Rings," A1.

90 Ibid.

91 Biggs, "Oprah Visit Stirs Excitement in City."

92 The Facing History and Ourselves website is located at <www.facinghistoryandourselves.org>.

93 Kumar, " 'Fear and Pride,' " B1.

94 Landis, "Franklin School Readies for Third Trip to Memphis."

95 Cornish, "Mission of National Civil Rights Museum Questioned."

96 Ibid.

97 Callahan, "8 People Added to National Civil Rights Museum Board."

98 Lollar, "National Civil Rights Museum Announces 40th Anniversary."

99 Garris, "New Construction Award 2003."

100 Garlington, "Library's New Name Honors Civil Rights Pioneer Hooks."

101 Ibid.

102 Bellah et al., *Habits of the Heart*, 153.

103 Saito, "Reiterated Commemoration," 355.

CHAPTER THREE

1 Molotch, Freudenburg, and Paulsen, "History Repeats Itself, but How?"

2 Ibid.; Rushing, "Globalization and the Paradoxes of Place"; Dreier, Mollenkopf, and Swanstrom, *Place Matters*.

3 Imrie, Pinch, and Boyle, "Identities, Citizenship and Power"; Suttles, "Cumulative Texture."

4 Molotch, "Growth Machine Links," 248, uses the term "place-building" in a meaning similar to Aguilar-San Juan's, ("Saying Vietnamese," 41) use of "place-making" and Florida's (*Rise of the Creative Class*, 6) reference to "place" as "the central organizing unit of our time." I use the term "place building" to include place making and place as a central organizing unit.

5 Zukin, *Landscapes of Power*, 16.

6 Rose, *Interstate*, 101.

7 Molotch, "Growth Machine Links," 248.

8 Rose, *Interstate*, 106.

9 Ibid., 116; Gotham, "Political Opportunity, Community Identity, and the Emergence of a Local Anti-Expressway Movement."

10 Marwick, *Sixties*, 451.

11 Heller, "Tentative Answer," 1031.

12 "That's Alright, Mama," recorded on 5 July 1954, received international media attention as the first rock and roll record at a "global" simulcast on its fiftieth anniversary in 2004. But Elvis was a "local" recording phenomenon at the time of this first paid appearance at Overton Park.

13 Sigafoos, *Cotton Row to Beale Street*, 109.

14 Marie Handy Ruffin Papers.

15 Tilly and Faudree, *Yesterday's Evergreen*, 17–18.

16 Gottdiener, *Social Production of Urban Space*, 6.

17 Goldfield, *Region, Race, and Cities*, 43.

18 Sigafoos, *Cotton Row to Beale Street*, 59–61.

19 Boyer, *Urban Masses and Moral Order*, 265.

20 Rose, *Interstate*, 5–6.

21 Boyer, *Urban Masses and Moral Order*, 239.

22 Cuba and Hummon, "Place to Call Home," 14.

23 Falk, *Rooted in Place*; Reed, *Enduring South*; Willie Morris, *North toward Home*; Twelve Southerners, *I'll Take My Stand*.

24 Brundage, "White Women," 124.

25 Peter Taylor, *Old Forest and Other Stories*.

26 Ibid., 50.

27 Cuba and Hummon, "Place to Call Home," 113.

28 Jackson, "Memphis, Tennessee."

29 Chamber of Commerce, "Expressways to Prosperity."

30 At this time three bridges crossed the Mississippi at Memphis—the Frisco Bridge, constructed in 1892 for train traffic and the first bridge crossing the Mississippi River south of St. Louis; the Harahan Bridge, a double-tracked rail bridge completed in 1916 and changed to accommodate cars; and the Memphis-Arkansas Bridge completed in 1949, still in use for automobiles and trucks. The "new" bridge, part of I-40 north of downtown, is the Hernando de Soto Bridge designed in the shape of the letter M.

31 Harland Bartholomew and Associates, "Report upon the Comprehensive Plan."

32 Strauss, "Revisiting Overton Park," 1262–64.

33 Tilly and Faudree, *Yesterday's Evergreen*, 17–18.

34 Charles Newman, letter to author, 8 April 2004.

35 Strauss, "Revisiting Overton Park."

36 Marie Handy Ruffin Papers.

37 Brown-Saracino, "Social Preservationists."

38 "Good People of 'Gomorrah' "; *Press-Scimitar* clippings.

39 Charlier, "Clear-Cuts under Attack," A1.

40 Wolff, "Group Upset Zoo Took Out 139 Trees."

41 The organization's website is located at <www.shelbyfarmspark.org>.

42 Pearson, "45 Years Later"; James and Martin, "Resource Protection."

43 Branston, "Bass Pro Shops or Cabela's Might Be a Good Fit."

44 Clark, "Urban Amenities," 104.

45 Callahan, "Should Shelby Farms Be a Cash Cow?"; Florida, *Rise of the Creative Class*.

46 Florida cited in Smart City Consulting, *Case for Shelby Farms Park*.

47 Smart City Consulting, *Case for Shelby Farms Park*.

48 Ibid.

49 The magazine is located at <www.mensfitness.com>.

50 Ruiz, "America's Most Obese Cities."

51 Smart City Consulting, *Case for Shelby Farms Park*.

52 Branston, "Bass Pro Shops or Cabela's Might Be a Good Fit."

53 Dando, "Riverfront Development Could Add 30,000-Plus Jobs."

54 Websites for the organizations are located at <www.friendsforourriverfont.org>; <www.memphisriverfront.com>.

55 Sorkin, *Variations on a Theme Park*, refers to the emergence of "a city without a place attached to it."

56 "Group Plans to Turn Shelby Farms into 'Model' Park."

57 Murdock, "Shelby Farms to Be a '21st-Century Park.'"

58 The organization's website is located at <www.shelbyfarmspark.org>.

59 Cuba and Hummon, "Place to Call Home," 113.

CHAPTER FOUR

1 Grogan and Proscio, *Comeback Cities*.

2 U.S. Census Bureau, "Percent of People below Poverty Level."

3 Editorial Projects in Education, "Diplomas Count."

4 Florida, *Rise of the Creative Class*.

5 Blue Ribbon honorees are those selected to at least four of the magazine's exclusive lists. FedEx appeared on five in 2005: Fortune 100 Best Companies to Work For, America's Most Admired Companies, World's Most Admired Companies, the Fortune 500, and the Fortune Global 500. The company has won awards for innovation in information technology, including induction in the U.S. Small Business Administration's Golden Anniversary Hall of Fame, as a company that began small and grew into an international leader in its field.

6   Robertson, "FedEx Chief Reflects on 25 Years of Memphis Business."

7   Roberts, "Catch the Taxiway"; Roberts, "Airport's Global Reach Makes It Region's Top Force for Prosperity."

8   Khan, "Sites for U.S. Logistics."

9   Memphis Business Journal, *Book of Lists 2006*.

10 Sheffield, "Pidgeon Park Poised for New Development."

11 Sigafoos, *Cotton Row to Beale Street*, 72, 144.

12 Wood, *Southern Capitalism*.

13 Sigafoos, *Cotton Row to Beale Street*, 36.

14 Factorage, an international system linking planters and merchant-creditors, was used in the seventeenth, eighteenth, and nineteenth centuries to market tobacco, sugar, cotton, rice, and other crops from the Americas. Woodman, *King Cotton*.

15 Social Register of Memphis, 1925.

16 Brownell, *Urban Ethos*, 47; Sigafoos, *Cotton Row to Beale Street*, 100.

17 Flanary, "Business Papers of Samuel B. Williamson, Napoleon Hill, and Noland Fontaine."

18 Sigafoos, *Cotton Row to Beale Street*, 65.

19 Ibid., 66.

20 Memphis Business Journal, *Book of Lists 2006*, 130.

21 Roberts, "Catch the Taxiway."

22 Ron Smith, "Seam Begins Peanut Trading"; <www.theseam.com>.

23 <www.mallorygroup.com>.

24 Horton, "Mallory Alexander International."

25 Brownell, *Urban Ethos*, 47.

26 Malizia, "Organizing to Overcome Uneven Development," 87.

27 Persky, "The South," 17; Carlton, "Revolution from Above," 473.

28 Cowie, *Capital Moves*.

29 Woods, *Development Arrested*, 29.

30 Cowie, *Capital Moves*, 7.

31 Roediger, *Wages of Whiteness*.

32 Cowie, *Capital Moves*, 76.

33 Gavin Wright, *Old South New South*, 79–80.

34 Bonacich, "Theory of Ethnic Antagonism."

35 Brown, "Role of Employers in Split Labor Markets," 657.

36 Ibid., 662.

37 Cobb, *Selling of the South*; Persky, "The South"; Lyson, *Two Sides to the Sunbelt*.

38 Roscigno et al., "Education and the Inequalities of Place," 2123.

39 Cowie, *Capital Moves*, 73.

40 Honey, *Southern Labor and Black Civil Rights*; Biles, *Memphis in the Great Depression*; Cobb, *Selling of the South*; Brownell, *Urban Ethos*, 50; Rushing, "Cold War Racial Politics."

41 Brownell, *Urban Ethos*, 23.

42 Gramsci, *Selections from the Prison Notebooks*.

43 Biles, *Memphis in the Great Depression*, 45.

44 Ibid.

45 Honey, *Southern Labor and Black Civil Rights*, 48.

46 Biles, *Memphis in the Great Depression*, 19.

47 The North Lawndale community's experience with deindustrialization and concentrations of poverty became the subject of a *Chicago Tribune* series published in 1985
titled "The Millstone."

48 Honey, "A Dream Deferred."

49 Ibid.

50 Joan Beifuss, *At the River I Stand*.

51 Cowie, *Capital Moves*, 93.

52 In 1992, the empty International Harvester buildings were used to hold interior sets
for the filming of *The Firm*, based on a John Grisham novel.

53 Finger, "Lost Memphis."

54 Moe and Wilkie, *Changing Places*, 86.

55 Jackson, "Memphis, Tennessee," 183.

56 Center City Commission, *Downtown Memphis 1978*, 4.

57 Maki, " 'City' at Sears Crosstown?"

58 Ashby, "Downtown Alleyways Receive Needed Bricks and Mortar."

59 Tennessee Governor's Economic and Jobs Conference, *Focus*; Tennessee Governor's
Economics and Jobs Conference, *Memphis Jobs Conference Progress Report*.

60 Tennessee Governor's Economic and Jobs Conference, *Focus*, 85.

61 The nine states that do not have state income taxes are Alaska, Florida, Nevada, New
Hampshire, South Dakota, Tennessee, Texas, Washington, and Wyoming.

62 Vogel and Larson, "North Carolina's Research Triangle"; Cortright and Mayer, "Signs
of Life."

63 Branston, "Memphis Tomorrow"; <www.memphistomorrow.org>; <www.memphis
bioworks.org>.

64 Wailoo, *Dying in the City of the Blues*, 122.

65 2005 IOP Annual Report; 2006 IOP Annual Report; <www.stjude.org>.

66 Wailoo, *Dying in the City of the Blues*, 126.

67 Ibid., 121–22.

68 Sullivan, "Financial Times"; Jensen, "Viewpoint"; Bennett, "New Urbanism and Uptown Gentry."

69 <www.uptownmemphis.org>.

70 <www.henryturley.com>; <www.uptownmemphis.org>.

71 Elliott, Gotham, and Milligan, "Framing the Urban."

72 Uptown Square Fact Sheet located at <www.lauderdalecourts.com / press / lc–fact–
sheet.pdf>.

73 Jensen, "Viewpoint."

74 Maki, "MHA to Redevelop 600 Housing Units at Dixie Homes."

75 Sullivan, "Financial Times."

76 Connolly, "Bioworks Foundation Earns Recognition."

77 American City Business Journals, "Brainpower of America's Largest Cities."

78 Memphis is the only metropolitan area in Tennessee that continues to have two

separate school systems. The Shelby County system is a smaller system having fewer low-income students and a higher percentage of white students.

79 Editorial Projects in Education, "Diplomas Count."

80 Day and Newburger, "Big Payoff."

81 <www.memphischamber.com>.

82 Downing, "Old Plant Site Reclaimed"; <www.epa.gov / brownfields>.

83 URS and NexGen, "PILOT Evaluation Program Project."

84 Sautet, "On my Mind."

85 Ibid.

86 Aldinger, "International Paper Wins 15-Year, $15M Tax Freeze"; Maki, "City's Changed —for Better, Says IP Chief."

87 Sheffield, "New York Firms to Acquire ServiceMaster."

88 Hardy and Bee, "2 Cities Enjoy Vibrant Scene."

89 Williams, "Bass Pro Casts Big Vision."

90 Walzer and Jacobs, *Public-Private Partnerships*, 26.

CHAPTER FIVE

1   McIlwaine, *Memphis down in Dixie*, 15.

2   Hall, *Cities in Civilization*, 553.

3   Ibid.

4   Ibid.

5   Ibid., 7.

6   Mulherin, "Taking Care of Business?," 22.

7   Barlow, *Looking Up at Down*, 4–5.

8   Dixon, *I Am the Blues*, 3–4.

9   Daniel, *Lost Revolutions*, 165.

10 Ibid., 148.

11 Blank, "Legacy's Cloudy through Lens of Race."

12 Connell and Gibson, "World Music," 357.

13 Griswold and Wright, "Cowbirds, Locals, and the Dynamic Endurance of Regionalism," 1414–15.

14 Ash Amin, "Placing Globalization," 133; Massey, "Power Geometry," 66.

15 Giddens, "Affluence, Poverty and the Idea of a Post-Scarcity Society"; Massey, "Power Geometry"; Ash Amin, "Placing Globalization"; Peacock, *Grounded Globalism*.

16 Appadurai, "Disjuncture and Difference."

17 Lefebvre, *Writings on Cities*, 148.

18 Gnuschke and Wallace, "Economic Impact of the Music Industry," 19.

19 Ibid., 27.

20 Hannigan, *Fantasy City*, 4–5; Grunwald, "Birthright to the Blues."

21 Gnuschke and Wallace, "Economic Impact of the Music Industry," 19.

22 George W. Lee, "Poetic Memories of Beale Street," 65.

23 Neil, "Beale Street Remembered," 39.

24 Ibid.

25 Ibid.

26 George W. Lee, "Poetic Memories of Beale Street," 65; Whitney Smith, "Uncovering the History of Beale Street."

27 Rufus Thomas interview, 7.

28 Vasco Smith, "1948: Swingin' at the Handy Theatre."

29 Rufus Thomas interview, 8–9.

30 "Identity Crisis," *Memphis*, 4.

31 George W. Lee, *Beale Street*, 13–14.

32 Lt. George W. Lee interview.

33 Biles, *Memphis in the Great Depression*, 40–41.

34 Handy, *Father of the Blues*.

35 Jackson, "Memphis, Tennessee," 178.

36 Sigafoos, *Cotton Row to Beale Street*, 125.

37 Hall, *Cities in Civilization*, 558; Harkins, *Metropolis of the American Nile*, 119.

38 Biles, *Memphis in the Great Depression*, 42.

39 Harkins, *Metropolis of the American Nile*, 119.

40 Hutchins, "Beale Street As It Was," 63.

41 "New Beale Street," 24–27.

42 Ibid., 24.

43 Ibid., 25.

44 McKee and Chisenhall, *Beale Black and Blue*, 87.

45 Burch, "Men Offer Recollections of Old Beale."

46 Whitney Smith, "Uncovering the History of Beale Street."

47 Turley, "Beale Street Relinquished," 45.

48 Moe and Wilkie, *Changing Places*.

49 Architect-Engineer Associates, *Blue Light District of Beale Street*.

50 Marwick, *Sixties*, 451.

51 Cited in Marwick, *Sixties*, 451.

52 Otto Lee interview.

53 *Press-Scimitar*, "Owners Protest Beale St. Plan."

54 Turley, "Beale Street Relinquished," 46.

55 Palmer, "Beale Street Redeemed."

56 Fair, "Clothier to the King," 74.

57 Ibid.

58 <www.lanskybros.com>.

59 Joan Beifuss, *At the River I Stand*, 148.

60 Ibid.

61 Ibid., 322–23; *Press-Scimitar*, "Riot Quelled but Sniping Continues."

62 Stanfield, *In Memphis*, 8.

63 Soja, *Postmodern Geographies*, 6.

64 M. Taylor, *Harlem between Heaven and Hell*, 2; Harvey, "From Space to Place and Back Again," 22.

65 Johnson and Russell, *Memphis*, 62.

66 Ibid., 4.

67 Crook, "Beale Street," 30.

68 Whitney Smith, "Uncovering the History of Beale Street."

69 Turley, "Beale Street Relinquished," 48; Robbins, "For Sale"; Martin, "Beale Street Reborn?," 61.

70 Moe and Wilkie, *Changing Places*, 85.

71 BeVier, "Where Have the People Gone?"

72 Turley "Beale Street Relinquished," 48.

73 Ibid.

74 BeVier, "Where Have the People Gone?"

75 Ibid.

76 Vaughan, "Some Want Beale Street Like It Was."

77 Harkins, *Metropolis of the American Nile*, 152.

78 Bowman, *Soulsville, U.S.A.*

79 Blank, "Legacy's Cloudy through Lens of Race."

80 Mulherin, "Taking Care of Business?," 20–22.

81 Bakke, "University of Memphis and the Heart of Elvis Week," 23.

82 Connell and Gibson, "World Music," 353.

83 Bakke, "University of Memphis and the Heart of Elvis Week," 23.

84 Bowman, *Soulsville, U.S.A.*

85 Bill Morris, "Playing for Keeps," 18.

86 Mulherin, "Taking Care of Business?," 20.

87 Blank, "The Artist Used Black and White."

88 Urry, "Sociology of Space and Place," 12.

89 Gnuschke, "Elvis Is Still Big Business in Memphis," 4.

90 Center City Commission, *Downtown Memphis 1978*, 4.

91 Tennessee Governor's Economic and Jobs Conference, *Focus*, 85–86.

92 Ibid., 87–88.

93 Center City Commission, *Downtown Memphis 1978*, 8; Schmidt, "Again, River Holds Key to Revival of Memphis."

94 Clubb, "Orpheum Rescue Raised Curtain on Long Run Downtown Revival."

95 Gnuschke and Wallace, "Economic Impact of the Music Industry," 19.

96 Roberts, "Taste of Memphis."

97 Gnuschke and Wallace, "Economic Impact of the Music Industry," 127.

98 Grazian, *Search for Authenticity in Urban Blues Clubs*, 17.

99 Boyd, "Reconstructing Bronzeville," 107. See also Kearns and Philo, *Selling Places*; and Kotler, Haider, and Rein, *Marketing Places*.

100 Judd and Fainstein, *Tourist City*, 12–13; Boyd, "Reconstructing Bronzeville."

101 Hannigan, *Fantasy City*, 6.

102 Peterson, "In Search of Authenticity," 1084–85.

103 Hannigan, *Fantasy City*, 6, 9.

104 Goldberger, "Rise of the Private City," 145–46.

105 <http://www.nba.com/grizzlies/fedexforum/opening—announcement—040729.html>.

106 Peterson, "In Search of Authenticity."

107   Johnson, "After a Night on Beale Street."

108   Grazian, *Search for Authenticity in Urban Blues Clubs*, 13.

109   Maki, "Downtown Hotel Project Secures Financing."

110   Maki, "More Blues for Beale Street," C2.

111   Recent feature films made in Memphis include *40 Shades of Blue*, 2004; *21 Grams*, 2002–3; *Cookie's Fortune*, 1998; and *People vs. Larry Flint*, 1996. For a complete list, see <www.memphis.filmcomm.org>.

112   Forman, *'Hood Comes First*, xviii–xix, 26.

113   John Beifuss, " 'Hustle' Anthem Up for Oscar"; Hofler, "Favorite Son"; Germain, " 'Hard' Day's Oscar."

114   Chris Davis, "Truth Hurts."

115   Cohen, "Southern Sensibilities Inspire 'Hustle and Flow' Writer-Director Craig Brewer."

116   John Beifuss, "When He Directs, Memphis Is in Focus."

117   Thomas, " 'Hustle' Song No Rapper's Delight."

118   Thomas, "File Oscar under History to Hide From."

119   Pun used in headline for Hunt article.

120   Dowd, "Pastor."

121   Bozell, "And the Award Goes to . . . Pimps!"

122   Hunt, "Bad Rap," P7.

123   Snyder, " 'Pimp' Was Quite a Moment."

124   Yolanda Jones, "Memphis Music Awards Gala Turns Out a Cluster of Stars."

125   Ibid.

126   Harrison and Gnuschke, "Overview of Film Production Incentives," 13.

127   Tobia, "Silk Stocking Cinema"; Film Production Advisory Committee, "Tennessee Film and Television Production Study."

128   John Beifuss, "Movie Team Scouts Memphis."

129   Urry, "Sociology of Space and Place."

CHAPTER SIX

1   Craig, *Ain't I a Beauty Queen?*, 12.

2   Griswold and Wright, "Cowbirds, Locals, and the Dynamic Endurance of Regionalism"; Putnam, *Bowling Alone*.

3   Collins, *Interaction Ritual Chains*, 43; Erik Olin Wright, "Continuing Relevance of Class Analysis."

4   Lynch, *Dress, Gender and Cultural Change*, 10; Ostrander, *Women of the Upper Class*.

5   Giddens, *Consequences of Modernity*, 2

6   Giddens, "Affluence, Poverty and the Idea of a Post-Scarcity Society," 367–68.

7   Langman and Cangemi, "Globalization and the Liminal."

8   Manning, "Spectacle."

9   McLean, "Cotton Carnival and Cotton Makers Jubilee," 10.

10   Bakhtin, *Rabelais and His World*.

11   Deegan, *American Ritual Dramas*, 24.

12 Giddens, *Consequences of Modernity*, 21; Waters, *Globalization*, 3.

13 Massey, "Power Geometry," 61.

14 Brown-Saracino, "Social Preservationists"; Bourdieu, *Distinction*.

15 Catherine Bell, *Ritual*.

16 Cotton Carnival also suspended festivities during World War II, 1942–45.

17 McLean, "Cotton Carnival and Cotton Makers Jubilee," 127.

18 Ibid., 148.

19 Dent, "Crown and Sceptre."

20 Allen J. Scott, "Cultural Economy of Cities," 323.

21 Erik Olin Wright, "Continuing Relevance of Class Analysis"; Kendall, "Class in the United States"; James Scott, *Domination and the Arts of Resistance*, 324–25.

22 Thanks to Perre Magness for the Williams reference in *Carnival Memphis: The Party with a Purpose*.

23 Marling, *Debutante*, 7.

24 In 2007, the queen was a college sophomore and the king was a retired grandfather.

25 Comus is the oldest continually active Mardi Gras organization in New Orleans and is considered the first Carnival krewe.

26 Rita Jones, "History of Memphis."

27 Magness, *Carnival Memphis*, 162, 166; Murphey, "Land of Cotton."

28 Dillman, "Southern Women," 16.

29 R. W. Connell, *Gender and Power*, 187; Wyatt-Brown, *Southern Honor*.

30 R. W. Connell, *Gender and Power*, 185.

31 The Mallory-Neely house, now listed on the National Register of Historic Places and operated as a city museum in Victorian Village downtown, was the residence of an antebellum banker named Kirtland, a Civil War–era cotton factor named Babb, and late-nineteenth-century cotton factors Mallory and Neely. Cotton factor (and former Confederate officer) James Neely bought the house in 1883. His daughter, Daisy, married cotton factor Barton Lee Mallory (the son of another cotton factor and former Confederate officer) in 1900. The couple returned to the home to rear three children, including William Neely Mallory and Barton Lee Mallory Jr., whose children and grandchildren occupy leadership positions in today's Memphis business community and head international corporations (Social Register of Memphis 1925; McIlwaine, *Memphis down in Dixie*, 287).

32 Magness, *Carnival Memphis*, 199.

33 <www.tournamentofroses.com>.

34 Banner, *American Beauty*, 251.

35 Magness, *Carnival Memphis*, 164.

36 Synnott, *Body Social*.

37 Kendall, *Power of Good Deeds*, 2; Adams and Bettis, "Commanding the Room in Short Skirts."

38 Domhoff, *Who Rules America?*

39 Bourdieu, "Forms of Capital."

40 Kendall, *Power of Good Deeds*, 6.

41 Ibid., 26.

42 Wilson and Musick, "Who Cares?," 696.

43 Kendall, *Power of Good Deeds*, 26–27.

44 Author's interview with Clyde Venson, 2 May 2007.

45 Weldon Johnson also wrote "Lift Every Voice and Sing," sometimes referred to as the Negro National Anthem.

46 In representations of African American women, the "Mammy" stereotype is an asexual image of the black woman as a worker, presented in contrast to the hypersexualized image of the black "Jezebel" and the image of the "protected" idealized white woman.

47 Magness, *Carnival Memphis*, 10.

48 Biles, *Memphis in the Great Depression*, 67

49 Honey, *Southern Labor and Black Civil Rights*.

50 Foner and Lewis, *From the Foundation of the CIO*, 192; Honey, *Southern Labor and Black Civil Rights*, 70; McLean, "Cotton Carnival and Cotton Makers Jubilee," 44.

51 In the Old Testament book of Genesis, Ham, the son of Noah, was cursed by his father for seeing him naked and not covering him when he was intoxicated. The curse on the "sons of Ham" has been interpreted as the creation of the first black person and condemning him to be the "slave of slaves" (Bay, "Remembering Racism").

52 Du Bois, *Philadelphia Negro*.

53 Sanders Duke Wilson, "Cotton Maker's Jubilee," 3.

54 An African American musical parody titled *Sons of Ham* played vaudeville in the early 1900s and created a different form of protest.

55 Du Bois, *Philadelphia Negro*, 325

56 Craig, *Ain't I a Beauty Queen?*, 166.

57 "Beale Street's Hero."

58 Venson Papers.

59 Trotter, "African American Fraternal Associations," 361.

60 Carnes, *Secret Ritual and Manhood*.

61 Trotter, "African American Fraternal Associations"; Myrdal, *American Dilemma*, 957.

62 Craig, *Ain't I a Beauty Queen?*, 14.

63 Bourdieu, *Algerians*, 161; Lamont and Lareau, "Cultural Capital," 159.

64 James Scott, *Domination and the Arts of Resistance*.

65 Piven and Cloward, *Poor Peoples' Movements*, 188–89.

66 Craig, *Ain't I a Beauty Queen?*, 45; James Scott, *Domination and the Arts of Resistance*.

67 Sanders Duke Wilson, "Cotton Maker's Jubilee," 4.

68 Woods, *Development Arrested*, 288.

69 Craig, *Ain't I a Beauty Queen?*, 8–14.

70 Takaki, "Aesculapius Was a White Man," 200; Hooks, *Ain't I a Woman*.

71 Omi and Winant, *Racial Formation*.

72 Hooks, "Representations of Whiteness," 20.

73 Craig, *Ain't I a Beauty Queen?*, 14.

74 Locke, "New Negro," 962.

75 Ibid.

76 Gates, "Trope of a New Negro," 140.

77 The symbolism of cotton, patriarchy, and oppression has been problematic for white cotton mill workers in the South, who were referred to as "lintheads," a reference to cotton fibers that attached to their hair. The term was used with scorn and derision in the 1930s, and the term and its implications for identity have reemerged in twenty-first-century discussions of heritage tourism and community development in at least one economically depressed former mill town (Fink, "When Community Comes Home to Roost").

78 Sanders Duke Wilson, "Cotton Maker's Jubilee," 8.

79 Ferris, "Mules," 512.

80 McIlwaine, *Memphis down in Dixie*, 286.

81 Wall, "Mules and Men and Women," 66.

82 Hooks, *Ain't I a Woman*.

83 Radford-Hill, "Keepin' It Real."

84 Sharpley-Whiting, *Pimps Up, Ho's Down*, 51.

85 Hooks, *Ain't I a Woman*, 70.

86 Craig, *Ain't I a Beauty Queen?*

87 Ibid., 166.

88 Keyes, "Empowering Self, Making Choices, Creating Spaces," 266.

89 Sharpley-Whiting, *Pimps Up, Ho's Down*, 8.

90 Author's interview with Clyde Venson, 2 May 2007.

91 William Julius Wilson, *Truly Disadvantaged*.

92 Sharpley-Whiting, *Pimps Up, Ho's Down*.

CHAPTER SEVEN

1   Michael Bell, "Ghosts of Place," 815.

2   Entrikin, *Betweenness of Place*; Reed, *One South*, 57.

3   Gordon, *It Came from Memphis*, 6; Griffin and Thompson, "Appalachia and the South," 304.

4   Kellner, "Theorizing Globalization," 293.

5   Scherzer, "Southern Cities," 705.

6   Ash Amin, "Good City," 1012.

7   Saito, "Reiterated Commemoration," 355.

8   Kelley, "Can We Get Together?"

9   Savitch and Vogel, "Suburbs without a City," 758.

10 Locker, "Nashville Reaped Benefits of Plan Eyed for Memphis."

11 Ibid.

12 Cashiola, "Creative Merger."

13 Savitch and Vogel, "Suburbs without a City," 750.

14 Ibid.

15 Ibid., 763.

16 Ibid.

17 Ibid., 760.

18 Wrenn, *Crisis and Commission Government*; Goings and Page, "African Americans versus the Memphis Street Railway Company," 133.

19 Lauterbach, " 'Follow That Dream' "; Van Riper, "Long Live the King."

20 "Elvis Presley Enterprises' Parent Going Private."

21 Williams, "Graceland and All That Pizazz."

22 Cobb, "Beyond the 'Y'all Wall,' " 2.

23 Forman, *'Hood Comes First*, xviii–xix, 26.

24 Roberts, "Cottoning to China."

25 Malone, "FedEx Focuses on China"; FedEx, "FedEx Announces Domestic Express Services in China."

26 Roberts, "Port o' Call"; Sheffield, "Pidgeon Park Poised for New Development."

27 Russell, "Wise Choice"; Thamel, "Memphis and Calipari Go to Hoop in China."

28 Capps, "Bredesen Brass, Business, Lobbyists Head to China."

29 Gieryn, "Space for Place in Sociology."

30 Appadurai, "Production of Locality."

BIBLIOGRAPHY

ARCHIVAL SOURCES

Memphis and Shelby County Room, Benjamin L. Hooks Central Library, Memphis, Tenn.

Architect-Engineer Associates. *The Blue Light District of Beale Street, Memphis, Tennessee: An Architectural and Historical Survey for the Memphis Housing Authority.* Nashville: Architect-Engineer Associates, 1974.

Crook, James David. "Beale Street: Rattling the Skeleton in Memphis' Closet." *Memphis*, October 1976, 29–32.

Flanary, Barbara. "The Business Papers of Samuel B. Williamson, Napoleon Hill, and Noland Fontaine."

"'The Good People of 'Gomorrah.'" *Mid-South* (published by *Memphis Commercial Appeal*), 12 September 1976, 7.

Halle, A. Arthur. *Authentic History and Growth of the Memphis Cotton Carnival Association.* Memphis: Cotton Carnival Association, 1952.

Harland Bartholomew and Associates. "A Report upon the Comprehensive Plan—Memphis, Tennessee." St. Louis, Mo., 1955.

Kessler, George E. "Forrest Park: Map." Memphis Park Department, 1902.

Martin, Tom. "Beale Street Reborn? The Battle of Beale Street Has Finally Begun." *Memphis*, August 1979, 59–68.

Mitchell, Sybil C. "Confederate Parks: A Point of Contention." *Tri-State Defender*, 6 August 2005, 3A. Vertical file on parks.

Neil, Kenneth. "Beale Street Remembered." *Memphis*, August 1979.

Palmer, Robert. "Beale Street Redeemed." *Memphis*, April 1978, 47–48.

Sayre, Heather. Arthur Halle Collection.

Social Register of Memphis. Penn-Renshaw, 1925.

Stanfield, J. Edwin. *In Memphis: More Than a Garbage Strike.* Atlanta: Southern Regional Council, 1968, suppl. I, 1.

Turley, Susan. "Beale Street Relinquished." *Memphis*, August 1979, 45–56.

U.S. Department of the Interior. *Beale Street Historic District*. Washington, D.C.: U.S. Department of the Interior, 1967.

Dr. R. Q. and Ethyl H. Venson Cotton Makers Jubilee Collection

Mississippi Valley Collections, McWherter Library, University of Memphis, Memphis, Tenn.

    Beale Street Box

        BeVier, Thomas. "Where Have the People Gone?" *Press-Scimitar*, 1973. Clipping, box 62047.

        Burch, Peggy. "Men Offer Recollections of Old Beale." *Press-Scimitar*, 1973. Clipping, box 62047.

        Mulherin, Joe. "Taking Care of Business? The Elvis Legend Lives On, but the City Doesn't Seem to Know What to Do with It." *Memphis*, August 1979, 20–22.

        Robbins, Jerry L. "For Sale: 27 Acres of Cleared Land—All Downtown." *Press-Scimitar*, 27 January 1975. Clipping.

        Vaughan, Johnnie. 1973. "Some Want Beale Street Like It Was, but What Was It?" *Press-Scimitar*, 9 October 1973. Clipping, box 62047. Center City Commission. *Downtown Memphis 1978: An Annual Report of the Center City Commission*. Memphis: Center City Commission, 1978.

    Chamber of Commerce. "Expressways to Prosperity: A Review of 1957 and a Forecast for 1958." Pamphlet. Memphis: Chamber of Commerce, 1958.

    Forrest Monument Association. *The Forrest Monument: Its History and Dedication*. Memphis: Forrest Monument Association, 1905.

    McFarland, L. B. *Memoirs and Addresses*. Memphis, 1922.

    "The New Beale Street." *Ebony*, September 1950, 22–24.

    Oral History Research Office Project, Memphis State University

        Jones, Rita. "History of Memphis: Interview with Mrs. Mollie Darnell Mallory." 1984.

        Lee, Lt. George W. Interview by Jack Hurley and speech, Memphis, 23 April 1967.

        Lee, Otto. Interview by Jack Hurley, Memphis, 3 March 1967. Jazz and Blues in Memphis Collection.

        Thomas, Rufus. Interview by Robert Palmer and David Less, Memphis, 28–29 October 1976. Jazz and Blues in Memphis Collection.

        Wilson, Sanders Duke. "The Cotton Maker's Jubilee: Interview with Mrs. Ethyl Venson," Memphis, 30 November 1984.

    Press-Scimitar clippings, box 2076

    Marie Handy Ruffin Papers

    Tennessee Governor's Economic and Jobs Conference. *Focus: Assets, Liabilities and Recommendations*. Memphis: The Conference, 1979.

    ———. *The Memphis Jobs Conference Progress Report*. 1981.

Author's Collection

    Kemet Jubilee. Kemet Jubilee Program, 2005. Contributed by Clyde Venson.

Abbott, Andrew. *Discipline and Department.* Chicago: University of Chicago Press, 1999.

——. "History and Sociology: The Lost Synthesis." *Social Science History* 15, no. 2 (1991): 201–38.

Abu Lughod, Janet. *New York, Chicago, Los Angeles: America's Global Cities.* Minneapolis: University of Minnesota Press, 1999.

Adams, Jane, and D. Gorton. "Southern Trauma: Revisiting Caste and Class in the Mississippi Delta." *American Anthropologist* 106, no. 2 (June 2004): 334–45.

Adams, Natalie, and Pamela Bettis. "Commanding the Room in Short Skirts: Cheering As the Embodiment of Ideal Girlhood." *Gender and Society* 17, no. 1 (2003): 73–91.

Adderley, Kenneth Roger. "Monument on the Mississippi: Background, Development, and the Rising Significance of the National Civil Rights Museum." M.A. thesis, University of Memphis, 1997.

Aguilar-San Juan, Karin. "Saying Vietnamese: Community and Place in Orange County and Boston." *City and Community* 4, no. 1 (2005): 37–65.

Aldinger, Jane. "International Paper Wins 15-Year, $15M Tax Freeze for Headquarters Move." *Memphis Business Journal,* 11 August 2005.

American City Business Journals. "The Brainpower of America's Largest Cities." <www.bizjournals.com / specials / pages / 12.html>.

Amin, Ash. "The Good City." *Urban Studies* 43, no. 5–6 (2006): 1009–23.

——. "Placing Globalization." *Theory, Culture and Society* 14, no. 2 (1997): 123–37.

Amin, Samir. *Accumulation on a Grand Scale.* Vol. 1. New York: Monthly Review Press, 1974.

Appadurai, Arjun. "Disjunction and Difference in the Global Cultural Economy." *Theory, Culture and Society* 7, no. 2 (1990): 295–310.

——. "The Past As a Scarce Resource." *Man,* n.s., 16 (1981): 201–19.

——. "The Production of Locality." In *Counterworks: Managing the Diversity of Knowledge,* edited by Richard Fardon, 204–25. London: Routledge, 1995.

Arrighi, Giovanni. *Adam Smith in Beijing.* New York: Verso, 2007.

Ashby, Andrew. "Downtown Alleyways Receive Needed Bricks and Mortar." *Memphis Daily News,* 27 March 2006. <downtownmemphis.com>.

"The Assassination." *Time,* 12 April 1968, 18.

Ayers, Edward. "Portraying Power." In *Jumpin' Jim Crow: Southern Politics from Civil War to Civil Rights,* edited by J. Dailey, G. E. Gilmore, and B. Simon, 301–3. Princeton: Princeton University Press, 2000.

——. *What Caused the Civil War: Reflections on the South and Southern History.* New York: W. W. Norton, 2005.

Bahr, Howard, and Theodore Caplow. "Middletown As an Urban Case Study." In *A Case for the Case Study,* edited by Joe R. Feagin, Anthony M. Orum, and Gideon Sjoberg, 80–120. Chapel Hill: University of North Carolina Press, 1991.

Bailey, D'Army. "The Confederates of Memphis (and Negroes Who Have More Important Things to Do)." *Black Commentator,* 27 October 2005. <www.blackcommentator.com>.

Bakhtin, Mikhail. *Rabelais and His World*. Bloomington: Indiana University Press, 1984.

Bakke, John P. "The University of Memphis and the Heart of Elvis Week." *Business Perspectives* 14, no. 3 (Summer 2002): 23–25.

Banner, Lois W. *American Beauty*. New York: Knopf, 1983.

Barlow, W. *Looking Up at Down: The Emergence of Blues Culture*. Philadelphia: Temple University Press, 1989.

Bay, Mia. "Remembering Racism: Rereading the Black Image in the White Mind." *Reviews in American History* 27, no. 4 (1999): 646–56.

"Beale Street's Hero." *Time*, 25 May 1936, 54, 56.

Beifuss, Joan. *At the River I Stand*. Memphis: St. Luke's Press, 1990.

Beifuss, John. " 'Hustle' Anthem Up for Oscar: 2 Best Actor Roles Made in Memphis." *Memphis Commercial Appeal*, 1 February 2006, A1.

———. "Memphis Gets Two Thumbs Up: Movie Team Scouts Memphis for a Place to Do Business." *Memphis Commercial Appeal*, 23 March 2007, A1.

———. "On the Set of 'Black Snake.' " *Memphis Commercial Appeal*, 11 October 2005, M1.

———. "Out of This World: Memphis Rappers' Performance, Victory Electrify Oscars Audience." *Memphis Commercial Appeal*, 7 March 2006, M1, M7.

———. "When He Directs, Memphis Is in Focus; Brewer Wants to Make Chances for Other Local Talent As He Creates His Films." *Memphis Commercial Appeal*, 1 January 2006, V2.

Bell, Catherine. *Ritual: Perspectives and Dimensions*. New York: Oxford University Press, 1997.

Bell, Michael Mayerfeld. "The Ghosts of Place." *Theory and Society* 26 (1997): 813–36.

Bellah, Robert N., Richard Madsen, William M. Sullivan, Ann Swidler, and Steven M. Tipton. *Habits of the Heart*. Berkeley: University of California Press, 1985.

Bennett, Abby Jean. "New Urbanism and Uptown Gentry: Entrepreneurial Development in Memphis, Tennessee." M.A. thesis, University of Memphis, 2005.

Biggs, Jennifer. "Oprah Visit Stirs Excitement in City; Diva Takes Impromptu Tour of Memphis Sites." *Memphis Commercial Appeal*, 7 June 2006, A9.

Biles, Roger. "Memphis." In *Encyclopedia of Southern Culture*, edited by Charles Reagan Wilson and William Ferris, 1460. Chapel Hill: University of North Carolina Press, 1989.

———. *Memphis in the Great Depression*. Knoxville: University of Tennessee Press, 1986.

Billings, Dwight B., Jr. *Planters and the Making of a "New South."* Chapel Hill: University of North Carolina Press, 1979.

Binkley, Bonnie. "Split Labor Markets in the South: The Memphis Firestone Experience." Unpublished manuscript, University of Memphis, 2002.

Bishir, Catherine. "Landmarks of Power: Building a Southern Past in Raleigh and Wilmington, North Carolina, 1885–1915." In *Where These Memories Grow: History, Memory, and Southern Identity*, edited by W. Fitzhugh Brundage, 139–68. Chapel Hill: University of North Carolina Press, 2000.

Black, Earl, and Merle Black. *The Rise of Southern Republicans*. Cambridge, Mass.: Harvard University Press, 2002.

Blank, Christopher. "The Artist Used Black and White; Many Still See Red." *Memphis Commercial Appeal*, 18 August 2002, A1.

Boggs, Carl. *The Two Revolutions: Antonio Gramsci and the Dilemmas of Western Marxism*. Boston: South End Press, 1984.

Bonacich, Edna. "A Theory of Ethnic Antagonism: The Split Labor Market." *American Sociological Review* 37, no. 5 (1972): 547–59.

Bond, Beverly, and Janann Sherman. *Memphis in Black and White*. Mount Pleasant: Arcadia Publishing, 2003.

Bourdieu, Pierre. *The Algerians*. Boston: Beacon Press, 1961.

———. *Distinction: A Social Critique of the Judgment of Taste*. Translated by R. Nice. Cambridge, Mass.: Harvard University Press, 1984.

———. "The Forms of Capital." In *Education: Culture, Economy and Society*, edited by A. Halsey, H. Lauder, P. Brown, and A. Stuart Wells, 46–58. Oxford: Oxford University Press, 1997.

Bowman, Robert. *Soulsville, U.S.A.: The Story of Stax Records*. New York: Schirmer Trade Books, 1997.

Boyd, Michelle. "Reconstructing Bronzeville: Racial Nostalgia and Neighborhood Redevelopment." *Journal of Urban Affairs* 22, no. 2 (2000): 107–22.

Boyer, Paul. *Urban Masses and Moral Order in America, 1820–1920*. Cambridge, Mass.: Harvard University Press, 1978.

Bozell, L. Brent. "And the Award Goes to . . . Pimps!" *Pittsburgh Tribune Review*, 12 March 2006.

Bradshaw, York, and Michael Wallace. "Informing Generality and Explaining Uniqueness: The Place of Case Studies in Comparative Research." *International Journal of Comparative Sociology* 32, no. 1–2 (1991): 154–71.

Branston, John. "Bass Pro Shops or Cabela's Might Be a Good Fit for the Pyramid or Shelby Farms." *Memphis Flyer*, 12 December 2004. <http://www.memphisflyer.com>.

———. "In a City on the Move, a Civil War Issue Refuses to Die." *New York Times*, 4 August 2005, A13.

———. "Man on Horseback: Political Correctness Is Only One of the Problems with Forrest Park." *Memphis Flyer*, 29 July 2005. <http://www.memphisflyer.com>.

———. "Memphis Tomorrow: A Behind-the-Scenes Group Works to Shape the City's Future." *Memphis Flyer*, 14 October 2005. <http://www.memphisflyer.com>.

Brown, Cliff. "The Role of Employers in Split Labor Markets: An Event-Structure Analysis of Racial Conflict and AFL Organizing, 1917–1919." *Social Forces* 79, no. 2 (2000): 653–81.

Brownell, Blaine. *Urban Ethos in the South, 1920–1930*. Baton Rouge: Louisiana State University Press, 1975.

Brown-Saracino, Japonica. "Social Preservationists and the Quest for Authentic Community." *City and Community* 3, no. 2 (2004): 135–56.

Brundage, W. Fitzhugh. "White Women and the Politics of Historical Memory in the New South, 1880–1920." In *Jumpin' Jim Crow: Southern Politics from Civil War to Civil Rights*, edited by J. Dailey, G. E. Gilmore, and B. Simon, 115–39. Princeton: Princeton University Press, 2000.

Burch, Peggy. "Expanding the Legacy: Museum Gets Bigger, Opens View to City's Painful Past." *Memphis Commercial Appeal*, 28 September 2002, A1.

Busbee, James. "Mississippi's Man of Letters." *Memphis Flyer*, 29 September 1997. <http://weeklywire.com/ww/09-29-97/memphis—socvr.html>.

Callahan, Jody. "8 People Added to National Civil Rights Museum Board." *Memphis Commercial Appeal*, 22 February 2008, B1.

———. "Should Shelby Farms Be a Cash Cow?" *Memphis Commercial Appeal*, 22 September 2002, A1.

Capers, Gerald M., Jr. *The Biography of a River Town: Memphis, Its Heroic Age.* Chapel Hill: University of North Carolina Press, 1939.

Capps, Milt. "Bredesen Brass, Business, Lobbyists Head to China." *Nashville Post*, 8 August 2007. <http://www.nashvillepost.com>.

Carlton, David. "The Revolution from Above: The National Market and the Beginnings of Industrialization in North Carolina." *Journal of American History* 77 (September 1990): 445–75.

Carnes, Mark C. *Secret Ritual and Manhood in Victorian America.* New York: Literary Guild of America, 1989.

Cash, W. J. *The Mind of the South.* New York: A. A. Knopf, 1941.

Cashiola, Mary. "Creative Merger." *Memphis Flyer*, 10 January 2008. <http://www.memphisflyer.com>.

Centre for Contemporary Cultural Studies. *Unpopular Education: Schooling and Social Democracy in England Since 1944.* London: Hutchinson, 1981.

Chacko, Elizabeth. "Understanding the Geography of Pellagra in the United States: The Role of Social and Place-Based Identities." *Gender, Place and Culture* 12, no. 2 (2005): 197–212.

Chambers, Douglas B. "This Dreamer Cometh: The National Civil Rights Museum." *American Visions* 14, no. 5 (October 1999): 40.

Charlier, Tom. "Clear-Cuts under Attack." *Memphis Commercial Appeal*, 13 July 2005, A1.

Childers, T. "Memphis." *American Heritage*, October 1998, 96–115.

Clark, Terry Nichols. "Urban Amenities: Lakes, Opera, and Juice Bars: Do They Drive Development?" *Research in Urban Policy* 9 (2004): 103–40.

Clubb, Deborah. "Orpheum Rescue Raised Curtain on Long Run Downtown Revival." *Memphis Commercial Appeal*, 1 January 2002, A1.

Cobb, James C. "Beyond the 'Y'all Wall': The American South Goes Global." In *Globalization and the American South*, edited by James C. Cobb and William Stueck, 1–18. Athens: University of Georgia Press, 2005.

———. *The Most Southern Place on Earth.* New York: Oxford University Press, 1992.

———. *The Selling of the South: The Southern Crusade for Industrial Development, 1936–1980.* Urbana: University of Illinois Press, 1993.

Cobb, James C., and William Stueck, eds. *Globalization and the American South.* Athens: University of Georgia Press, 2005.

Cohen, Sandy. "Southern Sensibilities Inspire 'Hustle and Flow' Writer-Director Craig Brewer." *International News* (Associated Press Worldstream), 5 January 2006.

Cohn, D. *God Shakes Creation.* New York: Harper Brothers, 1935.

Collins, Randall. *Interaction Ritual Chains.* Princeton: Princeton University Press, 2004.

Connell, John, and Chris Gibson. "World Music: Deterritorializing Place and Identity." *Progress in Human Geography* 28, no. 3 (2006): 342–61.

Connell, R. W. *Gender and Power: Society, the Person and Sexual Politics.* Sydney: Allen and Unwin, 1987.

———. *Masculinities*. Berkeley: University of California Press, 1995.

Connolly, Daniel. "Bioworks Foundation Earns Recognition for Training of Workers in Science Fields." *Memphis Commercial Appeal*, 23 March 2007, D2.

Cornish, Audie. "Mission of National Civil Rights Museum Questioned." *All Things Considered*, National Public Radio, 16 December 2007. <http://www.npr.org>.

Cortright, Joseph, and Heike Mayer. "Signs of Life: The Growth of Biotechnology Centers in the United States." Center on Urban and Metropolitan Policy, June 2002. <http://www.brookings.edu>.

Coski, John M. *The Confederate Battle Flag*. Cambridge, Mass.: Harvard University Press, 2005.

Cowie, Jefferson. *Capital Moves: RCA's Seventy-Year Quest for Cheap Labor*. New York: New Press, 1999.

Cox, Karen L. *Dixie's Daughters: The United Daughters of the Confederacy and the Preservation of Confederate Culture*. Gainesville: University of Florida Press, 2003.

Craig, Maxine Leeds. *Ain't I a Beauty Queen? Black Women, Beauty, and the Politics of Race*. Oxford: Oxford University Press, 2002.

Crosby, Molly Caldwell. *The American Plague: The Untold Story of Yellow Fever, the Epidemic That Shaped Our History*. New York: Berkley Books, 2006.

Cuba, Lee, and David M. Hummon. "A Place to Call Home: Identification with Dwelling, Community, and Region." *Sociological Quarterly* 34, no. 1 (1993): 111–31.

Dando, Mary. "Riverfront Development Could Add 30,000-Plus Jobs." *Memphis Business Journal*, 13 June 2003. <http://www.bizjournals.com/memphis/stories/2003/06/16/focus4.html>.

Daniel, Pete. *Lost Revolutions: The South in the 1950s*. Chapel Hill: University of North Carolina Press and the Smithsonian, 2000.

Davis, Chris. "Truth Hurts." *Memphis Flyer*, 15 July 2005. <http://www.memphisflyer.com>.

Davis, Rod. "Here Are Remembered Heroic Lives; At the National Civil Rights Museum, Hard History Bears an Inspiring Human Face." *San Antonio Express-News*, 4 December 2004, 1M.

Day, Jennifer C., and Eric C. Newburger. "The Big Payoff: Educational Attainment and Synthetic Estimates of Work-Life Earnings." Current Population Reports, U.S. Census, July 2002. <http://www.census.gov/prod/2002pubs/p23-210.pdf>.

DeCell, K. "In the Beginning." *Memphis*, April 1986, 13–22.

DeCosta-Willis, Miriam. *The Memphis Diary of Ida B. Wells*. Boston: Beacon Press, 1995.

Deegan, Mary Jo. *American Ritual Dramas: Social Rules and Cultural Meanings*. New York: Greenwood Press, 1989.

Dent, Amanda. "Crown and Sceptre: Grand Coronation Ball." *RSVP Memphis*, August 2006, 26.

Dillman, Caroline Matheny. "Southern Women: In Continuity or Change?" In *Women in the South: An Anthropological Perspective*, edited by Holly F. Matthews, 8–17. Athens: University of Georgia Press, 1989.

Dirlik, Arif. *The Postcolonial Aura: Third World Criticism in the Age of Global Capitalism*. New York: Westview Press, 1997.

Dixon, Willie. *I Am the Blues: The Willie Dixon Story*. New York: Da Capo Press, 1990.

Dollard, John. *Caste and Class in a Southern Town*. New Haven: Yale University Press, 1957 [1937].

Domhoff, William G. *Who Rules America?* Upper Saddle River, N.J.: Prentice-Hall, 1998.

Dowd, James. "Pastor: Three 6 Mafia Are Pawns of the Devil." *Memphis Commercial Appeal*, 13 March 2006, B1.

Downing, Shirley. "Old Plant Site Reclaimed for Playground." *Memphis Commercial Appeal*, 23 June 2006, CRB1.

Dreier, Peter, John Mollenkopf, and Todd Swanstrom. *Place Matters: Metropolitics for the Twenty-First Century*. Lawrence: University Press of Kansas, 2001.

Dries, Bill. "No Rest for a Weary Warrior: A Century Later, Statue Still on Culture Front Line." *Memphis Commercial Appeal*, 16 May 2005, B1.

Du Bois, W. E. B. *Black Reconstruction*. New York: Harcourt, Brace, 1935.

———. *The Philadelphia Negro: A Social Study*. Philadelphia: University of Pennsylvania Press, 1996 [1899].

———. *The Souls of Black Folk*. Mineola, N.Y.: Dover Publications, 1994 [1903].

Dunaway, Wilma A. *The First American Frontier*. Chapel Hill: University of North Carolina Press, 1996.

Dwyer, Owen J. "Location, Politics, and the Production of Civil Rights Memorial Landscapes." *Urban Geography* 23, no. 1 (2002): 31–56.

Eden, Ami. " 'Sites of Conscience' Get Boost from Libeskind, Parley." *Forward*, 25 July 2003.

Editorial Projects in Education (EPE Research Center). "Diplomas Count: An Essential Guide to Graduation Policy and Rates." *Education Week*, 22 June 2006. <http://www.edweek.org>.

Elliott, James R., Kevin Fox Gotham, and Melinda J Milligan. "Framing the Urban: Struggles over HOPE VI and the New Urbanism in an Historic City." *City and Community* 3, no. 4 (2004): 373–94.

"Elvis Presley Enterprises' Parent Going Private." *Memphis Business Journal*, 1 June 2007. <http://www.bizjournals.com>.

Entrikin, J. Nicholas. *The Betweenness of Place: Towards a Geography of Modernity*. London: MacMillan, 1991.

Erikson, Kai. *Everything in Its Path: A Destruction of Community in the Buffalo Creek Flood*. New York: Simon and Schuster, 1976.

Fair, S. "Clothier to the King." *New York Times*, 23 September 2001, 74.

Falk, William W. *Rooted in Place: Family and Belonging in a Southern Black Community*. New Brunswick, N.J.: Rutgers University Press, 2004.

Feagin, Joe. *Free Enterprise City: Houston in Political-Economic Perspective*. New Brunswick, N.J.: Rutgers University Press, 1988.

Feagin, Joe R., Anthony M. Orum, and Gideon Sjoberg, eds. *A Case for the Case Study*. Chapel Hill: University of North Carolina Press, 1991.

FedEx. "FedEx Announces Domestic Express Services in China." FedEx press release, 20 March 2007. <http://www.fedex.com/cn—english/about/pressreleases/20070320—507.html>.

Ferris, William. "Mules." In *Encyclopedia of Southern Culture*, edited by Charles Reagan Wilson and William Ferris, 511–12. Chapel Hill: University of North Carolina Press, 1989.

Film Production Advisory Committee. "Tennessee Film and Television Production Study." Nashville: Tennessee Film, Entertainment and Music Commission, 2006. <http://www.filmnashville.org>.

Finger, Michael. "Big Empties." *Memphis Flyer*, 4 December 1997. <http://www.memphis flyer.com/backissues/issue459/cvr459.htm>.

———. "Lost Memphis: An Album of Almost-Forgotten Images of Our City." *Memphis*, November 2002. <http://www.memphismagazine.com/backissues/november2002/lostmemphis.htm>.

Fink, Leon. *The Maya of Morganton: Work and Community in the Nuevo New South*. Chapel Hill: University of North Carolina Press, 2003.

———. "When Community Comes Home to Roost: The Southern Milltown As Lost Cause." *Journal of Social History* 40, no. 1 (2006): 119–45.

Florida, Richard. *The Rise of the Creative Class: And How It's Transforming Work, Leisure, Community and Everyday Life*. New York: Basic Books, 2002.

Foner, Phillip S., and Ronald L Lewis, eds. *From the Foundation of the CIO to the AFL-CIO Merger, 1936–1955*. Vol. 7 of *The Black Worker*. Philadelphia: Temple University Press, 1983.

Fontenay, Blake. "Struggle to Find a Compromise Proves Past Is Not Dead or Past." *Memphis Commercial Appeal*, 8 May 2005, V1.

Forman, Murray. *The 'Hood Comes First: Race, Space, and Place in Rap and Hip-Hop*. Middletown: Wesleyan University Press, 2002.

Foucault, Michel. *Discipline and Punish*. New York: Vintage Books, 1995 [1975].

Foucault, Michel, and J. Miscowiec. "Of Other Spaces." *Diacritics* 16, no. 1 (1986): 22–27.

Franklin, V. P. *Living Our Stories, Telling Our Truths*. New York: Scribner, 1995.

Friedman, Thomas L. *The World Is Flat: A Brief History of the Twenty-First Century*. New York: Farrar, Straus and Giroux, 2005.

Garlington, Lela. "Brother against Brother—After a Skirmish, Confederate Sons Elect Leaders, Then Let Out Rebel Yells." *Memphis Commercial Appeal*, 2 August 2002, B1.

———. "Library's New Name Honors Civil Rights Pioneer Hooks: System Had Shunned Family in Old Days." *Memphis Commercial Appeal*, 28 October 2005, B1.

Garris, Leah B. "New Construction Award 2003: A Novel Plan." *Buildings*, October 2003. <http://www.buildings.com>.

Gates, Henry Louis, Jr. "The Trope of a New Negro and the Reconstruction of the Image of the Black." *Representations* 24 (Autumn 1988): 129–55.

Geertz, Clifford. *The Interpretation of Cultures*. New York: Basic Books, 1973.

Germain, David. " 'Hard' Day's Oscar: Memphis Rappers Celebrate Win for 'Hustle' Song." *Memphis Commercial Appeal*, 6 March 2006, A1, A7.

Giddens, Anthony. "Affluence, Poverty and the Idea of a Post-Scarcity Society." *Development and Change* 27 (1996): 365–77.

———. *The Consequences of Modernity*. Cambridge: Polity Press, 1990.

Gieryn, Thomas F. "A Space for Place in Sociology." *Annual Review of Sociology* 26 (2000): 463–96.

Gladney, Margaret Rose, ed. *How Am I to Be Heard? Letters of Lillian Smith*. Chapel Hill: University of North Carolina Press, 1993.

Gnuschke, John E. "Elvis Is Still Big Business in Memphis." *Business Perspectives* 14, no. 3 (Summer 2002): 2–7.

Gnuschke, John E., and Jeff Wallace. "Economic Impact of the Music Industry in Memphis and Shelby County." *Business Perspectives* 16, no. 3 (Fall 2004): 18–27.

Goffman, Erving. *Stigma*. New York: Prentice-Hall, 1963.

Goings, Kenneth, and Brian D. Page. "African Americans versus the Memphis Street Railway Company: Or, How to Win the Battle but Lose the War, 1890–1920." *Journal of Urban History* 30, no. 2 (2004): 131–51.

Goldberger, Paul. "The Rise of the Private City." In *Breaking Away: The Future of Cities*, edited by Robert F. Wagner and Julia Vitullo-Martin, 135–47. New York: Twentieth Century Foundation, 1996.

Goldfield, David. *Cotton Fields and Skyscrapers: Southern City and Region, 1607–1980*. Baton Rouge: Louisiana State University Press, 1982.

———. *Region, Race, and Cities: Interpreting the Urban South*. Baton Rouge: Louisiana State University Press, 1997.

Gordon, Robert. *It Came from Memphis*. New York: Simon and Schuster, 1995.

Gotham, Kevin Fox. "Marketing Mardi Gras: Commodification, Spectacle and the Political Economy of Tourism in New Orleans." *Urban Studies* 39, no. 10 (2002): 1735–56.

———. "Political Opportunity, Community Identity, and the Emergence of a Local Anti-Expressway Movement." *Social Problems* 46 (1999): 332–54.

———. "Tourism from Above and Below: Globalization, Localization and New Orleans's Mardi Gras." *International Journal of Urban and Regional Research* 29, no. 2 (2005): 309–26.

Gotham, Kevin Fox, and William G. Staples. "Narrative Analysis and the New Historical Sociology." *Sociological Quarterly* 37, no. 3 (1996): 481–501.

Gottdiener, Mark. *The Social Production of Urban Space*. Austin: University of Texas Press, 1985.

Gramsci, Antonio. *Selections from the Prison Notebooks*. Edited and translated by Quintin Hoare and Geoffrey Nowell Smith. New York: International Publishers, 1971.

Grantham, Dewey W. *The Life and Death of the Solid South*. Lexington: University of Kentucky Press, 1988.

Grazian, David. *The Search for Authenticity in Urban Blues Clubs*. Chicago: University of Chicago Press, 2003.

Greenemeier, Larry. "Chief of the Year—FedEx CIO Rob Carter Delivers Speed, Flexibility, Efficiency." *Information Week*, 5 December 2005, 34.

Griffin, Larry J. "Temporality, Events, and Explanation in Historical Sociology." *Sociological Methods and Research* 20, no. 4 (1992): 403–27.

Griffin, Larry J., and Ashley B. Thompson. "Appalachia and the South—Collective Memory, Identity, and Representation in Appalachia and the South." *Appalachian Journal* 29, no. 3 (2002): 296–327.

Griffin, Larry J., and Don H. Doyle, eds. *The South As an American Problem*. Athens: University of Georgia Press, 1995.

Griswold, Wendy, and Nathan Wright. "Cowbirds, Locals, and the Dynamic Endurance of Regionalism." *American Journal of Sociology* 109, no. 6 (2004): 1411–51.

Grogan, Paul, and Tony Proscio. *Comeback Cities: A Blueprint for Urban Neighborhood Revival*. New York: Basic Books, 2000.

"Group Plans to Turn Shelby Farms into 'Model' Park." *Memphis Business Journal*, 20 July 2007. <http://www.bizjournals.com/memphis/stories/2007/07/16/daily32.html>.

Grunwald, Michael. "Birthright to the Blues; Memphis Scene Isn't What It Used to Be, Purists Lament." *Boston Globe*, 15 November 1997, A1.

Gustafson, Per. "Meanings of Place: Everyday Experience and Theoretical Conceptualizations." *Journal of Environmental Psychology* 21, no. 1 (2001): 5–16.

Hall, Peter. *Cities in Civilization: Culture, Innovation, and Urban Order*. London: Weidenfeld and Nicolson, 1998.

Handy, W. C. *Father of the Blues: An Autobiography*. New York: Da Capo Press, 1969.

Hannerz, Ulf. *Cultural Complexity: Studies in the Social Organization of Meaning*. New York: Columbia University Press, 1992.

——. "Flows, Boundaries and Hybrids." 1997. <http://www.transcomm.ox.ac.uk/working%20papers/hannerz.pdf>.

Hannigan, John. *Fantasy City*. New York: Routledge, 1998.

Hardy, Terri, and Mary Lynne Vellinga Bee. "2 Cities Enjoy Vibrant Scene: In Indianapolis and Memphis, Palaces for Sport Energize Downtown Fortunes." *Sacramento Bee*, 25 September 2006, A1.

Harkins, John E. *Metropolis of the American Nile*. Oxford: Guild Bindery Press, 1991.

Harrison, Faye V. "The Persistent Power of 'Race' in the Cultural and Political Economy of Racism." *Annual Review of Anthropology* 24 (1995): 47–74.

Harrison, Hasket D., and John E. Gnuschke. "An Overview of Film Production Incentives." *Business Perspectives* 17, no. 3 (Fall/Winter 2005): 4–13.

Harvey, David. *The Condition of Postmodernity*. Cambridge: Blackwell, 1990.

——. "From Managerialism to Entrepreneurialism: The Transformation in Urban Governance in Late Capitalism." *Geografiska Annaler* 71, no. B1 (1989): 3–17.

——. "From Space to Place and Back Again: Reflections on the Condition of Postmodernity." In *Mapping the Futures: Local Culture, Global Change*, edited by Jon Bird, Barry Curtis, Tim Putnam, George Robertson, and Lisa Ticker, 3–29. London: Routledge, 1993.

Haynes, Debra Elliott. "Civil Rights Museum Grows into Second Decade." *Memphis Commercial Appeal*, 23 September 2001.

Heller, Agnes. "A Tentative Answer to the Question: Has Civil Society Cultural Memory?" *Social Research* 68, no. 4 (2001): 1031–40.

Hill, Esther. "Maya Angelou: Resolving the Past, Embracing the Future." In *Conversations with Maya Angelou*, edited by Jeffrey M. Elliot, 109–14. Jackson: University Press of Mississippi, 1989.

Hobsbawm, Eric, and Terence Ranger, eds. *The Invention of Tradition*. New York: Cambridge University Press, 1983.

Hodos, Jerome. "Globalization, Regionalism, and Urban Restructuring: The Case of Philadelphia." *Urban Affairs Review* 37 (2002): 358–79.

Hofler, Robert. "Favorite Son." *Daily Variety*, 23 October 2005, Special Section 1, A6.

Holt, Douglas B. *How Brands Become Icons: The Principles of Cultural Branding*. Cambridge, Mass.: Harvard Business School Publications, 2004.

Honey, Michael. "A Dream Deferred." *The Nation*, 3 May 2004. <http://www.thenation.com/docprint.mhtml?i=20040503&s=honey>.

——. *Southern Labor and Black Civil Rights*. Champaign: University of Illinois Press, 1993.

Hooks, Bell. *Ain't I a Woman*. Cambridge, Mass.: South End Press, 1981.

——. "Representations of Whiteness in the Black Imagination." In *White Privilege*, edited by Paula S. Rothenberg, 19–23. New York: Worth Publishers, 2002.

Horton, Tommy. "Mallory Alexander International: More Than a Warehouse." *Cotton Farming*, March 2006. <http://www.cottonfarming.com>.

Hunt, Beverly. "A Bad Rap: Oscars No Place for Misognynistic, Demeaning 'Pimp.'" *Albany (N.Y.) Times Union*, 6 February 2006, P7.

Hurston, Zora Neale. *Their Eyes Were Watching God*. New York: Harper Collins, 1990 [1937].

Hutchins, Fred L. "Beale Street As It Was." *West Tennessee Historical Society Papers* (1972): 56–63.

Imrie, Rob, Steven Pinch, and Mark Boyle. "Identities, Citizenship and Power in the Cities." *Urban Studies* 33, no. 8 (1996): 1255–61.

Jackson, Kenneth. "Memphis, Tennessee: The Rise and Fall of Main Street." In *American Places: Encounters with History*, edited by William E. Leuchtenburg, 169–83. New York: Oxford University Press, 2000.

Jacobs, A. J. "Symbolic Urban Spaces and the Political Economy of Local Collective Memory: A Comparison of Hiroshima and Nagoya, Japan." *Journal of Political and Military Sociology* 31, no. 2 (2003): 253–78.

James, Steven E., and Tim Martin. "Resource Protection in the World's Largest Urban Park: A Model for Partnership between Parks, Higher Education, and the Community." *George Wright Forum* 17, no. 2 (2000): 86–91. <http://www.georgewright.org>.

Jaschik, Scott. "Confederates Defeat Vanderbilt." *Inside Higher Education*, 5 May 2005. <www.insidehighered.com>.

Jedlowski, Paolo. "Memory and Sociology." *Time and Society* 10, no. 1 (2001): 29–44.

Jensen, Larry. "Viewpoint: St. Jude Helps Put City on Bioscience Map." *Memphis Commercial Appeal*, 10 October 2004, B7.

Johnson, Eugene J., and Robert D. Russell. *Memphis: An Architectural Guide*. Knoxville: University of Tennessee Press, 1990.

Johnson, Jeff. "After a Night on Beale Street, Real Blues Is Welcome Respite." *Chicago Sun-Times*, 5 April 2004, Features, 44.

Jones, Jacintha. "It's Not a War, So Let's Be Civil, Lowery Says." *Memphis Commercial Appeal*, 30 July 2005, A1.

Jones, Yolanda. "Freedom Rings—Winners Recall Pioneers; Local Dignitaries Join Global Luminaries to Celebrate at Rights Gala." *Memphis Commercial Appeal*, 4 November 2005, A1.

——. "Memphis Music Awards Gala Turns Out a Cluster of Stars." *Memphis Commercial Appeal*, 23 October 2005, B1–B2.

Judd, Dennis R., and Susan S. Fainstein, eds. *The Tourist City*. New Haven: Yale University Press, 1999.

Kane, Thomas H. "Mourning the Promised Land: Martin Luther King Jr.'s Automortography and the National Civil Rights Museum." *American Literature* 76, no. 3 (2004): 549–77.

Kearns, Gerry, and Chris Philo. *Selling Places: The City As Cultural Capital, Past and Present.* Oxford: Pergamon Press, 1993.

Kelley, Michael. "Can We Get Together? Tax Woes Pump Up Consolidation Talk." *Memphis Commercial Appeal,* 4 May 2008, V1, V3.

Kellner, Douglas. "Theorizing Globalization." *Sociological Theory* 20, no. 3 (2002): 285–305.

Kendall, Diana. "Class in the United States: Not Only Alive but Reproducing." *Research in Social Stratification and Mobility* 24, no. 1 (2006): 89–104.

———. *The Power of Good Deeds: Privileged Women and the Social Reproduction of the Upper Class.* Lanham: Rowman and Littlefield, 2002.

Key, V. O. *Southern Politics in State and Nation.* New York: Vintage Books, 1949.

Keyes, Cheryl L. "Empowering Self, Making Choices, Creating Spaces: Black Female Identity via Rap Music Performance." In *That's the Joint! The Hip-Hop Studies Reader,* edited by Murray Forman and Mark Anthony Neal, 265–81. New York: Routledge, 2004.

Khan, Karim. "Sites for U.S. Logistics: Business Facilities." *The Location Advisor,* September 2004. <http://www.businessfacilties.com>.

Kotler, Philip, Donald Haider, and Irving Rein. *Marketing Places.* New York: Free Press, 1993.

Kuhn, Thomas S. *The Structure of Scientific Revolutions.* Chicago: University of Chicago Press, 1962.

Kumar, Ruman Banerji. " 'Fear and Pride': Spring Break Trip Recounts Civil Rights Struggle." *Memphis Commercial Appeal,* 19 March 2005, B1.

Lamont, Michele, and Annette Lareau. "Cultural Capital: Allusion, Gaps and Glissandos in Recent Theoretical Developments." *Sociological Theory* 6, no. 2 (1988): 153–68.

Landis, Debra. "Franklin School Readies for Third Trip to Memphis." *State Journal Register,* 7 March 2005, 19.

Langman, Lauren, and Katie Cangemi. "Globalization and the Liminal: Transgression, Identity and the Urban Primitive." *Research in Urban Policy* 9 (2004): 141–76.

Lauterbach, Preston. " 'Follow That Dream': EPE Is Proposing a $250 Million Graceland Expansion on Elvis Presley Boulevard. What Will It Mean for Memphis?" *Memphis Flyer,* 10 January 2008. <http://www.memphisflyer.com>.

Lee, George W. *Beale Street: Where the Blues Began.* New York: Ballou, 1934.

———. "Poetic Memories of Beale Street." *West Tennessee Historical Society Papers* (1969): 64–73.

Lee, Richard. "International Paper Leaves Stamford, Conn., for Memphis, Tenn." *Stamford Advocate,* 17 August 2005.

Lefebvre, Henri. *Writings on Cities.* Translated by Eleonor Kofman and Elizabeth Lebas. Oxford: Blackwell, 1996.

Lewis, Peirce F. "Axioms for Reading the Landscape." In *The Interpretation of Ordinary Landscapes: Geographical Essays,* edited by Donald W. Meinig, 11–32. New York: Oxford University Press, 1979.

Lichter, Daniel T. "Race, Employment Hardship, and Inequality in the American Nonmetropolitan South." *American Sociological Review* 54 (1989): 436–46.

Locke, Alain. "The New Negro." In *The Norton Anthology of African American Literature,* edited by Henry Louis Gates Jr. and Nellie Y. McKay, 961–70. New York: W. W. Norton, 1997 [1925].

Locker, Richard. "Nashville Reaped Benefits of Plan Eyed for Memphis." *Memphis Commercial Appeal*, 4 May 2008, V1, V3.

———. "Tourism Zone Bill Gets Nod." *Memphis Commercial Appeal*, 8 June 2007, A1.

Logan, Raymond. *The Negro in American Life and Thought: The Nadir, 1877–1901*. New York: Dial Press, 1954.

Lollar, Michael. "Events Mark 40 Years since Death of MLK." *Memphis Commercial Appeal*, 5 March 2008, B2.

Love, Jimmy. "Slinging Mud at Forrest Just Besmirches Walter Bailey." *Memphis Commercial Appeal*, 15 May 2005, V3.

Lynch, Annette. *Dress, Gender and Cultural Change*. Oxford: Berg, 1999.

Lyne, Jack. "ServiceMaster 'PILOTing' HQ, 500 Quality Jobs into Memphis." *Site Selection Incentive Deal of the Month*, November 2006. <http://www.siteselection.com>.

Lyson, Thomas. *Two Sides to the Sunbelt: Growing Divergence between the Rural and Urban South*. New York: Praeger Press, 1989.

Magness, Perre. *Carnival Memphis: The Party with a Purpose*. Memphis: Carnival Memphis, 2006.

Maki, Amos. "A 'City' at Sears Crosstown?: Mixed-Use Complex Planned; Sale Possible in December." *Memphis Commercial Appeal*, 30 November 2005, C1.

———. "City Council to Get Audit of Pilot Program." *Memphis Commercial Appeal*, 15 June 2006, C1.

———. "City's Changed—for Better, Says IP Chief; Locals Cheer News of HQ's Move from Connecticut." *Memphis Commercial Appeal*, 17 August 2005, A1.

———. "Downtown Hotel Project Secures Financing." *Memphis Commercial Appeal*, 1 December 2005, A1, A5.

———. "I-69's Path Laced with Economic Benefits." *Memphis Business Journal*, 10 December 2004. <http://www.bizjournals.com/memphis/stories/2004/12/13/story3.html>.

———. "MHA to Redevelop 600 Housing Units at Dixie Homes." *Memphis Business Journal*, 1 July 2005. <http://www.bizjournals.com/memphis/stories/2005/07/04/story2.html>.

———. "More Blues for Beale Street." *Memphis Commercial Appeal*, 14 January 2006, C1–C2.

———. "Not Competitive—Report: Workers Lack Skills, Education." *Memphis Commercial Appeal*, 22 June 2006, C1.

———. "One Beale Sings 'Wow': Luxury Condos, Hotel Proposed for River Landing." *Memphis Commercial Appeal*, 3 December 2005, A1, A12.

———. "Westin Beale Fills a Tall Order." *Memphis Commercial Appeal*, 10 December 2005, C1.

Malizia, Emil. "Organizing to Overcome Uneven Development: The Case of the U.S. South." *Review of Radical Political Economics* 10, no. 3 (1978): 87–94.

Malone, Robert. "FedEx Focuses on China." *Forbes*, 9 September 2006. <http://www.forbes.com>.

Manning, Frank E. "Spectacle." In *Folklore, Cultural Performances and Popular Entertainments*, edited by Richard Bauman, 291–99. New York: Oxford University Press, 1992.

Marling, Karal Ann. *Debutante: Rites and Regalia of American Debdom*. Lawrence: University Press of Kansas, 2004.

Marwick, Arthur. *The Sixties: Cultural Revolution in Britain, France, Italy and the United States*. Oxford: Oxford University Press, 1998.

Massey, Doreen. "Power Geometry and a Progressive Sense of Place." In *Mapping the Futures: Local Culture, Global Change*, edited by Jon Bird, Barry Curtis, Tim Putnam, and Lisa Tickner, 59–69. New York: Routledge, 1993.

McIlwaine, Shields. *Memphis down in Dixie*. New York: E. P. Dutton, 1948.

McKee, Margaret, and Fred Chisenhall. *Beale Black and Blue: Life and Music on Black America's Main Street*. Baton Rouge: Louisiana State University Press, 1981.

McLaurin, Melton A. "Commemorating Wilmington's Racial Violence of 1898: From Individual to Collective Memory." *Southern Cultures* 6, no. 4 (2000): 35–57.

McLean, Robert Emmett. "Cotton Carnival and Cotton Makers Jubilee: Memphis Society in Black and White." M.A. thesis, George Mason University, 1994.

McMichael, Philip. "Slavery in Capitalism: The Rise and Demise of the U.S. Ante-Bellum Cotton Culture." *Theory and Society* 20, no. 3 (1991): 321–49.

Memphis Business Journal. *Book of Lists 2006*. Charlotte, N.C.: American City Business Journals, 2006.

Memphis Convention and Visitors Bureau. "The Economic Impact of Travel in Memphis and Shelby County." Memphis: Memphis Convention and Visitors Bureau, 2003.

Memphis Regional Chamber of Commerce. *Memphis Region Sourcebook*. Charlotte, N.C.: Michael Gallis and Associates, 2001.

Mills, C. Wright. *The Sociological Imagination*. Oxford: Oxford University Press, 1959.

Moe, Richard, and Carter Wilkie. *Changing Places: Rebuilding Community in the Age of Sprawl*. New York: Henry Holt and Company, 1997.

Mohl, R. A. "City and Region: The Missing Dimension in U.S. Urban History." *Journal of Urban History* 25, no. 1 (1998): 3–21.

Molotch, Harvey. "Growth Machine Links: Up, Down, and Across." In *The Urban Growth Machine: Critical Perspectives Two Decades Later*, edited by Andrew E. G. Jones and David Wilson, 247–66. Albany: State University of New York Press, 1999.

Molotch, Harvey, William Freudenburg, and Krista E. Paulsen. "History Repeats Itself, but How? City Character, Urban Tradition, and the Accomplishment of Place." *American Sociological Review* 65, no. 6 (2000): 791–823.

Morris, Bill. "Playing for Keeps: Elvis Presley and the Evolution of Memphis; Elvis Is Still Big Business in Memphis." *Business Perspectives* 14, no. 3 (Summer 2002): 18–19.

Morris, Willie. *North toward Home*. New York: Vintage Books, 1967.

Mumford, Louis. *The City in History*. New York: Harcourt, Brace and World, 1961.

Murdock, James. "Shelby Farms to Be a '21st-Century Park.'" *Architectural Record*, 30 August 2007. <http://www.archrecord.construction.com/news/daily/archives/070830shelby.asp>.

Murphey, Lance. "The Land of Cotton: The Carnival Queen Camilla Brinner." *Memphis Commercial Appeal*, 4 December 2005, V6.

Myrdal, Gunnar. *An American Dilemma*. Vol. 2. New York: Harper and Brothers, 1994.

Odum, Howard W. *Southern Regions of the United States*. Chapel Hill: University of North Carolina Press, 1936.

Olick, Jeffrey, and J. Robbins. "Social Memory Studies: From 'Collective Memory' to the Historical Sociology of Mnemonic Practices." *Annual Review of Sociology* 24 (1998): 105–40.

Omi, Michael, and Howard Winant. *Racial Formation in the United States: From the 1960s to the 1980s.* New York: Routledge and Kegan Paul, 1986.

Orum, Anthony. *Power, Money, and the People: The Making of Modern Austin.* Austin: Texas Monthly Press, 1987.

Orum, Anthony, and Xiangming Chen. *The World of Cities: Places in Comparative and Historical Perspective.* New York: Blackwell Publishing, 2003.

Osborne, Brian S. "Landscapes, Memory, Monuments, and Commemoration: Putting Identity in Its Place." Paper commissioned by the Department of Canadian Heritage for the Ethnocultural, Racial, Religious and Linguistic Diversity and Identity Seminar, 2001. <http://www.canada.metropolis.net/events/ethnocultural/publications/putinden.pdf>.

Ostrander, Susan A. *Women of the Upper Class.* Philadelphia: Temple University Press, 1984.

"Owners Protest Beale St. Plan." *Press-Scimitar,* 17 February 1967, 17.

Park, Carolyne. "Center City Commission Seeks Feedback on Downtown's Future." *Memphis Business Journal,* 17 February 2006. <http://www.Memphis.bizjournals.com>.

Partnership for Prosperity. "Much to Be Proud Of, Much to Be Done." Memphis: Memphis Regional Chamber of Commerce, 2002. <http://www.memphischamber.com/PartnershipForProsperity.pdf>.

Paulsen, Krista E. "Making Character Concrete: Empirical Strategies for Studying Place Distinction." *City and Community* 3, no. 3 (2004): 243–62.

Peacock, James L. *Grounded Globalism: How the U.S. South Embraces the World.* Athens: University of Georgia Press, 2007.

Peacock, James L., Harry L. Watson, and Carrie R. Matthews, eds. *The American South in a Global World.* Chapel Hill: University of North Carolina Press, 2005.

Pearson, Gene. "45 Years Later, It's Time for a Shelby Farms Plan." *Memphis Commercial Appeal,* 21 April 2005, B7, Guest Column.

Peck, Chris. "New Day Lures Oprah—and Us." *Memphis Commercial Appeal,* 13 November 2005, V4.

Persky, Joe. "The South: A Colony at Home." *Southern Exposure* 1 (1973): 14–22.

Peterson, Richard A. "In Search of Authenticity." *Journal of Management Studies* 42, no. 5 (2005): 1083–98.

Piven, Frances Fox, and Richard Cloward. *Poor Peoples' Movements: Why They Succeed, How They Fail.* New York: Pantheon Books, 1977.

Portes, Alejandro, and Alex Stepick. *City on the Edge: The Transformation of Miami.* Berkeley: University of California Press, 1993.

Powdermaker, Hortense. *After Freedom: A Cultural Study in the Deep South.* Madison: University of Wisconsin Press, 1993 [1939].

Putnam, Robert. *Bowling Alone.* New York: Simon and Schuster, 2000.

Radford-Hill, Sheila. "Keepin' It Real: A Generational Commentary on Kimberly Springer's 'Third Wave Black Feminism?'" *Signs* 27, no. 4 (2002): 1083–89.

Ragin, Charles C. *The Comparative Method.* Berkeley: University of California Press, 1987.

Reed, John Shelton. *The Enduring South*. Chapel Hill: University of North Carolina Press, 1975.

——. *My Tears Spoiled My Aim*. Columbia: University of Missouri Press, 1993.

——. *One South*. Baton Rouge: Louisiana State University Press, 1982.

——. "On Narrative and Sociology." *Social Forces* 68, no. 1 (1989): 1–14.

——. *Southern Folk Plain and Fancy: Native White Social Types*. Athens: University of Georgia Press, 1986.

Risher, Wayne. "Civil Rights Museum Opens Eyes to History." *Memphis Commercial Appeal*, 29 September 1991.

Roberts, Jane. "Airport's Global Reach Makes It Region's Top Force for Prosperity." *Memphis Commercial Appeal*, 28 March 2008, D1.

——. "Catch the Taxiway." *Memphis Commercial Appeal*, 26 June 2006, A1.

——. "Cottoning to China: Tennessee's Biggest Customer Makes $500 Million Deal." *Memphis Commercial Appeal*, 19 May 2007, C1.

——. "Port o' Call—Far-West Canadian Harbor Closes Distance between Memphis, Pacific Markets." *Memphis Commercial Appeal*, 30 September 2007, C1.

——. "A Taste of Memphis: Airport Travelers Can Sample Fare the City's Proud to Brag About." *Memphis Commercial Appeal*, 2 December 2005, C1.

Robertson, Rob. "FedEX Chief Reflects on 25 Years of Memphis Business." *Memphis Business Journal*, 15 October 2004, 1, 50.

——. "Memphis Labor Pool Unmotivated, Unattractive to Outsiders, Study Shows." *Memphis Business Journal*, 7 July 2005.

Robinson, William I. *Promoting Polyarchy*. New York: Cambridge University Press, 1996.

Roediger, David. *The Wages of Whiteness: Race and the Making of the American Working Class*. New York: Verso, 1991.

Rofe, Matthew W. " 'I Want to Be Global': Theorising the Gentrifying Class As an Emergent Elite Global Community." *Urban Studies* 40, no. 12 (2003): 2511–26.

Roscigno, Vincent J., Donald Tomaskoic-Devey, and Martha Crowley. "Education and the Inequalities of Place." *Social Forces* 84, no. 4 (2006): 2121–45.

Rose, Mark H. *Interstate: Express Highway Politics, 1939–1989*. Knoxville: University of Tennessee Press, 1990.

Rossiter, Clinton. *The American Presidency*. New York: Harcourt and Brace, 1960.

Rousey, Dennis C. "Yellow Fever and Black Policemen in Memphis: A Post-Reconstruction Anomaly." *Journal of Southern History* 51, no. 3 (1985): 357–74.

Ruiz, Rebecca. "America's Most Obese Cities." *Forbes*, 26 November 2007. <http://www.forbes.com/2007/11/14/health-obesity-cities-forbeslife-cx—rr—1114obese.html>.

Rushing, Wanda. "Cold War Racial Politics and Global Impression Management: North Carolina Economic Development As a Case Study." *Current Sociology* 48, no. 2 (2000): 51–69.

——. "Globalization and the Paradoxes of Place: Poverty and Power in Memphis." *City and Community* 3, no. 1 (2004): 65–80.

——. "Rural Empowerment Zones and Enterprise Communities: The Impact of Globalization Processes and Public Policy on Economic Development." *Journal of Poverty* 4, no. 4 (2000): 45–63.

——. "'Sin, Sex, and Segregation': Social Control and the Education of Southern Women." *Gender and Education* 14, no. 2 (2002): 167–79.

Russell, Greg. "A Wise Choice." *University of Memphis Magazine* (Summer 2007): 20–23.

Saito, Hiro. "Reiterated Commemoration: Hiroshima As National Trauma." *Sociological Theory* 24, no. 4 (2006): 353–76.

Sassen, Saskia, ed. *Global Cities, Linked Cities.* New York: Routledge, 2002.

Sautet, Frederic. "Local Tax Incentives in Action: The Payment-in-Lieu-of-Tax Program in Memphis, Tennessee." Mercatus Center, George Mason University, June 2006. <http://www.mercatus.org>.

——. "On My Mind: Don't Tempt Me." Mercatus Center, George Mason University, June 2006. <http://www.mercatus.org>.

Savage, Kirk. "The Politics of Memory: Black Emancipation and the Civil War Monument." In *Commemorations: The Politics of National Identity,* edited by John R. Gillis, 127–49. Princeton: Princeton University Press, 1994.

Savitch, H. V., and Ronald K. Vogel. "Suburbs without a City: Power and City-County Consolidation." *Urban Affairs Review* 39, no. 6 (July 2004): 758–90.

Schein, Richard H. "The Place of Landscape: A Conceptual Framework for Interpreting an American Scene." *Annals of the Association of American Geographers* 87, no. 4 (1997): 660–80.

Scherzer, Kenneth A. "Southern Cities—How Exceptional?" *Journal of Urban History* 26, no. 5 (2000): 692–706.

Schmidt, William E. "Again, River Holds Key to Revival of Memphis." *New York Times,* 4 July 1986, A10.

Schudson, Michael. "How Culture Works: Perspectives from Media Studies on the Efficacy of Symbols." *Theory and Society* 18, no. 2 (1989): 153–80.

Schuman, Howard, Barry Schwartz, and Hannah D'Arcy. "Elite Revisionists and Popular Beliefs." *Public Opinion Quarterly* 69, no. 1 (2005): 2–29.

Schwartz, Barry. "Social Change and Collective Memory: The Democratization of George Washington." *American Sociological Review* (April 1991): 221–36.

Schwartz, Barry, and Howard Schuman. "History, Commemoration, and Belief: Abraham Lincoln in American Memory, 1945–2001." *American Sociological Review* 70, no. 2 (2005): 183–203.

Scott, Allen J. "The Cultural Economy of Cities." *International Journal of Urban and Regional Research* 21 (1997): 323–39.

Scott, James C. *Domination and the Arts of Resistance: Hidden Transcripts.* New Haven: Yale University Press, 1990.

Share, Don. *Union.* Lincoln, Nebr.: Zoo Press, 2002.

Sharpley-Whiting, T. Denean. *Pimps Up, Ho's Down: Hip Hop's Hold on Young Black Women.* New York: New York University Press, 2007.

Sheffield, Christopher. "New York Firms to Acquire ServiceMaster." *Memphis Business Journal,* 20 March 2007.

——. "Pidgeon Park Poised for New Development." *Memphis Business Journal,* 12 March 2007.

Sigafoos, Robert A. *Cotton Row to Beale Street: A Business History of Memphis.* Memphis: Memphis State University Press, 1979.

Sitton, Ron. "Beale Street Culture Blues." *Southern Culture* 1, no. 4 (1999). <www
.southerner.net>.

Sjoberg, Gideon, Norman Williams, Ted R. Vaughan, and Andrée F. Sjoberg. "The Case
Study Approach in Social Research: Basic Methodological Issues." In *A Case for the Case
Study*, edited by Joe R. Feagin, Anthony M. Orum, and Gideon Sjoberg, 27–79. Chapel
Hill: University of North Carolina Press, 1991.

Skocpol, Theda, and Jennifer Lynn Oser. "Organization Despite Adversity: The Origins
and Development of African American Fraternal Associations." *Social Science History*
28, no. 3 (2004): 367–537.

Smart City Consulting. *The Case for Shelby Farms Park: Creating a Great American Park*,
2005. <http://www.memphismojo.com/shelbyfarms>.

Smith, David A., and Michael F. Timberlake. "World City Networks and Hierarchies,
1977–1997." *American Behavioral Scientist* 44, no. 10 (2001): 1656–78.

Smith, Jon, and Deborah Cohn, eds. "Introduction: Uncanny Hybridities." In *Look Away!
The U.S. South in New World Studies*. Durham: Duke University Press, 2004.

Smith, Michael P. *Transnational Urbanism*. New York: Blackwell Publishing, 2001.

Smith, Ron. "The Seam Begins Peanut Trading." *Southwest Farm Press*, 9 August 2005.
<http://www.southwestfarmpress.com>.

Smith, Vasco. "1948: Swingin' at the Handy Theater." *Memphis Magazine*, November 1999.
<http://www.memphismagazine.com>.

Smith, Whitney. "Uncovering the History of Beale Street." *Memphis Commercial Appeal*, 20
February 1983, B1.

Snyder, Gabriel. " 'Pimp' Was Quite a Moment." *Daily Variety*, 6 March 2006, 36.

Soja, Edward. *Postmodern Geographies*. London: Verso, 1989.

Sorkin, Michael, ed. *Variations on a Theme Park: The New American City and the End of
Public Space*. New York: Hill and Wang, 1992.

Stanfield, J. Edwin. *In Memphis: Mirror to America?* Atlanta: Southern Regional Council,
1968.

Strauss, Peter. "Revisiting Overton Park: Political and Judicial Controls over
Administrative Actions Affecting the Community." *UCLA Law Review* 39 (June 1992):
1251–1329.

Sullivan, Paul. "Financial Times: A Fresh Approach to the Art of Healing." *Gabbe Group*, 3
June 2006. <http://www.216.198.218.233/wpcontent/uploads/2006/06/FT%20
Jonas%20060306.pdf>.

Suttles, Gerald D. "The Cumulative Texture of Local Urban Culture." *American Journal of
Sociology* 90, no. 2 (1984): 283–304.

Synnott, Anthony. *The Body Social*. New York: Routledge, 1993.

Takaki, Ronald. "Aesculapius Was a White Man: Race and the Cult of True
Womanhood." In *The "Racial" Economy of Science*, edited by Sandra Harding, 201–9.
Bloomington: Indiana University Press, 1993.

Taylor, Monique M. *Harlem between Heaven and Hell*. Minnneapolis: University of
Minnesota Press, 2002.

Taylor, Peter. *The Old Forest and Other Stories*. New York: Picador, 1996.

———. *A Summons to Memphis*. New York: Ballantine Books, 1986.

Taylor, Peter J., and Robert E. Lang. "U.S. Cities in the 'World City Network.'" Brookings Institution, February 2005. <www.brookings.edu>.

Thamel, Pete. "Memphis and Calipari Go to Hoop in China." *New York Times*, 20 September 2007. <http://www.nytimes.com>.

Thomas, G. Scott. "America's Smartest Cities." *Bizjournals*, 12 June 2006. <http://www.bizjournals.com>.

Thomas, Wendi C. "File Oscar under History to Hide From." *Memphis Commercial Appeal*, 7 March 2006, A2.

———. "'Hustle' Song No Rapper's Delight." *Memphis Commercial Appeal*, 2 March 2006, A2.

Tilly, Betty, and Pat Faudree. *Yesterday's Evergreen: Today's Mid-Town Memphis*. Memphis: Metropolitan InterFaith Association, 1980.

Tobia, P. J. "Silk Stocking Cinema." *Nashville Scene*, 1 June 2006. <http://www.nashvillescene.com>.

Trotter, Joe W. "African American Fraternal Associations in American History: An Introduction." *Social Science History* 28, no. 3 (2004): 355–66.

Twelve Southerners. *I'll Take My Stand*. New York: Harper and Brothers, 1930.

"Two New Interstates to Speed Traffic Flow through Memphis." *Memphis News Bureau*, 19 February 2004. <http://www.memphisnewsbureau.org/newsroom/000077.html>.

Urry, John. "The Sociology of Space and Place." In *The Blackwell Companion to Sociology*, edited by Judith R. Blau, 3–15. Malden, Mass.: Blackwell, 2001.

URS Corporation and NexGen Advisors. "PILOT Evaluation Program Project: Evaluation Report," 2005. <www.shelbycountytn.gov/FirstPortal/dotShowDoc/dotContent/Government/CountyServices/PlanningandDevelopment/PILOT—Eval—%20Rrt—Final.pdf>.

U.S. Census Bureau. *County and City Data Book: 2007*. <http://www.census.gov>.

———. "Percent of People below Poverty Level in the Past 12 Months." *American Community Survey*, 2003. <http://www.census.gov>.

———. *State and Metropolitan Area Data Book: 2006*. <http://www.census.gov>.

Van Riper, Tom. "Long Live the King." *Forbes*, 15 August 2007. <http://www.forbes.com>.

Vogel, Ezra, and Andrea Larson. "North Carolina's Research Triangle: State Modernization." In *Comeback*, edited by Ezra F. Vogel, 240–62. New York: Simon and Schuster, 1985.

Wagner-Pacifici, Robin, and Barry Schwartz. "The Vietnam Veterans Memorial: Commemorating a Difficult Past." *American Journal of Sociology* 97, no. 2 (2005): 376–420.

Wailoo, Keith. *Dying in the City of the Blues: Sickle Cell Anemia and the Politics of Race and Health*. Chapel Hill: University of North Carolina Press, 2001.

Wall, Cheryl A. "Mules and Men and Women: Zora Neale Hurston's Strategies of Narration and Visions of Female Empowerment." *Black American Literature Forum* 23, no. 4 (1989): 661–80.

Wallerstein, Immanuel. "American Slavery and the Capitalist World-Economy." In Immanuel Wallerstein, *The Capitalist World Economy*, 202–22. London: Cambridge University Press, 1979.

——. "What Can One Mean by Southern Culture?" In *The Evolution of Southern Culture*, edited by Newman Bartley, 1–13. Athens: University of Georgia Press, 1988.

Walzer, Norman, and Brian D. Jacobs. *Public-Private Partnerships for Local Economic Development*. Westport, Conn.: Greenwood, 1998.

Warner, Margaret. "Local Control versus National Interest: The Debate over Southern Public Health, 1878–1884." *Journal of Southern History* 50, no. 3 (1984): 407–28.

Warner, R. Stephen. "Oenology: The Making of *New Wine*." In *A Case for the Case Study*, edited by Joe R. Feagin, Anthony M. Orum, and Gideon Sjoberg, 174–99. Chapel Hill: University of North Carolina Press, 1991.

Waters, Malcolm. *Globalization*. London: Routledge, 1995.

Weinbaum, Eve S. *To Move a Mountain: Fighting the Global Economy in Appalachia*. New York: New Press, 2004.

Welty, Eudora. *The Eye of the Story*. New York: Random House, 1977.

——. *One Writer's Beginnings*. Cambridge, Mass.: Harvard University Press, 1984.

Whyte, William Foote. *Street Corner Society*, 3rd ed. Chicago: University of Chicago Press, 1993.

Williams, David. "Bass Pro Casts Big Vision: Hotel, Marina, Inclinator in Retailer's Concept, and There's Talk of a Theme Park at Proposed Pyramid Site." *Memphis Commercial Appeal*, 25 February 2006, A5.

——. "Graceland and All That Pizazz—Ambitious Expansion Hinges on Public Funds." *Memphis Commercial Appeal*, 2 June 2007, A1.

——. "The Last Pyramid Show a Rock and Roll Farewell." *Memphis Commercial Appeal*, 4 February 2007, A1.

Williamson, Joel. *The Crucible of Race*. New York: Oxford University Press, 1984.

Wilson, John, and Marc Musick. "Who Cares? Toward an Integrated Theory of Volunteer Work." *American Sociological Review* 62, no. 5 (1997): 694–713.

Wilson, William H. *The City Beautiful Movement*. Baltimore: Johns Hopkins University Press, 1989.

Wilson, William Julius. *The Truly Disadvantaged: The Inner City, the Underclass, and Public Policy*. Chicago: University of Chicago Press, 1990.

Wolff, Cindy. "Old Forest Furor—Group Upset Zoo Took Out 139 Trees to Build Teton Trek." *Memphis Commercial Appeal*, 5 March 2008, B1.

Wood, Phillip J. *Southern Capitalism: The Political Economy of North Carolina, 1880–1980*. Durham: Duke University Press, 1986.

Woodman, Harold D. *King Cotton and His Retainers: Financing and Marketing the Cotton Crop of the South, 1800–1925*. Lexington: University of Kentucky Press, 1968.

Woods, Clyde. *Development Arrested: The Blues and Plantation Power in the Mississippi Delta*. New York: Verso, 1998.

Woodward, C. Vann. *The Burden of Southern History*, 3rd ed. Baton Rouge: Louisiana State University Press, 1993.

——. *Origins of the New South, 1877–1913*. Baton Rouge: Louisiana State University Press, 1951.

Wrenn, Lynette Boney. *Crisis and Commission Government in Memphis: Elite Rule in a Gilded Age City*. Knoxville: University of Tennessee Press, 1998.

Wright, Erik Olin. "The Continuing Relevance of Class Analysis: Comments." *Theory and Society* 25, no. 1 (1996): 693–716.

Wright, Gavin. *Old South New South: Revolutions in the Southern Economy since the Civil War.* New York: Basic Books, 1986.

Wright, Richard. *Black Boy.* New York: Viking Press, 1991.

———. *12 Million Black Voices.* New York: Viking Press, 1941.

Wyatt-Brown, Bertram. *Southern Honor: Ethics and Behavior in the Old South.* New York: Oxford University Press, 1982.

Zukin, Sharon. *Landscapes of Power.* Berkeley: University of California Press, 1991.

INDEX